REAGAN

AN AMERICAN STORY

REAGAN

AN AMERICAN STORY

Adriana Bosch

with a foreword by
David McCullough

TV Books

TV Books ✦ New York

To my family which sustains me.
And to my father who always backs me.

Publisher's Cataloging-in-Publication Data
Bosch, Adriana.
     Reagan: an American story / Adriana Bosch; with a foreword by David
McCullough. — 1st ed.
     p. cm.
     Includes index.

     1. Reagan, Ronald. 2. Presidents—United States—Biography. 3. Gover-
nors—California—Biography. 4. United States—Politics and government—
1981-1989. I. Title.

E877.B67 1998   973.927'092
                             QBI98-278

Major funding for *The American Experience* is provided by the Alfred P.
Sloan Foundation. National corporate funding is provided by Liberty
Mutual and Scotts/Miracle-Gro. Additional funding provided by public
television viewers.

Endsheet Photomosaic™ illustration by Robert Silvers for *The American
Experience*. Content from American Memory, National Digital Library
Program, Library of Congress.

TV Books

TV Books, L.L.C.
Publishers serving the television industry.
1619 Broadway, Ninth Floor
New York, NY 10019

Text design and production by Joe Gannon.
Manufactured in the United States by Royal Book Manufacturing.

Contents

✦ Foreword *by David McCullough* 7

✦ Introduction: In Search
of Ronald Reagan *by Austin Hoyt* 11

CHAPTER 1 ✦ Reagan 19

CHAPTER 2 ✦ Lifeguard. 25

CHAPTER 3 ✦ The World of Make-Believe 36

CHAPTER 4 ✦ The World Of Reality. 51

CHAPTER 5 ✦ When Ronnie Met Nancy 70

CHAPTER 6 ✦ An Education in Politics 80

CHAPTER 7 ✦ California Here He Comes 101

CHAPTER 8 ✦ Candidate. 113

CHAPTER 9 ✦ Happy Days Are Here Again 142

CHAPTER 10 ✦ John Hinkley's Bullet 160

CHAPTER 11 ✦ The Ranch in the Sky 176

CHAPTER 12 ✦ Staying the Course 183

CHAPTER 13 ✦ Evil Empire. 197

CHAPTER 14 ✦ Slouching Toward Armageddon 217

CHAPTER 15 ✦ Morning in America. 241

CHAPTER 16 ✦ Geneva: When the Aging Lion
Met the Young Tiger. 253

CHAPTER 17   ✦   Lady Liberty's Leading Man 269

CHAPTER 18   ✦   His Finest Hour 279

CHAPTER 19   ✦   Iran-Contra: The Darkest Time. 292

CHAPTER 20   ✦   Peace in Our Time 315

CHAPTER 21   ✦   Sunset. 332

                 ✦   Index 342

                 ✦   Acknowledgements. 349

                 ✦   Photo Credits 350

                 ✦   About *The American Experience* 351

                 ✦   About the Authors 352

Foreword

David McCullough

We all hear and read a great deal about how wealthy we are as a nation. We're told our productivity is ahead of everybody else's, that more of our people are educated than any other nation's, that we live longer, have better retirement funds. But I wonder how often we stop to realize—and appreciate—how rich we Americans are in story.

This year, *The American Experience* is celebrating its tenth anniversary. In those ten years, over one hundred shows have been presented to audiences in the millions—an average of almost seven million viewers an episode. It is the country's only regularly scheduled historical documentary series, and what stories it can tell.

The American Experience brings to television the work of the best documentary filmmakers of our time and in many cases their best work—David Grubin's "LBJ," Charles Guggenheim's "D-Day," Tom Lennon's "Battle of the Bulge," Austin Hoyt's "Carnegie," Ric Burns's "The Donner Party." *The American Experience* also brings to light stories about less well-known events and figures. Ed Gray and Janet Graham's marvelous "Orphan Trains" was scholarly groundbreaking, fine filmmaking that resulted in genuine historic discovery. Sam Pollard and Joyce Vaughn's powerful "Going Back to T-Town," about the race riots in Tulsa, Oklahoma, is another example of first-rate scholarship, investigation and interpretation. Again and again, the interviews done for our films, the research in archives and film and photograph collections, have turned up important new history, things of significance that have not been said or seen before.

This book, *Reagan*, is the first of a series of six titles to be developed directly from the films of *The American Experience*. Ronald Reagan, the fortieth president of the United States, held office from January 1981 to January 1989—eight highly eventful, crucial years, a time of high prosperity and painful recession, of much star-spangled optimism and the terrible, over-hanging fear that the world might be blown to pieces. It was then, too, that the Cold War all but ended, a turning point in history, the importance of which can hardly be overstated.

What distinguishes this book and film project are the exclusive interviews with so many protagonists in the drama, including Mikhail Gorbachev, as well as members of the President's own family: Nancy, Maureen, Ron and Patti. Indeed, this is the first film biography of Ronald Reagan in which his family agreed to appear.

Several themes emerge in the telling of the story. One is that Reagan was so often underestimated. Who would have ever thought that a movie star could twice be elected governor of our largest state, let alone twice be elected President? Another theme is the extent of his religious conviction, beginning in boyhood.

Never in the history of the country had there been a President with his background. There had been lawyers aplenty, farmers, teachers, soldiers, but never an actor—which left a lot of people wondering. Asked once near the end of his second term if he had learned anything as an actor that was of use to him in the presidency, he replied, "There have been times . . . when I have wondered how you could do the job if you hadn't been an actor."

As a movie star, Ronald Reagan nearly always played the hero—a good-looking, likable fellow who stood for all the old American virtues of honesty, courage and big-hearted optimism. Then, as governor and as President, Ronald Reagan showed that in the real-life drama of politics he was no celluloid contrivance. That he responded as he did after the attempt on his life probably did more than anything could have to verify the true, appealing, human substance of the man.

But there was also the limited attention span and the jelly beans—easy subjects for ridicule. His economic theories struck many as zany. But to millions of Americans, the greatest worry was Reagan's headlong, militant anti-Communism.

Of his virtues it could also be said that he never bragged about himself, never whined and never lost faith in American strength and creativity. As no President since FDR, he demonstrated the power of fixed objectives in combination with extraordinary charm. And he was perceived as lucky—no small attribute in a leader.

Whether it was the decisions he made that brought on the end of the Cold War, or whether it was his luck to have been in office as history played itself out, are questions that will be debated for years to come. But there is no question that he wanted to end the Cold War. He took advantage of opportunities when they came, he spent a staggering sum, and the Cold War did end.

— West Tisbury, Massachusetts
January 1998

In Search of Ronald Reagan

Austin Hoyt
Executive Producer, "Reagan"

The idea of doing a biography on Ronald Reagan for *The American Experience* was that of Peter McGhee, Vice President for National Productions at WGBH. The decision was made in 1994. Reagan had been out of office only five years. The dust of history was far from settled. But Peter saw a rare opportunity to make, not just chronicle, history—to embark on a journey in search of Ronald Reagan the man, and the meaning of the Reagan presidency.

I had met Ronald Reagan thirty years ago, in December 1967, at the front door of Yale's Timothy Dwight College, where he had come to speak to the students. I was there to document the encounter for the Public Broadcast Laboratory's "PBL" program, the precursor of PBS. In response to campus animosity, the college master had posted a notice asking students to "remember he was a guest of the college and to comport themselves accordingly. But," he added, "this does not imply any surrender of our convictions." For four days, students badgered Governor Reagan mercilessly over his backing of the Vietnam War and lukewarm endorsement of civil rights. I was pleased they pushed him so hard. It would make for better television. *The New York Times* headline was, "Reagan Keeps Smiling at Yale Despite Sneers and Hostile Air."

At the end of the week, addressing Reagan at a forum at the law school, a student tried a knockout punch. "Yesterday you had lunch with the political science faculty," he began. "One member noted that unlike other public figures you asked no questions or in any other way attempted to learn from these men. Does this mean you are closed to learning, especially from academic experts?" There were murmurs amid the painful silence. "Well, I don't know which member of the luncheon group that was," Reagan responded, "but I would think in all fairness that he might also add that at no time was I free of the questions that had been asked of me, and as a guest, I felt I should answer what was being asked." The auditorium erupted with sustained applause.

Though I would have several encounters with Ronald Reagan after the one at Yale in 1967, that was my introduction to the disarming charm and rhetorical power of Reagan.

The process for *The American Experience* began when my colleague and the author of this volume, Adriana Bosch, contacted the Office of Ronald Reagan in Los Angeles and sent them a copy of the biography of Dwight D. Eisenhower that she and I had done for *The American Experience*. We were informed that President and Mrs. Reagan liked it and would cooperate with us. That was more than flattering. It was crucial. Probably all the people we would contact who had served Reagan when he was governor or President would call his office to find out if the Reagans trusted us. Needless to say, this willingness to cooperate was not contingent upon any right to review our scripts at any stage, nor would we have agreed to any such request.

One of the advantages of producing something so soon after Reagan had left office is that the key participants and eyewitnesses, at least to his presidency, are still alive. One of the risks in a project at this point in time is that people will hold back critical comments of a man who remains enormously popular and who is ill.

We interviewed 51 people on camera—including Mikhail Gorbachev, Margaret Thatcher, even John Barletta, his Secret Service agent at the ranch—and spoke to many more. They gave us a wealth of first-person stories and anecdotes. We were especially lucky to have the cooperation of two biographers who are candid about Reagan's frailties: Edmund Morris, whose own authorized biography of the President is soon to be published, and Lou Cannon, who has written three biographies of Ronald Reagan.

It was a pity that Tip O'Neill, Reagan's adversary as Speaker of the House, was not alive. We turned to Christopher Matthews, O'Neill's press aide, who has remained critical of many of Reagan's policies, although he admires Reagan as a very effective politician. We thought we'd talk to the Russians, his adversaries in the Cold War. They would muss him up a bit. It turns out that very soon after Mikhail Gorbachev met Reagan in Geneva in 1985 he began to like Reagan. This was the word we got in Moscow from Alexander Bessmertnykh and Sergei Tarasenko, high officials in the Foreign Ministry responsible for U.S. affairs on Reagan's watch.

We missed Gorbachev when we were in Moscow, but caught up with him in New York. I was granted half an hour for the interview. Gorbachev's final comment was, "He is really a very big person. A very great political leader, and, well, the rest is up to you."

Indeed it was. So what to make of Ronald Reagan?

His son Ron, who we found to be a very frank, amiable and insightful fellow, warned us, "You're not going to figure him out. That's the first thing you need to know. *I* haven't figured him out. I don't know anybody who has figured him out." Lou Cannon remembered when someone asked Reagan on the eve of his election, "What is it, Governor, that people see in you?" Reagan's response was, "Would you laugh if I told you that they look at me and they see themselves?"

How true my colleague Adriana and I found that to be. People did see in Reagan a reflection of themselves. When I asked Nancy Reagan if Ronald Reagan was at heart a peacemaker or a cold warrior, she replied without hesitation, "Peacemaker, of course." That is how she wanted to see him. George Shultz stressed Reagan's negotiating skills. The Secretary of State believed in negotiations. Sergei Tarasenko of the Soviet Foreign Ministry called Reagan "perhaps the last romantic of his generation." Tarasenko struck me as an incurable romantic. Reagan's speechwriter Tony Dolan, responsible for the "Evil Empire" speech, placed Reagan among America's most intellectual presidents. Dolan is very cerebral. And on it went. The search for Ronald Reagan was not going to be easy.

"Go to the ranch," Edmund Morris urged. "That's where you'll find his soul." He described the ranch house as small and simple, with a fireplace but no central heating. "That's him," Morris said. "The fancy Los Angeles life is Nancy." In the barn at the ranch all the chain saws and pole saws, his brush cutting tools, were lined up in an orderly manner. And the post hole diggers. What impressed me most about the ranch were the fence posts made of telephone poles. Reagan and his sidekicks Dennis Le Blanc and Barney Barnett sawed all the posts, lined them up, and dug all the holes. First around the patio, then around the pond, then the pasture, and finally they tackled the orchard. That was a lot of digging, sawing and aligning. And those fences are a beautiful sight. Reagan, Dennis told me, would never ask anyone to do something he would not do himself. That tells you something of the man.

And what about the woman behind the man? Nancy was at the ranch when we arrived. She had arranged to have Dennis show us around. Dennis was one of the elite of the California Highway Patrol who trained with the Secret Service and was detailed to protect Governor Reagan. He is a big handsome guy who I imagine would be difficult to push around. Dennis was with us when we were filming on the back forty. A Secret Service agent drove up—a beefy guy who looked like Yul Brynner and sported a pistol on his hip. "Dennis," he said, "It's supper time. Rainbow wants you at the ranch house," referring to Nancy by her code name (the President's is "Rawhide"). Of course Nancy was his boss, but still, I've never seen a guy disappear so fast. That was my first glimpse of the power of Nancy Reagan.

Nancy consented to an interview, the first she had given since she left the White House. There was a lot she did not want to talk about, which is her right, but we were pleased with some of her anecdotes which we could not have gotten from anyone else. Later, she felt she had not done well on camera and wanted very much to redo the interview. We disagreed and when she relented her last words were, "I just want to do what's right for Ronnie."

We learned, in the making of the film, of Reagan's disgust with a drunken father, how as a child of an alcoholic, he learned to shut out the unpleasant—the explanation, perhaps, to why he denied for so long that he traded arms to Iran for hostages. He found solace in his mother's church, the Disciples of Christ. He was a lifeguard on the Rock River in the summers as a student, and his subsequent political life, as Edmund Morris told us, was devoted to the general theme of rescue. As an actor and later as President, he needed to be engaged as a performer in a production. He saw himself once on a television monitor and said, "Oh, there he is." He often found it hard to distinguish fantasy from reality. From a childhood of adversity he forged a determined character. Beneath the affable exterior, his long time advisor Martin Anderson observed, is "a solid steel tempered bar."

That gives a glimpse of the man. But what about the President?

Reagan was nearly 70 when he was inaugurated, the oldest President in American history. For the previous twenty years, ever since Eisenhower, the presidency of every one of his predecessors had ended in failure. Many pundits felt the office was unmanageable, too much for anyone to handle, much less an actor turned president. And the problems which America faced when Reagan came into office in January 1981 were enormous: an economy in shambles, an emboldened Soviet adversary and a crisis of self-confidence.

Reagan had little use for the details of government, tended to over-delegate and grew increasingly disengaged. But he almost always rose to the occasion and pursued his ideals with great determination.

Through the force of his rhetoric and his capable staff, Reagan pushed through Congress his conservative program—cuts in taxes and domestic spending and a military buildup, winning what he called "the biggest political victory in half a century." He saw the nation through its worst recession since the Great Depression and then through its greatest economic expansion in peacetime history. But he failed to curb the growth of government, leaving behind a trillion-dollar budget and a huge deficit. Under Ronald Reagan, for the first time in the twentieth century the United States became a debtor nation.

He succeeded in reviving the American spirit. Edmund Morris puts it well: "He rescued America from a period of poisonous self doubt." When he left the White House in 1989, he was one of the most popular Presidents in history.

The passion of his lifetime, ever since he battled Communists in Hollywood as a member of the Screen Actors Guild, was a hatred of Communism and the Soviet Union. I don't think he had a master plan to bring down the Soviet Union. But he did sense, as he told Lou Cannon and others at *The Washington Post* during the Republican primary in 1980, that his proposed defense buildup would not accelerate the arms race because the Soviet Union would not be able to compete. He seems to have had an uncanny intuition on this. His declared policy was to build up America's defenses and then negotiate from a position of strength. It came as a surprise to me to learn how much Reagan abhorred nuclear weapons and wanted to eliminate their threat. But Administration insiders told us he wanted more than to negotiate arms reductions. He wanted to win the Cold War.

The Soviet Union collapsed on George Bush's watch, but the turning point came on Reagan's. There were actually two turning points. One was when he deployed Pershing and cruise missiles in Western Europe in 1983, thwarting the Soviet Union's efforts to split the NATO alliance. The other was a hastily arranged summit at Reykjavik, Iceland, in 1986 when he refused Gorbachev's demands to limit research on the Strategic Defense Initiative. Reykjavik seemed like a failure at the time, but as Gorbachev told me in New York, their discussions brought them "to the top of the hill and from the top of the hill you can see a long way."

Scholars will debate for decades what role Ronald Reagan played in the end of the Cold War. Many give the primary credit to Gorbachev. I too came to feel that Gorbachev played a major role in ending the Cold War—he lost it. As Anthony Lewis of the *The New York Times* told me, "He lost it gracefully, and how lucky we all are that he did." Gorbachev was intelligent enough to realize the need to reform Communism and to reach a new understanding with the West. But he could not control the reforms he initiated. When they spiraled out of control, the Soviet Union disintegrated.

Ronald Reagan wanted to win the Cold War, he threatened the Soviets with his arms buildup, he supported anti-Communist insurgencies around the world, he committed the CIA to keep Solidarity alive in Poland, and he predicted to the British Parliament that Marxism-Leninism would end up "in the ash heap of history." Poland was freed, the Berlin Wall came down, and the Soviet Union collapsed. Maybe you can't prove a cause-and-effect relationship, but to deny one seems foolish.

To the extent that "Reagan" the film and *Reagan* the book are biographies, it doesn't matter what credit you give him. You understand the man through his commitment. If character is revealed through action, Reagan's determination, his willful optimism, his faith in America and Western ideals are revealed in his battle against big government and Communism, the crusades of his lifetime.

CHAPTER 1

Reagan

On July 4, 1986, Lady Liberty's one-hundredth birthday, Ronald Reagan stood on the deck of the *John F. Kennedy*. As he pushed the button that sent a laser beam across the New York harbor to light the refurbished symbol of the American promise, the skies above erupted in the biggest display of fireworks in history. Midway into his second presidential term, Ronald Reagan was at the height of his popularity. He had become as one with America's great symbol: the embodiment of the nation's most cherished myths.

"He was a man for whom the American dream became a luminous reality," wrote journalist and Reagan biographer Lou Cannon, "the wholesome citizen hero who inhabits our democratic imaginations, an 'Everyman' who was slow to anger, but willing to fight for right, and correct wrongdoing when aroused."[1]

"Reagan was a bit of a mystic," his close aide Lyn Nofziger said, "very much a Christian and very much a man who believes in the Almighty and in a plan that the Almighty may have. And he thought that America was sent here between two oceans for a very specific purpose, which was literally to be a beacon of freedom to the rest of the world."[2]

He had come to office in 1980 to rescue America from, in the words of biographer Edmund Morris, "a period of poisonous self-doubt," to restore the nation's confidence, to demonstrate to Americans that they had a role, a special role of moral leadership in the world, something that they had forgotten in the dark decades of the 1970s and 1960s.[3] When he left office in 1989, he left an America that was militarily stronger, wealthier and more confident.

Yet he also left behind an America saddled with a national debt exceeding $1 trillion, a country in which many social problems remained unsolved or had grown worse, a society that many felt had become less compassionate, and where the gap between rich and poor had widened.

"The sad thing about the Reagan era was, there were cuts in domestic programs but certainly no cuts in government spending enough prevent this enormous growth in deficits . . . to the point now where one of the chief costs of government is paying off the debt that was incurred," Christopher Matthews told *The American Experience*.[4] "I can't tell you what history is going to say 100 years from now about Ronald Reagan's presidency," concurred ABC correspondent Sam Donaldson ," but, if you talk about today, we're still paying for tripling the national debt. We're still paying . . . for what went on during [the Reagan] years."[5] "A hundred years from now, there's no doubt that ending the Cold War will be on Reagan's historical tombstone," countered Richard Norton Smith. "We'll forget the change of the mood of the country. We'll forget the economic indices of the Reagan era. But we will remember that he ended a forty-year nightmare, in which a mushroom cloud loomed over all of our heads."[6] "If you seek his monument, look for what we don't see," George Will added eloquently. "We don't see the Berlin Wall. We don't see "the iron curtain from Stetin to Trieste."[7]

The only actor ever to become President, Ronald Reagan rose in politics through the power of his rhetoric, bursting onto the political scene in 1964 with a speech on behalf of conservative Republican Barry Goldwater. The "Great Communicator," Reagan used the presidency as a place of moral leadership, a "bully pulpit" to mobilize the American people with his unwavering optimism, and to convert them to his own convictions—his aversion to big government, and his hatred of Communism. But this most ideological of Presidents was also a pragmatist, a skillful politician who understood the value of compromise. Chief of Staff James Baker told *The American Experience*, "President Reagan wanted to succeed and he knew that to succeed in politics, particularly with a Democratic Congress, he would have to compromise. He said to me many times, 'I would much prefer to get 80 percent of what I want than to go off the cliff with the flag flying.'"[8]

Ronald Reagan was indeed a man of paradoxes, a mystery that has yet to be unraveled despite the efforts of scores of aides, biographers, even his own family. As his son Ron told us, "I haven't figured him out, I don't know anybody who has figured him out."[9]

He was an idealist who believed in America's inherent goodness, in freedom and its ultimate triumph. Yet sometimes he acted with the expediency of a Machiavelli. Under the "Reagan Doctrine," he confronted Communism throughout the world, aiding dictators and democrats, Islamic fundamentalists and African warlords, faithful to the timeless maxim that "the enemy of my enemy is my friend."[10]

He cut the benefits of millions and watched Americans suffer through the hardest economic times since the Great Depression, yet he would respond compassionately to the hardship of individuals by writing them personal checks from the Oval Office.

He called the Soviet Union "the focus of evil," but negotiated arms reductions agreements with its leaders. He abhorred nuclear weapons, but built them by the thousands. He repeatedly stated that "a nuclear war cannot be won and must be fought," but took the world to the brink by deploying Pershing missiles in Europe in the fall of 1983, scaring millions worldwide including the founder of Physicians for Social Responsibility, Dr. Helen Caldicott, who feared that "Reagan could push the [nuclear] button."[11]

He seldom went to church, but was deeply religious—he had faith in the power of prayer and believed that the hand of God determines human events. He believed in Armageddon—the inevitable and final confrontation between good and evil—yet an incurable optimist, he did everything in his power to try to prevent it. He preached family values, but was himself a detached father who failed to reach his children.[12]

Reagan was not a learned man. His lack of command of factual details—even on important issues—and frequent "gaffes" —misstatements or factual errors—lead many to think that he was not intelligent. But as his aides report, he had a formidable memory, and an uncanny ability to listen to a debate, reducing issues to their essence and formulating them in terms that were simple and crystal clear. "This guy was very smart," Reagan's advisor Martin Anderson told *The American Experience*. "And there's one piece of hard evidence if anyone disbelieves that. We have here in the archives of the Hoover Institution some handwritten drafts of major speeches that Ronald Reagan wrote all by himself. Ask any intellectual, the real test of how well a person thinks or how much you know, or how you can assimilate and put together information is to sit down with a blank piece of paper and a black pen and write it yourself in your own hand. Try it. That is really a very powerful test of overall intelligence. And the record has survived."[13]

"Reagan was certainly smart enough to be President," Lou Cannon concluded, "and his temperament was ideally suited to the job. He didn't rattle, he could shut out the clamor . . . shut out what was going on around him and focus at the business at hand. . . . That's a big thing if you are in that Oval Office."[14]

He was gentlemanly and considerate, but he was also tough and determined, and as many an adversary discovered, a formidable foe. Columnist George Will told *The American Experience*, "the stricken fields of American politics are littered with the bleached bones of those who underestimated Ronald Reagan."[15]

Mostly he is remembered as simple, aging President, whose humor and charm captivated much of America. Less known is the younger man: the fast-talking, quick and aggressive conservative governor and candidate, whose mind, in the words of a biographer, "worked like clockwork."

Tip O'Neill's aide Christopher Matthews, who met Reagan in the early days of his presidency when he still had most his old vigor, recalls him as "tough and confrontational, feisty and streetwise, . . . more like James Cagney than Jimmy Stewart."[16] Martin Anderson best described him as a "nice soft silky pillow, . . . but if you took a hard punch, you would find in the middle a solid tempered steel bar. That was the real Ronald Reagan. That was the essence of Ronald Reagan."[17]

This essence, which Reagan biographer Edmund Morris has called Reagan's "atman"—a Hindu term meaning a strong inner core—was forged against the adversity of a poor, nomadic and isolated childhood, a childhood which began in the plains of rural western Illinois, where Reagan spent the first years of his life.

NOTES

[1] Lou Cannon, *Role of a Lifetime* (California Journal Press, 1991), pp. 32–34.

[2] Lyn Nofziger, Interview with Author.

[3] Richard Norton Smith, Interview with Author.

[4] Christopher Matthews, Interview with Author.

[5] Sam Donaldson, Interview with Author. Though the budget deficit has been brought under control, the national debt arising from the accumulation of deficits during the 1980s has yet to be paid.

[6] Richard Norton Smith, Interview with Author.

[7] George Will, Interview with Author. The reference is to Winston Churchill's famous "Iron Curtain" speech at Fulton College, Missouri, in May 1946.

[8] James Baker III, Interview with Author.

[9] Ronald Prescott Reagan, Interview with Austin Hoyt.

[10] Henry Kissinger, *Diplomacy* (New York: Touchstone, 1995), p. 774.

[11] Helen Caldicott, Interview with Austin Hoyt.

[12] Ronald Prescott Reagan, Interview with Author.

[13] Martin Anderson, Interview with Author.

[14] Lou Cannon, Interview with Author.

[15] George Wills, Interview with Author.

[16] Christopher Matthews, Interview with Author.

[17] Martin Anderson, Interview with Author.

CHAPTER 2

Lifeguard

Ronald Reagan was born in a second-floor apartment on the main and only street of Tampico, Illinois, in such poor circumstances that years later, while visiting his birthplace, he visibly recoiled.[1]

It was 1911, the year the first studio opened in Hollywood and six years before America would fight its first world war. "Dutch," as the young Reagan was called, was the second son of Nelle and Jack Reagan. She was a pious Protestant of Scottish descent, he a second-generation Irish Catholic who suffered from what in those days was politely referred to as "a deep thirst."

"My dad was destined by God, I think, to be a salesman," Reagan wrote of Jack:

> He was endowed with the gift of blarney and the charm of a leprechaun. No one I ever met could tell a story better than he could. . . . My mother was a small woman with auburn hair and a sense of optimism as deep as the Cosmos, who raised me to believe that God has a plan for everyone and that everything happens for a purpose. . . . From him I learned the value of hard work and ambition, and maybe a little something about telling a story. From her, I learned the value of prayer, how to have dreams and believe I could make them come true. . . . While he was filled with dreams of making something of himself, she had a drive to help my brother [Neil] and me make something of ourselves."[2]

Jack and Nelle had been married two years when they arrived in Tampico in 1906. Jack had taken a position as a clerk at the local Pitney Store just opening on Main Street. He expected to prosper in Tampico, a shipping center on the Henepin Canal 100 miles northeast of the Mississippi River. But Tampico languished. Jack left, taking Nelle and his sons, three-year-old Dutch and six-year-old Neil, on a restless trek: Chicago 1914, Galesburg 1915, Monmouth 1918, back to Tampico in 1919, and finally to Dixon in 1920. From the age of four to the age of ten, Reagan lived the life of a nomad, every year a new school, a new town, neighbors and friends left behind. The little boy had nowhere to go except within.

"I'm sure that the fact our family moved so often left a mark on me," Reagan admitted in his autobiography:

> I was introverted and probably a little slow in making friends. In some way I think this reluctance to get close to people never left me completely. . . . I've never had trouble making friends, but I've been inclined to hold back a little of myself, reserving it to myself.[3]

Lyn Nofziger, a long time aide who describes himself "the last of the living Reaganites," observed: "There always seemed to be a kind of a veil between Reagan and the rest of the world. Not obvious or anything, but you kind of didn't get that last quarter-of-an-inch through there."[4]

Reagan treated everyone with equal kindness and friendliness, and no one had a special claim on him, not his closest advisor, not even his own children.

"He's a real gentleman," his son Ron told *The American Experience*,

[He] really does treat everybody, everybody the same way. With the same kindness and the same generosity. Now that's a good thing on one hand, if you're anybody. On the other hand, if you're a member of his family and you realize that you're being treated exactly the same way as the guy who just filled up your gas tank, you begin to wonder well, you know, what makes us special to you?[5]

Michael Deaver, who dedicated most of his adult life to the service of the Reagans, echoed Ron's observation:

He is kind to everybody; he treats everybody the same way. I don't think that it would make any difference if you were Queen Elizabeth or you were the gardener. Ronald Reagan would treat you the same. But . . . there are not a lot of people to get past that original kindness or warmth.[6]

"He's a friendly man who has one friend and he married her," added columnist George Will, who befriended the Reagans in Washington. "But beyond that to look for a second real friend, the kind of person he might open up to, I don't know who it would be."[7]

If there were other scars from the dark days of Reagan's early life, we did not find them. Never fond of introspection, Reagan's own childhood memories depict a mostly happy time. He wrote of the gaslit sidewalks of Chicago alive with people, of eggs and butterflies encased in a naturalists' attic, of Sunday family drives, of ice-skating in the cold wind, and of a summer spent in what he called a "Tom Sawyer–Huck Finn idyll," swimming in clear-bottom creeks and treacherous canals, hunting and fishing. "Those were the days were I learned the riches of rags."[8]

Even as small boy, Reagan, in the words George Will, "had a talent for happiness."[9] Biographer Edmund Morris observed that Reagan always thought of himself as Tom Sawyer, "a barefoot boy with a straw between his teeth and too much time on his hands, but the ugliness of Huck Finn's life, that's something he could not identify with." Richard Norton Smith, a former director of the Reagan Library, characterized this quality as "willful optimism," adding that,

> It's a paradox that the Reagan presidency is thought of as a paragon of old-fashioned, small-town, patriotic, flag-waving values—the epitome of what didn't exist for Reagan himself in his nomadic boyhood. Perhaps he spent the rest of his life imagining and inhabiting an America that he didn't really experience as a boy.[10]

Dutch was almost ten years old when the family finally settled down in Dixon, a town of 8,000 inhabitants, nineteen miles away from Tampico and about 100 miles west of Chicago. The town offered two main attractions, the Rock River and the Dixon Arch, built to commemorate the end of WWI. Each year, the town's three war veterans marched underneath it.

Dixon was a typical midwestern farm community. Local dairy farms supplied the Borden Milk Company, and farmers brought their corn and wheat to to be shipped from there to Chicago, Omaha and down South. On Saturday nights people gathered downtown to shop and talk.

Dixon prided itself on being the backbone of the country: "Main Street" America. Reagan would always regard Dixon as his home town, "a small universe where I learned standards and values that would guide me for the rest of my life. It was in Dixon where I really found myself."[11]

Nineteen twenty-two, the year the Reagans arrived in Dixon, was a time of progress and opportunity, "the Roaring Twenties," but also a time when many Americans clung to the 19th-century values of piety and rugged individualism, the old values of the nation, made more precious because they were beginning to be eclipsed by industrialization and the growth of cities.[12]

In the midst of the prosperity, even Jack Reagan found his break. After years as a salesman, he became manager and part-owner of "The Fashion Boot Shop." The shop advertised itself as being on the cutting edge of podiatry. Certainly no other shoe store in Dixon boasted a state-of-the-art X-ray machine or as a handsome proprietor who held forth with his good cheer and endless repertory of jokes and stories. But prosperity eluded Jack. Dixonians were conservative and mostly poor; the town was hardly the place to make a fortune selling shoes. And then there was "the black curse." Prohibition notwithstanding, Jack managed frequent detours to the local speakeasy, where he would binge on near-beer and moonshine whiskey.

Reagan's first encounter with his father's alcoholism came in early adolescence, a defining age for any young man. When he wrote about it in 1965, he referred to it as "a turning point . . . the moment of accepting responsibility."

I was eleven years old the first time I came home to find my father flat on his back on the front porch. . . . He was drunk, dead to the world. I stood over him for a minute or two. I wanted to let myself in the house and go to bed and pretend he wasn't there. [I saw his] arms spread out as if he were crucified, his hair soaked with melting snow. When I tried to waken him he just snored loud enough, I suspected, for the neighborhood to hear. . . . I bent over him, smelling the sharp odor of the whiskey from the speakeasy. I got a fistful of his overcoat. Opening the door I managed to drag him inside and get him to bed.[13]

Later in life, whenever Reagan spoke of his father, on the rare occasions he did, he could barely hide the contempt he felt. "The moral disdain behind what he would say was quite palpable," recalled Edmund Morris. "He thought of his father as a man with a weakness, who should have been strong enough to conquer it."[14]

Perhaps, as historian Robert Dallek has suggested, Reagan embraced the values of autonomy, independence and freedom—concepts that became the core of his political ideology—in reaction to his father's dependency on alcohol.[15] More immediately, however, Jack's alcoholism brought the young Reagan closer to his mother and to her church, the Disciples of Christ.

Nelle was remembered as "a lovely Christian lady who devoted all her life to helping other people."[16] Helen Lawton, her neighbor in Dixon, still remembers her bringing apples, crackers and the Bible to prisoners in the local jail.

Nelle staged morality plays, cautionary tales in which good battled and triumphed over evil. "Dutch" frequently performed in them, and learned to love the theater. As her son's age of consent approached, she helped him prepare for baptism. She gave him a book, *That Printer of Udells*, which Reagan later described to Edmund Morris as "the most important book he ever read."

It is the story of a young Christian man born in a rather ugly industrial midwestern town, who discovers through a series of bitter experiences with an alcoholic father that he has got the gift of oratory. He is able to inspire young people in the town toward good works. He always wears a brown suit. And through his good looks and his voice and his convictions he manages to create a whole social movement in this town. And at the end of the book, the young man, Dick Faulkner, goes off to Washington to take his message to the world. The message he takes to the world is that of practical Christianity. Independence, charity beginning at home, self-reliance, decency, fidelity, the sanctity of human Christian relationships, marriage, motherhood, parentage. All these simple beliefs instilled themselves in the young Ronald Reagan. He went to his mother when he finished that book, and he said, 'I want to be like that man.' So when he talked to me about *That Printer of Udells* he was talking about his religious crux. And I think in the Oval Office, sitting there in that brown suit, he was that young man that he'd read about all those years before.[17]

The Disciples of Christ Church was a religion based on the notion of practical Christianity. Followers like Nelle firmly believed in good works, the Bible, and that the hand of God guides human life.

The Disciples of Christ were Christians of the world, of the community. They believed in going out and behaving in a Christ-like Christian passion. It was not a spiritual transcendental religion, it was not intellectual. I don't think at any time in his life Reagan ever pondered the larger questions of human existence. His religion was that of a man who felt that he could make life better for his village, his town, his state, his country, by just behaving like a decent Christian.[18]

Reagan imbibed deeply from his mother's faith. Those closest to him attest to his spirituality, and his strong belief in predestination and the power of prayer. "He always believed that whatever happens it's for a reason," remembers his daughter Maureen, "and he has always been able to reach down inside and pull out a belief in a Supreme Being that has been able to get him through some of the hardest times."[19]

Reagan wrote of his own religious convictions:

> I've always believed that we were, each of us, put here for a reason. That there is a plan, a divine plan for all of us. In an effort to embrace that plan, we are blessed with the special gift of prayer, the happiness and solace to be gained by talking to the Lord.[20]

Reagan's adolescent life was anchored in his mother's church. He attended prayer meetings, taught Sunday school, continued to act in his mother's morality plays and in 1926 led an Easter service. He became, in the words of biographer and Reagan critic George Will, "as close to being a minister's kid as one can be without actually moving into the rectory."[21] He even dated the minister's daughter, Margaret "Mugs" Cleaver, a relationship that further deepened the rift between Reagan and his father. The Disciples of Christ advocated temperance, and Margaret strongly disapproved of drinking. Reagan lived in perpetual fear of the shame that his father's "dark curse" could bring on the family. He confronted Jack. Should he ever be drunk in front of Margaret or embarrass him any way, he told his father, he would never speak to him again.[22]

"Dutch" had found himself. By age fourteen, he had matured from a scrappy boy to a handsome, athletic young man. Determined to live the storybook life of an American youth, he played varsity football, was captain of the swim team and always had the lead in school dramas. In high school he was elected class president and school president.

He also wrote poetry and short stories, including one titled "Meditations of a Lifeguard":

> She's walking toward the dock now. She tips grace-fully over to the edge of the crowded pier and settles like a butterfly. The lifeguard strolls by, turns and strolls by again. Then he settles in the immediate region of the cause of all this sudden awakening. He assumes a manly worried expression, designed to touch the heart of any blonde, brunette or unclassified female. He has done all that is necessary. She speaks, and the sound of her voice is like balm to a wounded soul . . . .

Reagan was writing about himself. For seven consecutive summers beginning with high school and through his last year in college, "Dutch" Reagan was the lifeguard at Lowell Park, the local swimming hole two miles upstream from Dixon, on the Rock River.

On a summer afternoon, Lowell Park has a tranquil feel. The grassy shores slope gently into the slow flowing river, now vacant and dirty. Reagan's old lifeguard chair still stands as a lonesome remnant of a time long past, when the clear rushing waters were crowded with hundreds of swimmers escaping the searing heat of the midwestern plain. Above them all stood the ever vigilant "Dutch" Reagan.

Edmund Morris believes the Rock River was the central symbol of Reagan's youth. "'The Rock River flows for you tonight, Mr. President.' It was something a radio announcer said to him after he was elected. It came over the airwaves. I've never forgotten that. 'The Rock River flows for you tonight, Mr. President.'"[23]

Ronald Reagan would have many careers—actor, governor, president, but it was at Lowell Park where he first discovered the role he came to love best—hero.

Neighbor Helen Lawton still gets a glint in her eye when she reminisces about Reagan "walking up and down the ramp, handsome and bronzed, with his lifeguard sign on his swimsuit and a whistle around his neck."[24]

The job was not all glamour. Every morning at dawn Reagan trekked to the home of the Graybills, the family who owned the concession at Lowell Park. He took their van to pick up a 300-pound block of ice, then drove to get hamburgers and supplies for the foodstand. For as many as twelve hours a day, Reagan watched swimmers negotiate the currents of the Rock River. During his seven summers at Lowell Park, Reagan, an excellent swimmer and zealous lifeguard, pulled 77 people from the treacherous waters. He kept a record by cutting notches in a log. Dr. Lamar Wells, Reagan's Sunday school pupil, testified to the accuracy of the record. "Seventy-seven was his count, and there were 77 notches in the log out there," he told *The American Experience*.[25]

Years later, the log was carried away by the river current. But the memory remained.

> The poignant thing about the Rock River is that in his dotage, after he left the White House, when he began to lose his mind, the one thing he would still want to talk about was his days as a lifeguard on the Rock River. He had a picture in his office of the spot where he used to stand as a boy, and he would take all his visitors up to this picture and he would say, "You see, that's where I used to be a lifeguard. I saved 77 lives there."[26]

"Reagan's subsequent career," concluded Edmund Morris, "his political career, was dedicated to the general theme of rescue."

NOTES

[1] Conversation between Edmund Morris, Josh Clark and Austin Hoyt.

[2] Ronald Reagan, *An American Life* (New York: Simon and Schuster, 1990) p. 21–23

[3] *Ibid*, p.31

[4] Lyn Nofziger, Interview with Author.

[5] Ronald Prescott Reagan, Interview with Austin Hoyt.

[6] Michael Deaver, Interview with Author.

[7] George Will, Interview with Author.

[8] Ronald Reagan, *Where's the Rest of Me* (New York: Dell, 1981), p. 13.

[9] George F. Wills, Interview with Author.

[10] Richard Norton Smith, Interview with Author.

[11] Ronald Reagan, *Where's the Rest of Me,* p. 27 and *An American Life*, p. 26.

[12] Robert Dallek, Interview with Author.

[13] Ronald Reagan, *Where's The Rest of Me*, p. 7.

[14] Edmund Morris, Interview with Author.

[15] Robert Dallek, Interview with Author.

[16] Helen Lawton, Interview with Author.

[17] Edmund Morris, Interview with Author.

[18] Edmund Morris, Interview with Author.

[19] Maureen Reagan, Interview with Author.

[20] Ronald Reagan, Quoted in Patti Davis, *Angels Don't Die: My Father's Gift Of Faith* (New York: Harper Collins, 1995), p. ix.

[21] Gary Wills, *Reagan's America*. (New York: Penguin Books, 1988), p.22.

[22] Ronald Prescott Reagan, Interview with Austin Hoyt.

[23] Edmund Morris, Interview with Author.

[24] Helen Lawton, Interview with Josh Clark.

[25] Dr. Lamar Welles, Interview with Josh Clark.

[26] Edmund Morris, Interview with Author.

CHAPTER 3

The World of Make-Believe

In 1928, Ronald Reagan attended Eureka College, a school of 220 students run by the Disciples of Christ. It was also the school where his girlfriend Margaret Cleaver was enrolled.

Only 2 percent of Americans went to college in those years, and Reagan would always look at higher education as a great privilege. In 1980, during a campaign appearance at his old college, Reagan waxed poetically: "Everything good that happened to me—everything—started here on this campus."[1]

Reagan did it all at Eureka. He was reporter for the school paper; president of the Booster Club; he played varsity football for three years; he was head cheerleader for the basketball team; the school's number-one swimmer; feature editor of the school yearbook, a member of the student senate for two years; and president for one.[2]

His many extracurricular activities and his romance with "Mugs" Cleaver left little time for study, and he relied on his memory to get through his courses. "I majored in sociology and economics," he would later say of his experience at Eureka. "I got poor marks, [but] I copped the lead in most plays. And in football I won three varsity sweaters."[3]

As a freshman, he got a chance to test his eloquence during a student strike. Though he was, by his own admission, "far from a ringleader," on one crucial motion he mounted the lectern, moving with his own words the students and even faculty to approve it by acclamation. "Hell," he later wrote, "with two more lines I would have had them riding through 'every Middlesex village and farm without horses yet.' . . . It was heady wine."[4]

Reagan graduated from Eureka in 1932. It was the depths of the Great Depression, and 13 million Americans—25 percent of the adult population—were out of work.[5]

Later, when in the second year of his presidency the nation plunged into recession, Reagan never tired of telling the hardship the Reagan family had endured through the tough times of the Great Depression. No doubt their experience mirrored that of many Americans at the time. But for the Reagans recovery came sooner than for most. Even through the Dust Bowl years of the mid-1930s, Reagan was able to rescue his family from misery.

In the fall of 1932, Reagan headed to Chicago to look for a job in radio—his sights set high on a career in the dominant entertainment medium of the day. For four or five days, he knocked in vain on the doors of major radio stations, but broadcasters were disinclined to take a chance on the inexperienced twenty-one-year-old. He headed west, and kept knocking on doors, no matter how rural the town or how small the radio station. In February, "Dutch" got his first job, at WOC (World of Chiropractic) Radio in Davenport, as a sportscaster and staff announcer. His salary, $100 per month, was a fortune in 1932.

That spring, Reagan was promoted to WHO in Des Moines, Iowa, NBC's main radio station broadcasting to what Reagan called the "solar plexus of the country."[6] One hundred and fifty miles west of the Dixon of his youth, Ronald Reagan was saying goodbye to his town, his church, and even his high school sweetheart and fiancée "Mugs" Cleaver. On a trip to Europe she met an attorney and decided to marry him. If Reagan was hurt by Cleaver's rejection, he never let on. "As our lives traveled in diverging paths," he later wrote, "our lovely and wholesome relationship did not survive growing up."[7]

In Des Moines his salary tripled to $75 dollars per week, "big money in those days," and "Dutch" led the enviable life of a popular bachelor. He found a job for his older brother Neil and brought Nelle on frequent visits. At a nearby military academy, he learned to ride horses. Not long after, Reagan bought his first car, a beige Nash convertible. Handsome and well-dressed, he had his pick of the most eligible women and was welcome at Des Moines's most fashionable establishments. Neither a drinker, nor a gambler he was able to save money and to send some home. Only in his early twenties, he had already become the main breadwinner for his family back in Dixon.

"Those were wonderful days," he later wrote. "I was one of a profession just becoming popular and common—the visualizer for the armchair quarterback."[8]

And visualize he did. For five years, Dutch Reagan, baseball sportscaster for WHO, transported his listeners to the bleachers of Chicago's Wrigley Field and Comiskey Park with his vivid accounts of the Chicago Cubs and Chicago White Sox baseball games. Only Reagan wasn't at the baseball park, but sitting in his booth, back in Des Moines.

> Our baseball games would be broadcast without my even being present at the ball park, thanks to a system known as telegraphic report. In Chicago, in the press box, a telegraph operator would tap out each play. Sitting on the opposite side of a glass window from me in our studios in Davenport, another telegraph operator, hearing this dot and dash, would type out the message, slide it through a slot in the window, and I would translate it into the audible sounds of baseball.[9]

"I think that was a very good training ground for him," said one of Reagan's biographers, Lou Cannon. "Because if you look at where Reagan is really a master communicator, it is on radio. If you think about Reagan's career as an actor and as President and as a speaker, just generally, he was a powerful recreator. He recreated our experiences. Reagan was really best when he was recreating something."[10]

One of Reagan's favorite anecdotes, which sheds light on Reagan's imaginative prowess, took place during a Cubs game, and might have saved his budding career. While Reagan still relied on telegraph notes passed to him by his partner "Curly," at least half a dozen broadcasters were actually at the ball game and could call the plays as they happened on the field. Reagan, as he himself remembered, was usually half a pitch behind, and one mistake short of disaster. Years later, he could still vividly recall how he got out of a tight spot during a broadcast of a Chicago Cubs game:

> On this summer day the Cubs and Saint Louis [Cardinals] were locked in a scoreless tie: Dizzy Dean on the mound, Augie Galan at bat for the Cubs in the ninth inning. I saw Curly start to type so I finished the windup and had Dean send the ball on its way to the plate, took the slip from Curly, and found myself faced with the terse note: The wire has gone dead. I had a ball on the way to the plate and there was no way to call it back. At the same time, I was convinced that a ball game tied up in the ninth inning was no time to tell my audience we had lost contact with the game. . . . I knew of only one thing that wouldn't get in the score column and betray me—a foul ball. So I had Augie foul this pitch down the left field foul line. I looked expectantly at Curly. He shrugged helplessly, so I had Augie foul another one, and still another; then he fouled one back into the box seats. I described in detail the redheaded

kid who had scrambled and gotten the souvenir ball. He fouled one into the open deck that just missed a home run. He fouled for six minutes and forty-five seconds until I lost count. I began to be frightened that maybe I was establishing a new world record for a fellow staying at bat hitting fouls, and this could betray me. Yet I was into it so far I didn't dare reveal that the wire had gone dead. My voice was rising in pitch and threatening to crack—and then, bless him, Curly started typing. I clutched at the slip. It said: 'Galan popped out on the first ball pitched.'[11]

Ronald Reagan's talents as a recreator paid off handsomely. After 600 games, broadcast to millions across seven midwestern states, he had become a celebrity. Years later Hugh Sidey, presidential correspondent for *Time* magazine and a fellow midwesterner, shared his childhood recollections of Ronald Reagan with biographer Edmund Morris:

I remember Hugh Sidey telling me that when he was a child in Iowa in the '30s in the Dust Bowl years, he used to hear Ronald Reagan's voice coming over the airwaves—just doing baseball commentary—but he said there was something about that voice that gave me as a child the feeling that life was going to get better. He said, I don't know what it was, but there was something about the voice. So fundamentally first and foremost, Reagan was a voice. When I tried to explain that voice I always think of the phosphorus samples you see in jars, in chemistry when you're at school. That soft fuzziness, which is not dry. A softness on the edge and the outside, but if you slice it inside, there's this crosscut of silvery sheen, solidity.[12]

By then, "Dutch" Reagan was looking beyond Des Moines. "The town," wrote Anne Edwards, a Reagan biographer, "had caught Hollywood fever when film promoters came through shooting screen tests for possible future movie stars."[13]

"Dutch" Reagan, had also caught the fever but he was not about to take chances, and waited for the right opportunity to go to Hollywood. Arguing that a close acquaintance with the Chicago Cubs would fill him "with color and atmosphere for the coming baseball season," he convinced his bosses at WHO to let him join the Chicago Cubs at Catalina Island off the Santa Barbara coast for one month of spring training. His secret goal was to take a screen test.

After a month with the Cubs in Catalina, Reagan went to Hollywood for an interview with agent Bill Meiklejohn.

Wearing a beige linen suit and smoking a pipe, Reagan cut a dashing image. "I have another Robert Taylor sitting across from me," Meiklejohn told the Warner Brothers casting director Max Arnow. Perhaps an exaggeration, but close enough to get Reagan a six-month contract earning $200 per week. One requirement was that he drop the nickname "Dutch." Another was that he wear wide-neck shirts and his tie in a windsor knot in order to disguise his broad swimmer's shoulders. The thick myopic glasses he'd worn since childhood would have to be replaced by contact lenses.

When Reagan reported for duty at Warner Brothers in June 1937, he entered a complete and self-contained world—a world of make-believe.

Reagan later recalled the moment he stepped onto the set of his first film "Love is on the Air." "I was . . . surrounded by a wall of light (which) gave me a feeling of privacy that completely dispelled any nervousness I might have expected."

Reagan came to Hollywood at the height of the "studio system." Actors would sign contracts with major studios and be paid a salary to work exclusively for a given studio for a number of years.

> The studio system was wonderful for actors, especially actors starting out. They were guaranteed a paycheck. They were taught their craft. . . . Those that would climb the ladder climbed the ladder and those that didn't didn't.[14]

As *The American Experience* learned from biographers Edmund Morris, Lou Cannon and Robert Dallek, the studio system proved ideally suited to Reagan's character and temperament.

> He loved the studio system . . . . He loved being looked after. . . . Reagan has always liked to be looked after. He likes to have a Jack Warner in charge of the finances. He likes to have a wardrobe mistress and a supporting cast. He likes to be surrounded by the business of a great commercial enterprise. And that's where I think Ronald Reagan became a corporate person. Mr. General Electric was born in 1937 at Warner Brothers.[15]

> He was very much a corporate man. . . . He prided himself on a kind of fantasy world in which he identified himself with old-fashioned rugged individualism, sort of a western cowboy, one might say, the tough-minded American whose spoke his mind, who is independent . . . But in his own life, he was very much the product of a corporate America, of the studio system in Hollywood.[16]

He was the ultimate company man. He did these "B" films. Reagan used to say, "They didn't want them good, they want them Tuesday." He was perfect for this kind of movie production. First of all, these were, even by the standard of the day, let alone by modern standards, very low-budget films. They were produced on a very, very heavy schedule. Reagan was a good memorizer. He memorized his lines. He was very quick at memorization, so he didn't have to go over it scene after scene after he had messed up his lines. He worked hard, he showed up on time, he didn't drink, he didn't smoke. . . . He was a Boy Scout.[17]

In his first three years at Warner, Reagan made twenty "B" movies. He was private investigator, Brass Bancroft, who uncovered criminal money rings as well as Nazi infiltrators. "I fought in prisons. . . . I fought in a dirigible down at sea. . . . I fought in an airplane. . . . I swam with bullets hitting the water six inches from my face. . . . I even let them shoot a bottle out of my hand with a sling shot." He became, in his own words, "the Errol Flynn of the B's . . . as brave as Errol, but in a low-budget fashion."[18]

Historian Robert Dallek noted that Reagan loved the hero's role because he fantasized about himself as a heroic figure. It was a role that came very naturally to the young actor from the midwest.

The first time his mother sees him in the first film he plays in, she looks at the screen and she says, "That's my Dutch," and what she's speaking to is the idea that he's himself on the screen, that he's in a sense playing out the fantasy that he has, that he's very comfortable with.[19]

In his Hollywood career Ronald Reagan would make more than fifty films. Only once, in the last film he ever made, did he play the villain.[20]

Though he never rose to the stature of an Errol Flynn or a James Cagney at Warner Brothers, Reagan showed early promise as an actor. Fan mail was coming in; not an overwhelming amount, but enough to assure the studio that he had potential.[21] In 1940, the Audience Research Institute examined the marquee value of sixty newcomers and predicted that within three years Reagan would be among the top ten.[22]

He was soon earning $1,000 a week. He brought Nelle and Jack to California and bought them a home—the first one Reagan's parents ever owned. Neil also came to California in the 1940s, eventually becoming a prominent figure in the world of advertising.

As it suited an up-and-coming player, Reagan married Jane Wyman, his leading lady in the film "Brother Rat." A blonde with a perky attitude and "a button nose," Wyman had been cast in light comedy roles which hid her intensity, her ambition, and her commitment to acting. "She was first and foremost a career woman," said daughter Maureen Reagan, born in 1941, a year after the couple's marriage. Wyman, whose real name was Sarah Jane Fulks, had started her acting career 'hoofing it on the line' as a chorus girl at Paramount.[23] If Reagan was secure and content, Wyman was driven and suspicious. Already once divorced, she was also far more "street-smart" than her husband.

"I went around all the time with a mild form of hate eating into me," Hollywood biographer Ann Edwards quoted Wyman as saying, "I was constantly on the alert . . . for signs that someone was trying to spoil my job for me. I suspected the hairdresser for trying to ruin my looks . . . a press agent for trying to make me look silly in print . . . [but] I trusted Ronnie. For the first time in my life I truly trusted someone."[24]

To those fascinated with the lives of stars the Wyman–
Reagan marriage was a fairy-tale affair. "Reagan had all the
attributes of an American hero," wrote Edwards. "A young man
with ideals who treated women (mother, bride and leading
lady) reverently. The public assumed that the "blonde divorcée
had been redeemed, and what was required for a happy ending
was a stalwart, old-fashioned American husband."[25]

A favorite and frequent feature of fan magazines, Ron and
Jane became the darlings of the Warner Brothers publicity
machine, a valuable asset for an industry preoccupied with pro-
jecting a good image.

> They were always worried, the people around the stu-
> dios, that some breath of scandal involving their bright
> stars would cause people to stop turning up en masse at
> the box office, that the Legion of Decency would turn
> on them, or something like that. And Reagan and
> Wyman were real, you know. They were in love, they
> were wholesome. . . . People liked to look at them. And
> they, particularly Reagan, didn't ask too many ques-
> tions. If they wanted to celebrate the marriage, Reagan
> was willing, so they did.[26]

After the birth of Maureen, and later the adoption of her
brother Michael in 1945, the Reagans were promoted as the
perfect Hollywood family in countless features and photographs.

> Well now most of those pictures were taken by the
> studio. . . . I would suspect that I could go into about
> fifty or hundred homes and . . . and have people have
> exactly the same scrapbook I have.[27]

As the young actor learned his trade, he began to ascend the ladder of the studio system. He was cast as football hero George Gipp in "Knute Rockne: All American," a role he coveted, and which earned him the nickname "The Gipper."

"I've always suspected that there might have been many actors in Hollywood who could have played the part better, but none could have wanted to play it more than I did," Reagan later wrote.

When the film premiered at Notre Dame, Reagan was given the opportunity to pay back what he felt was an old debt. "Nelle cornered me and told me that Jack's dream of his life would be to make that trip," he later recalled. . . . He'd never seen a Notre Dame team play . . . he thought Pat O'Brien (who played Knute Rockne) was the greatest man since Al Smith. . . . [But] a chilling fear made me hesitate. We had all lived too long in fear of the black curse."[28]

In the end Nelle persuaded her son to invite Jack to the movie's premiere. Maureen Reagan recalled,

> My father was always guilty about the fact that he had these malevolent feelings towards his own father. And he said he was sitting at this on his desk and he looked over and Jack had this beatific smile on his face and it was like everything was okay. You know, he didn't have to feel guilty anymore, he had paid back.[29]

Reagan's generous gesture proved timely. In 1941, a year after his trip to Notre Dame, Jack Reagan died of a heart attack. Maureen shared with *The American Experience* a story her father once told her about his experience at Jack's funeral.

> The day of Jack's funeral, my father said that he was very sad, he was very depressed. . . . And as he was walking into the church, he heard Jack's voice and Jack told

him that everything was okay, that he was fine now, that he had no pain and he was at peace and my father said that, all of a sudden, all the sadness went away and he just took a deep breath and he knew that it was okay.[30]

Reagan's portrayal of football hero George Gipp paved his way out of the "B" movies.

In 1941 he played opposite Errol Flynn in "Santa Fe Trail," a film that biographer Lou Cannon called a "historical disgrace." Flynn played cavalryman J.E.B. Stuart and Reagan played his best friend, General George Armstrong Custer—no matter to the studio that the two men never met in their lives.[31] Reagan got the part only after John Wayne turned it down. For the duration of the production, Reagan imaginatively countered Flynn's constant scene-stealing maneuvers, and delivered a performance which boosted his film career.

By now Reagan was famous enough to be chosen to play Drake McHugh, a small-town rake, in the Hollywood adaptation of Henry Bellamann's best-selling novel, "King's Row." When he accepted the role, he had not yet read the script and was unaware of its demands. In the film, Drake McHugh's legs are unnecessarily amputated by a vindictive town doctor after a train accident. Reagan agonized over the performance.

"I felt I had neither the experience nor the talent to fake it. I simply had to find out how it really felt, short of actual amputation. . . . I was stumped. I commenced to panic as the day for shooting came nearer."[32]

On the day of the shooting Reagan climbed on to the bed, where a hole had been cut for his legs an hour before the scene was scheduled to be shot. "I can't describe even now my feelings as I tried to reach for where my legs could be. 'Randy,' . . . I screamed . . . . 'Where's the rest of me?'" Reagan was so proud of his delivery that twenty-five years later, he used the line as the title of his autobiography.

Drake McHugh was Reagan's most celebrated role and the one that brought him within reach of stardom. When the film was completed, Jack Warner signed Reagan for seven years and paid him $1 million.

By the time "Kings Row" was released, America was at war, and Ronald Reagan was called to duty. Ineligible for combat because of poor eyesight, Reagan only got as far as the Army Air Force First Motion Picture Unit in Culver City, nineteen miles from home. The studio hyped it up as if he'd truly left for war. *Modern Times*, a fan magazine, reported: "Reagan said to his wife and baby, 'So long, button nose, and went off to join his regiment."

Though Reagan never fired a shot in battle, he often donned his dress uniform to drum up support for America's war effort. No other 20th-century President—except for Dwight Eisenhower—would be seen so frequently in military uniform. Even as a soldier, Reagan never left the world of make-believe.

> He loved to wear a uniform. To act like a soldier. To salute properly. There was nothing he enjoyed more as President than saluting. As commander-in-chief, he would do that little extra flip to the salute, which you hardly ever see in the Armed Services anyway, it was a real Hollywood salute. But it meant a great deal to him.[33]

Serving his country from the safety of Culver City, Lieutenant Ronald Reagan became a soldier in Hollywood's wartime propaganda machine. He made war movies—"Rear Gunner," "For God and Country," "This is the Army"—and narrated training films. But he was also responsible for personnel and, as Camp Adjutant, helped run the First Motion Picture Unit. Most important, Reagan learned to value the sacrifices made by those less fortunate than him. Those who did not experience real combat had "an almost reverent feeling for the men who faced the enemy," he later said.[34]

As President, Reagan often invoked the feats of wartime heroes. In 1984, on the fortieth anniversary of D-Day, he brought tears to many eyes when spoke to "the boys of Point du Hoc," the U.S. Army Rangers who climbed the cliffs of Normandy. The horror of the allied landings at Omaha Beach became the moving story of one soldier, Private Zanata, as told to his daughter in wartime letters read by Ronald Reagan.

Sometimes he would sacrifice factual detail for dramatic effect. In his inaugural address, he spoke of the sacrifice of WWI veteran Martin Treptow, mentioning his burial in Arlington National Cemetery, when he knew fully well Treptow had been buried in Wisconsin. In a meeting with Israeli Prime Minister Yitzhak Shamir, he described the horror he had felt witnessing Nazi death camps in World War II and was promptly reminded by reporters that he had never left Los Angeles during the war. Reagan's romantic bent, his attraction to mythic heroism and his penchant for the dramatic frequently left him vulnerable to the charge that after many years in Hollywood he could no longer separate fact from fiction.[35]

NOTES

[1] Lou Cannon, *Reagan* (New York: Putnam), p. 41.
[2] "Peoria Journal Star," October 17, 1980. Quoted in Lou Cannon, *Reagan*, p. 41.
[3] Ronald Reagan, "How to Make Yourself Important," *Photoplay*, August 1942.
[4] Ronald Reagan, *Where's the Rest of Me*, p. 29.
[5] Gary Wills, *Reagan's America*, p. 69.
[6] Ronald Reagan, *Where's the Rest of Me*, p. 58.
[7] Ronald Reagan, *Where's the Rest of Me*, p. 45.
[8] Ronald Reagan, *Where's the Rest of Me*, p. 59.
[9] Ronald Reagan, *Where's the Rest of Me*, p. 65.
[10] Lou Cannon, Interview with Austin Hoyt.

[11] Ronald Reagan, *Where's the Rest of Me*, p. 67.

[12] Edmund Morris, Interview with Author.

[13] Anne Edwards, *Early Reagan: The Rise to Power* (New York: William Morrow and Company, Inc., 1987), p. 151.

[14] Maureen Reagan, Interview with Author.

[15] Edmund Morris, Interview with Author.

[16] Robert Dallek, Interview with Author.

[17] Lou Cannon, Interview with Author.

[18] Ronald Reagan, *Where's the Rest of Me*, p. 81.

[19] Robert Dallek. Interview with Author.

[20] Reagan made 53 feature movies, including "The Killers" for NBC in 1964, the only villain role he ever played.

[21] Anne Edwards, *Early Reagan*, p. 184.

[22] Steven Vaughn, *Ronald Reagan in Hollywood: Movies and Politics* (Cambridge: Cambridge University Press, 1994), p. 36.

[23] Maureen Reagan, Interview with Author.

[24] Jane Wyman, Quoted in Anne Edwards, *Early Reagan*, p. 193.

[25] Anne Edwards, *Early Reagan*, p. 201.

[26] Lou Cannon, Interview with Austin Hoyt.

[27] Maureen Reagan, Interview with Author.

[28] Ronald Reagan, *Where's the Rest of Me*, pp. 97–98.

[29] Maureen Reagan, Interview with Author.

[30] Maureen Reagan, Interview with Author.

[31] Lou Cannon, *Reagan*, p. 56.

[32] Ronald Reagan, *Where's the Rest of Me*, p. 5

[33] Edmund Morris, Interview with Author.

[34] Anne Edwards, *Early Reagan*, p. 270.

[35] Lou Cannon, *The Role of a Lifetime*, p. 11, calls the Treptow incident a portent of things to come. See also Gary Wills, *Reagan's America*, pp. 191–201.

Ronald "Dutch" Reagan as a boy in Dixon, Illinois, around the time of his baptism into his mother's Disciples of Christ church.

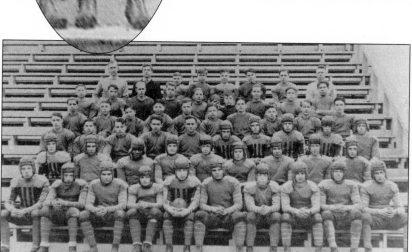

As a high school athlete in Dixon, Reagan played varsity football.

Nancy Davis as a child with her mother, Edith Lucket.

During his six summers as a lifeguard he was credited with saving seventy-seven swimmers from the treacherous currents of the Rock River in Lowell Park, Illinois.

Reagan often played the lead in school dramas. Here, he performs opposite his childhood sweetheart, Margaret "Mugs" Cleaver.

Reagan did it all at Eureka College. He was reporter for the school paper, president of the Booster Club, played varsity football for three years, was head cheerleader for the basketball team, the school's number-one swimmer, feature editor of the school yearbook, a member of the student senate for two years, and president for one.

Dutch Reagan, baseball sportscaster for WHO, transported his listeners to the bleachers of Chicago's Wrigley Field and Comiskey Park with his vivid accounts of Chicago Cubs and Chicago White Sox baseball games.

Reagan became a prominent actor in Hollywood in the 1930s and married Jane Wyman, his leading lady in the film "Brother Rat." Along with their daughter Maureen and adopted son Michael, they were idealized by the press as the epitome of the, all-American, wholesome family.

Communists in Hollywood became engaged in a struggle to gain a foothold in the movie industry in order to promote Communist ideas through the influence of motion pictures. Reagan first learned about Communists and their intentions as a member of a Hollywood union, the Screen Actors Guild. On November 10, two weeks after the House Un-American Activities Committee hearings, SAG voted to require any officer or board member to sign an affidavit "that he is not a member of the Communist Party nor affiliated with any such party."

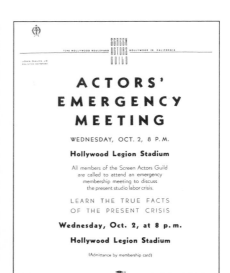

SCREEN ACTORS GUILD
7046 HOLLYWOOD BOULEVARD   HOLLYWOOD 28, CALIFORNIA

JOHN DALES, JR.
EXECUTIVE SECRETARY

ACTORS' EMERGENCY MEETING

WEDNESDAY, OCT. 2, 8 P. M.

Hollywood Legion Stadium

All members of the Screen Actors Guild
are called to attend an emergency
membership meeting to discuss
the present studio labor crisis.

LEARN THE TRUE FACTS
OF THE PRESENT CRISIS

Wednesday, Oct. 2, at 8 p. m.

Hollywood Legion Stadium

(Admittance by membership card)

Ronald Reagan, elected to six terms as president of the Screen Actors Guild, addresses a meeting.

Due to his testimony as a friendly witness in front of the House Un-American Activities Committee, Reagan's reputation in Hollywood would be forever tarnished. And his obsession with Communism may have exacted an even higher price. In 1948, Jane Wyman filed for divorce. "In recent months," Jane told the court, "my husband and I engaged in continual arguments on his political views."

When Ronald Reagan met Nancy Davis, she was a thirty-year-old actress under contract at MGM. A mutual friend asked Reagan to help Davis clear her name, which had been mistakenly included in a list of Communist sympathizers.

The year of his divorce from Jane Wyman was the worst year in his life. He was in a deep depression. Not only had he lost his wife, but his acting career seemed to be on the decline. Edmund Morris remembers him saying once over dinner, while telling the story of that awful year, "And then along came Nancy Davis and saved my soul." Shown here, they were married in an intimate ceremony in 1952.

For eight years between 1954 and 1962, Ronald Reagan paid a weekly visit to Americans in their living rooms as host of "General Electric Theater." During that time he travelled a road of transition from his roots in show business to the world of politics.

Reagan's contract stipulated that he spend ten weeks a year touring General Electric offices and factories across the country as a celebrity spokesman and morale-booster. In the process, Reagan got a political education few could even dream of.

By his own account, Reagan visited all 135 General Electric plants and met 250,000 employees. "At one plant I distributed ten thousand photos, and in two days I signed all of them."

Conservatism entered national politics in the early 1960s in the person of Barry Goldwater. He spoke for a growing number of mostly white, middle-class Americans, who rejected the prevailing consensus that government intervention could right America's wrongs—including ending segregation. Reagan became co-chairman of the Goldwater for President campaign in California.

On October 27, 1964 he spoke on national television on Goldwater's behalf. His speech, "A Time for Choosing," later became known among conservatives simply as "The Speech." It was an instant success. *Time* called it "the one bright spot in an otherwise dismal campaign." While it could not save Goldwater's candidacy (he was trounced by Johnson), it did raise more than $8 million for Goldwater and the Republican Party, and it catapulted Reagan into the political spotlight.

As Governor of California, Reagan was able to fulfill the promise he had made voters, saving taxpayers $2 billion dollars, and bringing the spiraling growth of state government under control. He learned the mechanics of government and how to get things done.

Governor Reagan playing with his son. But the magical moments, all the Reagan children agree, were few and far between, and never emotionally satisfying. Reagan was not only absent from home a lot of the time, he was also emotionally absent, absorbed in his work and in his wife. The Reagans' close marital relationship, which worked so well for Nancy and Ron, not only excluded the rest of the world, but also their children.

CHAPTER 4

The World of Reality

The war years had been boom years for Hollywood. Movie audiences increased from 80 to 100 million. Movie theaters operated round the clock. Profits more than tripled.[1] While producing comedies and light entertainment, the studios also did their part to boost public morale—releasing Oscar-winning films such as "Mrs. Miniver" and "Casablanca," along with countless war movies like "International Squadron" and Irving Berlin's "This Is the Army" (in which Reagan played a part.) Through its involvement in the war effort, the movie industry discovered its power to shape public opinion. At war's end, many actors, writers, directors and producers turned their attention to new issues—race relations and the atomic bomb among them. "No star would be caught dead at a commissary table without a cause," wrote Dorothy Parker with customary wry humor.

Like many others in Tinseltown, Captain Ronald Reagan's political awareness was heightened by the war. He had been a committed "internationalist," arguing against isolationism at every opportunity. A "near hopeless hemophiliac liberal," Reagan, by his own account, had "voted Democratic in every election . . . [and] had followed FDR blindly."[2]

"I was a New Dealer to the core," he later wrote. "I thought government could solve all our postwar problems just as it had ended the Depression and won the war."[3]

In late summer 1945, a few weeks after his release from the Army, Reagan took a brief vacation alone at Lake Arrowhead.[4]

There, he made an important decision. "With the tools I had:
my thoughts, my speaking abilities, my reputation as an actor,
I would try to bring about the regeneration of the world . . . [by]
blindly and busily joining every organization that would guarantee to save [it]. . . . This introduced me to the world of reality as opposed to make-believe."[5]

The actor turned political activist made his debut on
December 12, 1945, at a mass meeting in Hollywood Legion
Stadium sponsored by the Hollywood Independent Citizens'
Committee for the Arts, Sciences and Professions (HIC-
CASP), an organization with a reputation as a Communist
front. The purpose of the meeting was to call attention to the
looming threat of the atomic bomb, first dropped on Hiroshima
and Nagasaki only months before.

> He's involved in these leftist organizations where the
> Communists clearly were struggling for control. The
> Communists valued Hollywood. They probably overly
> valued it considerably and they made no bones about
> what they were trying to do. Reagan . . . would dismiss
> this, would dismiss the Communist conspiracy, the
> Communist threat . . . .I don't think it ever occurred to
> Reagan that there were people who might have the
> Soviet Union, rather than the United States of Amer-
> ica, as their agenda . . . . I think he was naive. I think
> he never thought about the Soviet Union at all.[6]

Communist activity in Hollywood has been traced back to
the mid-1930s, and particularly to 1937, when actors mobilized
on behalf of the Republican cause in the Spanish Civil War. In
the 1940s many Hollywood Communists had joined non-
Communists in "popular fronts" to fight Hollywood's propaganda war against the common Nazi enemy. But as the war

ended, and the Soviet-American alliance turned into the Cold War, members of the Communist party ended their wartime policy of cooperation and Communists in Hollywood became engaged in a struggle to gain a foothold in the movie industry in order to promote Communist ideas through the influence of motion pictures.

Reagan first learned about Communists and their intentions as a member of a Hollywood union, the Screen Actors Guild (SAG). He had been introduced to the Screen Actors Guild by his wife Jane Wyman and had quickly risen to become a member of the Guild's board. As a SAG Board member, and later as its president, he mediated a dispute between two rival unions. One of the unions, the Conference of Studio Unions, (CSU) was lead by a suspected Communist, Herb Sorrell.[7]

The mediation failed and Sorrell's union went on strike. In late September thousands of strikers massed at the gates of Warner Brothers. As the strike turned violent, Reagan became convinced that Sorrell and his union were more interested in promoting Communism in Hollywood than they were in protecting the rights of studio workers.[8] "The leadership does not want a settlement." Reagan concluded. "It stands to gain by continued disorder and disruption."

> This Conference of Studio Unions had a large number of Communists in its ranks and the fact that they were involved in physical violence at the studio gates, which he personally experienced, buses being overturned, windows smashed, stones thrown, bottles brandished, some bloodshed, the fact that he personally witnessed this, personally experienced it, associated it with red, as he would have said, red domination of the union—that's what turned him.[9]

"He believed they were a danger to our [union] as well as to the nation . . . ," SAG Executive Director Jack Dales told *The American Experience*. "I don't think the Communists really had the idea of taking over because they were a small minority. But they could try to make trouble, and trouble they made . . . ."[10]

Sorrel and Reagan went head to head. When Reagan crossed the picket line outside Warner Brothers, Sorrell called for a boycott of his movies.[11] Reagan was called a fascist. An anonymous phone caller threatened to disfigure his face so he could never act again. He began to carry a gun, and accepted police protection. He lost weight and he became an informant for the FBI.[12]

"These were eye-opening years for me," he later wrote. "Now I knew from first-hand experience how Communists used lies, deceit, violence, or any other tactic that suited them to advance the cause of Soviet expansionism."[13]

> I think Reagan felt personally betrayed when he discovered that there were Communists who were trying to taking over things. . . . He has a penchant to overdramatize things, and when he became convinced that . . . the Communist threat . . . was real he overdramatized it and overreacted to it.[14]

Hollywood contemporaries remember one couldn't talk to Reagan without him saying, "The Communists are going to take over."

From his position as president of the Screen Actors Guild Reagan battled Communists with the zeal of a movie hero. Jack Dales recalls that Reagan's effort was to deny Communists a foothold in the union.

> At one membership meeting at the Hollywood Legion where boxing matches used to be held, . . . he

addressed the audience, which was the [SAG] membership. He said, you know, of course, that we have some
Communists here. And he pointed. Somebody back
there, somebody up here, over there and over there.
They're going to try to make eleven or twelve people
sound like hundreds . . . . Don't be fooled . . . . And he
fought all the way. Very hard and very diligently.[15]

In the fall of 1947, Reagan testified as a friendly witness in
front of the House Un-American Activities Committee.
Although Reagan had been an FBI informant for some time, at
the HUAC hearings he refused to "name names."

> **Reagan:** . . . There has been a small group within the
> Screen Actors Guild which has consistently opposed
> the policy of the Guild board and officers of the Guild,
> as evidenced by the vote on various issues. That small
> clique referred to has been suspected of more or less fol-
> lowing the tactics we associate with the Communist
> Party.
>
> **Mr. Strippling:** Would you refer to them as a disrup-
> tive influence?
>
> **Reagan:** I would say that at times they have
> attempted to be a disruptive influence.
>
> **Strippling:** You have no knowledge yourself as to
> whether or not any of them are members of the Com-
> munist Party?
>
> **Reagan:** No, sir. I have no investigative force or any-
> thing and I do not know.

Reagan concluded his appearance with an attempt to recon-
cile his anti-Communism with his Democratic ideals.

Reagan: As a citizen I would hesitate, or not like, to see any political party outlawed on the basis of its political ideology. We have spent 170 years in this country on the basis that democracy is strong enough to stand up and fight against the inroads of any ideology. However if it is proven that an organization is an agent of a power, a foreign power, or in any way not a legitimate political party, and I think the Government is capable of proving that, if the proof is there, then that is another matter.

On November 10, two weeks after the hearings, SAG voted to require any officer or board member to sign an affidavit "that he is not a member of the Communist Party nor affiliated with any such party."

Despite the balancing act of his testimony, and his refusal to "name names," Ronald Reagan would be forever tarnished by his association with the HUAC and Hollywood's "blacklist"— ten writers and directors who were imprisoned for refusing to cooperate with the HUAC investigation and many others who were denied work for years to come.[16]

I don't think he descended the moral depths or anything . . . .But the fact is that the blacklist is a blemish. The blacklist is a terrible, terrible blemish on our country because it says, you're not going to be able to work because we don't agree with your views or we don't agree with the radical organization to which you belong and, while I don't think Reagan should be excoriated for doing what most people in positions of power did, I also don't think that's one of his finer moments either.[17]

Reagan's obsession with Communism may have exacted a

price even higher than his reputation. In June 1948, Wyman filed for divorce on the grounds of mental cruelty. "In recent months," Jane told the court, "my husband and I engaged in continual arguments on his political views. . . . Finally there was nothing in common between us . . . nothing to sustain our marriage." There might have been other hidden reasons behind the break-up—some have suggested Jane had an affair with Lew Ayres, her co-star in the film "Johnny Belinda."[18] But Wyman has never spoken publicly about her break-up with Reagan. Equally, Reagan maintained a gentleman's silence about his wife.

"I suppose there had been warning signs," he later wrote, "if only I hadn't been so busy."

Whatever else might have been going on, Ron and Jane had drifted apart. He was absorbed by politics, she by her acting career. In only a few years, Jane had reached true stardom, earning an Oscar nomination for her role as Ma Baxter in the film "The Yearling," and then winning the Oscar for her portrayal of a deaf-mute in the film "Johnny Belinda." On Oscar night Jane was accompanied by her leading man, Lew Ayres. Reagan went alone.

The world of make-believe which the Reagans had inhabited in the magical years of Hollywood in the 1930s and the early 1940s had not survived the harsher reality of the years after the war. In July 1949 their divorce became final.

Reagan was devastated. "No one in his family had ever been divorced," Maureen told *The American Experience*. "He didn't quite know how to deal with it."[19] "I thought this only happened to other people, and you read about it in the papers," Reagan later wrote.[20]

He never expected it. . . . I spent enough time on it
to believe that the story that I once thought apocryphal

is true, that Reagan came home and was told, this is over. The marriage is over. And that he was totally stunned by it, it was like he was hit by a ton of bricks and it was a very, very hard thing for him to accept or get over.[21]

Judge William Clark, one of the few Reagan aides who regards himself a friend of Ronald Reagan, confided to *The American Experience* that Reagan once told him that "he felt that his greatest failing in life had been his failure in his first marriage, . . . and he felt that he bore the full responsibility for the failing of that marriage. And it was said not so much as a confessional point as an admonition to us of the importance of family, of marriage."[22]

The year of his divorce from Jane Wyman was the worst year in Ronald Reagan's life. He was in a deep depression. Not only had he lost his wife, but his acting career seemed to be on the decline. Since his return to Warner Brothers in 1946, already in his mid-30s, Reagan had been cast—and miscast—in a string of mediocre films where he played the romantic lead.[23] He went to Britain to film "The Hasty Heart" with Richard Todd, who stole the movie from him. Shortly after his return he broke his leg in six places while stealing second base in an amateur baseball game and had to remain hospitalized for most of 1949.

"And by the time he'd hobbled . . . out of the hospital on crutches," explained Edmund Morris, "he was a changed man. And I remember him saying to us once over dinner, telling the story of that awful year. 'And then along came Nancy Davis and saved my soul.'"[24]

NOTES
[1] Thomas Schatz, *The Genius of the System: Hollywood Filmmaking in the Studio System* (New York: Henry Holt, 1996), p. 298.

[2] Ronald Reagan, *Where's the Rest of Me*. p. 139.

[3] Ronald Reagan, *An American Life*, p. 105.

[4] His wife, Jane Wyman, was busy filming "The Yearling."

[5] *Ibid*, p. 139–140.

[6] Lou Cannon, Interview with Austin Hoyt.

[7] Vaughn, *Ronald Reagan in Hollywood*, pp. 137–138. The Tenney Commission accused him of being a party member under the name Herbert Stewart and produced an alleged membership card and handwriting experts to prove it. Sorrell admitted taking money from Communists in 1945 and during a strike in 1937, and endorsing organizations thought to be fronts. But he denied belonging to the party.

[8] The Communist Party was very much interested in the success of the Conference of Studio Unions, Max Silver, a Los Angeles County Communist leader later admitted. The party was interested in establishing a nerve center that would be to some extent influenced by party policy and party people.

[9] Edmund Morris, Interview with Author.

[10] Jack Dales, Interview with Author.

[11] Reagan crossed the picket line while working on "Night Unto Night," Sorrell called a boycott of the movies of all actors who crossed the picket line, and Reagan was high on the list. Vaughn, *Ronald Reagan in Hollywood*, p. 143.

[12] This was confirmed by the White House in 1985, after a California newspaper broke the story.

[13] Ronald Reagan, *An American Life*, p. 115. By the time Reagan "discovered" Communism it was already a national issue. In the 1946 Congressional elections in California, Navy Lieutenant Commander Richard Nixon ran as the "Fighting Quaker" against Democratic incumbent Jerry Voorhis, labeling him "the candidate of the Kremlin." Though Nixon was never able to link Voorhis to any Communist organization, the attacks contributed to Voorhis's defeat. Anne Edwards, *Early Reagan*, p. 301.

[14] Lou Cannon, Interview with Author.

[15] Jack Dales, Interview with Author. By the early 1950s, according to Jack Dales, Reagan was convinced that the world would come to an end if the Communists got too much power. Anne Edwards, *Early Reagan*, p. 441.

[16] Of the nearly one thousand men and women who were blacklisted, less than one hundred were ever proven to have Communist connections.

[17] Lou Cannon, Interview with Austin Hoyt.

[18] She and Ayres were constant companions, wrote Anne Edwards, and were seen holding hands "unostentatiously but firmly." At one Hollywood party Jane allegedly blurted out, "Lew is the love of my life." Anne Edwards, *Early Reagan*, p. 354.

[19] Maureen Reagan, Interview with Author.

[20] Ronald Reagan, *Where's the Rest of Me*, p. 191.

[21] Lou Cannon, Interview with Austin Hoyt.

[22] Judge William Clark, Interview with Author.

[23] These included "The Voice of the Turtle," "That Hagen Girl," "John Loves Mary," and "The Girl from Jones Beach," the one box office success.

[24] Edmund Morris, Interview with Author.

CHAPTER 5

When Ronnie Met Nancy

When Ronald Reagan met Nancy Davis, she was a thirty-year-old actress under contract at MGM, the so-called "Tiffany" of Hollywood studios. The daughter of a well-known stage actress, Edith Lucket, Nancy had spent most of her life around the studio or the theater. Neither a brilliant actress nor a spectacular beauty, she nonetheless circulated among Hollywood's elite. She dated Clark Gable and counted among her friends the director John Huston, Spencer Tracy, Mary Martin and Katherine Hepburn.[1] She played opposite some of the best leading men of her day, James Mason in "East Side, West Side" (her first film, 1949), Glenn Ford in "The Doctor and the Girl," and Frederick March in "It's a Big Country" (1952).

Despite their vastly different backgrounds, Ronald Reagan and Nancy Davis shared an insecure and nomadic childhood.

"I was christened Ann Frances Robbins, though for some reason they always called me Nancy," she wrote of her early years.[2] Her father, Kenneth Robbins, abandoned her mother Edith when Nancy was still a baby. For a while, Edith brought Nancy with her as she toured on-stage. Then, at some unspecified age when Nancy was, in her own words, "out of diapers," Edith left her with a sister in Bethesda, Maryland, "to live a normal childhood," while she went on with her career. "It was a painful period for both of us," Nancy later wrote. "I missed her terribly."[3]

Life changed dramatically for Nancy on her tenth birthday. Her mother married Loyal Davis, a prominent Chicago neurosurgeon, and brought Nancy to live with them on Chicago's Lake Shore Drive. Dr. Davis's wealth and connections opened a new world for Nancy. She remained forever grateful to the man she always called Dr. Loyal, but came to regard as her father.[4]

Davis, a respected neurosurgeon, was upright and a political conservative. Edith was warm, caring, and by all accounts most charming. To her husband's and her daughter's delight, her parlor was one of the most popular salons in Chicago high society. Nancy enjoyed a gilded youth. She attended Girl's Latin, Chicago's best private school for girls. She then graduated from Smith College, one of New England's premier women's colleges, before embarking on her own Broadway career.

Ronnie and Nancy first met in 1949, when a mutual friend asked Reagan to help Davis clear her name, which had been mistakenly included in a list of Communist sympathizers. "Bells didn't ring or skyrockets explode," Reagan later wrote, "although I think perhaps they did. It was just that I buried the part of me where such things happened so deep, I couldn't hear them."[5]

Their first evening out they dined at La Rue's, a fancy restaurant on Sunset Strip, and later went to Ciro's, a popular nightclub where musicians Sophie Tucker and Xavier Cougat were opening that night. One date followed another. Sometimes they spent evenings at home, or with friends fellow actor Bill Holden and his wife. They became regulars at the fashionable Chasen's.

Nancy was in love. But, as she put it, "Ronnie was in no hurry to make a commitment. . . . He had been burned in his first marriage, and the pain went deep."[6] While she waited patiently for his wounds to heal, she acquired some wounds of her own. Years later, as Reagan advisor Lyn Nofzinger recalled, Nancy was still bothered by any mention of Jane Wyman.

[During the governor's] campaign of 1966, we'd gone
to a fund-raiser out in the San Fernando Valley, at a theater in the round, and two of the entertainers were Rowan
and Martin, [who were later on] "Laugh In," and they
were kidding back and forth extemporaneously, and one
of them said, "Ronald Reagan for President," and the
other said, "No, Jimmy Stewart for President and Ronald
Reagan for Vice President," and the other said, "And Jane
Wyman for First Lady," and the minute they said it they
knew they . . . shouldn't have said it. It was just . . . a
micro-second, [but] a very poignant one. And I looked
over at Nancy. She was sitting about two people away
from me, and she just froze, and she never enjoyed the rest
of that program. I learned from that one. One doesn't talk
about Jane Wyman [around] Nancy.[7]

Ronnie and Nancy were married in 1952 in an intimate ceremony. The only guests were the Holdens, who served as witnesses. Seven months later, Nancy gave birth to Patricia Ann
Reagan, who later changed her name to Patti Davis.

The Reagans embarked on one of the closest partnerships in
political history. Their "double act," as one biographer called it,
endured for the rest of their lives. "Reagan's White House years
have been the Reagans' years," George Will wrote in 1989.
"Their lives are thoroughly woven together."[8]

Stuart Spencer, who worked with the Reagans since the
beginning of Reagan's political career in 1965, observed,

It was a team. The two of them attacked the world
together. Discussed the world, discussed problems.
Everything they did together and there was nothing . . .
very little . . . that he ever discussed that she didn't
know about.[9]

The adoring way Nancy looked at her husband—which cynical journalists dubbed "the gaze," the hand-holding, the public kisses, the fact that he called her "mommy," and her high visibility, later became daily fodder for the press, which tended to deem all this devotion staged and exaggerated, and possibly indicative that Nancy wielded too much power in the Reagan White House. But, as *The American Experience* learned through interviews with Reagan's closest associates and their children, their love was real, and her influence—though indeed enormous—was misunderstood.

Michael Deaver, White House Deputy Chief of Staff, told *The American Experience*:

> There've been a lot of comments about Ronald and Nancy Reagan, and was it real . . . . And I think it's the most real love I've ever seen. What you see there is right. It is true. Reagan said once that his life began when he met Nancy, and I believe that to be true. I think that he became a fulfilled person. He became able to do many things that he wanted to do because of Nancy.[10]

Daughter Patti Davis explained:

> My parents have about as close a relationship as I've ever seen anyone have. They really, sort of complete each other. They're kind of two halves of a circle. . . . I think it's amazing to be witness to that kind of love and that kind of devotion between people. I've never loved anyone that much. I think it must be an amazing experience.[11]

Son Ronald Prescott Reagan added:

> They're very, very different people, Dad and Nancy, but in a way that complements the other very well. I mean . . . he's a guy who is almost impossible to dislike. He's a guy who always thinks the best of people. Can't believe that anybody who's ever met him, would ever want to do anything bad to him, would ever want to go behind his back, would ever want to stab him in the back. That's just not within his realm of thinking. He just can't conceive of it. Nancy on the other hand is far more cunning about that sort of stuff. She has no trouble understanding stabbing in the back.[12]

Nancy assigned herself the role of "protector" in Reagan's life. George Will commented: "She had one great concern, which was the happiness and political welfare of her husband. She was a very gifted politician. . . . Not infrequently, she asserted herself and made her feelings known."[13]

But, against public perception, Nancy, by most accounts, did not intervene in the day-to-day affairs of government.

> Nancy's a very smart woman. A very tough woman. A woman with good political instincts. [She] did not try to run the government. When she interfered, it was because she wanted to make sure that Reagan was being taken care of properly. She didn't like to see him overworked, overtired, and she was a very defensive kind of mother hen with him.[14]

> The best way to describe their relationship politically was that he was the CEO, he was the boss, and she was the Personnel Director. As they went through life, it was always Nancy that had to take a look at you. She'd research you. She'd find out about you, so

she spent all her time looking for people that would serve her man well.[15]

> She just sort of had her antenna up for people, for people who were cultivating him not because they agreed with his ideas or because they liked him or wanted to serve him, but because they wanted to take some advantage, and [she] sensed that. I don't know how she did it, but what was evident to people at a very, very early stage, very early in his career, [was] that Nancy looks out for his interest, and if you're going to try to hurt or screw Reagan, you know, you're going to have to deal with her.[16]

During his two terms as governor of California, when Reagan was in his mid-fifties, the "tough guys" in his Administration regarded Nancy as an unavoidable nuisance and even as a political liability whose "Hollywood ways" exposed the governor to bad press. Most of the people in Reagan's staff either feared Nancy or lacked the patience to handle her. A young staff member, Michael Deaver, assumed the role of "intermediary" between Reagan's staff and his sensitive and concerned wife. Between 1966 and 1985, he deftly "managed" Nancy Reagan, a task which became known as "the mommy watch."

Except for Donald Regan, who served as White House Chief of Staff between 1985 and 1987, Reagan's staff gradually learned to appreciate Nancy's role. As the President grew older and more distant from his job, Nancy, as Kenneth Duberstein told *The American Experience*, became an indispensable presence at the White House.

> She was an aide. Nancy knew Ronald Reagan better than [any] other living human being. She knew his

good days and his bad days. She knew how he had slept that night. She was Ronald Reagan's best friend, and she spent the most time with him. She understood him for the longest period, and she helped us explain, reveal, talk with us, guide us . . . on understanding Ronald Reagan the man and what his interests and goals were.[17]

Aside from her husband's welfare, Nancy was also keenly interested in his place in history. She wanted Reagan to be remembered as a man of peace. In 1983, she joined with National Security Advisor Robert McFarlane, Secretary of State George Shultz, and Deputy Chief of Staff Michael Deaver in an effort to "nurture a change in President Reagan's attitude toward the Soviet Union."[18]

She (did) everything possible to move it in that direction because she thought, not only did he want to do this but she . . . thought that he might be able to accomplish it, where somebody hadn't before because she knew his talents and his abilities. And so she . . . pushed that along.[19]

Long before they moved into the White House, Nancy Davis and Ronald Reagan were a Hollywood team. And life for them was not always a bed of roses. Though Reagan was enjoying great success as the president of the Screen Actors Guild and had been elected to six consecutive terms, by 1950 his acting career was failing fast. No longer a contract player and never a true star, Reagan had difficulty finding good roles. Though he realized his dream of starring in Westerns, he excelled more for his riding than his acting ability. He was upstaged by a chimpanzee in "Bedtime for Bonzo."[20] One of Reagan's last films,

"Hellcats of the Navy"—in which he played opposite Nancy—was considered a flop.

Maureen remembers that her father at the time was "as low as he could get. He could not understand why a career he loved so much and thought he was so good at, was slipping through his fingers."[21] "It hurt when the career dried up," Nancy later recalled. "But he rolled with it . . . . he'd get back to the deep belief that everything happens for a reason."[22]

Reagan was always very proud of his acting career. Years later, as presidential assistant Jim Kuhn revealed to *The American Experience*, any criticism of his acting ability still touched a raw nerve in Ronald Reagan.

> One Friday afternoon in the Oval Office, right before we left for Camp David, a family came in, I believe from Michigan, to say hello to the President and have their photos taken. And at the end of the brief meeting . . . the grandmother spoke up and wanted to pay a compliment to the President . . . . She said, "Mr. President, I think you're the greatest President in the history of the United States, but I never cared for you much as an actor." And I thought, "Oh, my God! Why did she say that?" You could tell Reagan was totally taken aback by it, and it really hit hard. Really hurt his feelings.[23]

Nancy remembers the early 1950s as "a difficult time for us. . . . If there was a time my husband needed me, it was then."[24] Except for the occasional guest appearance with George Burns and Gracie Allen in "Burns and Allen," Reagan was out of work for most of 1953. The Reagans were in debt. His agent offered him a job as an MC introducing the singing quartet "The Continentals," at "The Last Frontier Hotel" in Las Vegas.

"Ronnie hated the idea," Nancy wrote, "but the money was good and we were broke."[25]

Nancy came to Vegas with Ronnie, leaving three-month-old Patti with the housekeeper. "Every night when we got back to our room, we thought of it as just so many more weeks we could hold out in our waiting game."[26]

The waiting game ended when General Electric offered Reagan $150,000 a year to host their weekly television series, "General Electric Theater." "GE Theater" would not only make Reagan a rich man, it would launch his political career.

NOTES

[1] Nancy Reagan, *My Turn* (New York: Random House, 1989), pp. 78–79.

[2] *Ibid*, p. 67.

[3] Nancy Reagan, *My Turn*, p. 70.

[4] *Ibid*, p. 74–75. Dr. Davis formally adopted Nancy when she was fourteen. He felt she had "earned the name Davis."

[5] Ronald Reagan, *Where's the Rest Of Me*, p. 235.

[6] Nancy Davis, *My Turn*, pp. 96–97.

[7] Lyn Nofziger, Interview with Author.

[8] George Will, "How Reagan Changed America," *Newsweek*, January 1989, p. 14.

[9] Stuart Spencer, Interview with Author.

[10] Michael Deaver, Interview with Author.

[11] Patti Davis, Interview with Author.

[12] Ronald Prescott Reagan, Interview with Austin Hoyt.

[13] George F. Will, Interview with Author.

[14] Lyn Nofziger, Interview with Author.

[15] Stuart Spencer, Interview with Author. Reagan's management style—which consisted of assembling people and listening to their advice in order to make a decision—made Nancy's role as "Chief of Personnel" all the more important.

[16] Lou Cannon, Interview with Austin Hoyt. Many of Reagan's closest associates—including Lyn Nofziger, Judge William Clark, David Stockman, Richard Darman, and most notably, Donald Regan—became the target of Nancy's wrath. They all exited the White House through Nancy's influence, with the one exception of Stockman, whom Reagan "forgave" after Stockman's "betrayal" interview with Joe Greider in the *Atlantic Monthly* in 1981.

[17] Kenneth Duberstein, Interview with Author.

[18] Robert C. McFarlane, *Special Trust*, (New york: Soho Press, 1994), p. 295. Nancy's role in nudging Reagan toward closer relations with the Soviets is discussed in greater depth in Chapter 15.

[19] Michael Deaver, Interview with Author.

[20] Publicity photos of Reagan feeding a milk bottle to a monkey were of no help to Reagan in his attempt to convince voters that he should be taken seriously as a politician.

[21] Maureen Reagan, Interview with Author.

[22] Nancy Reagan, Interview with Austin Hoyt.

[23] Jim Kuhn, Interview with Josh Clark.

[24] Nancy Reagan, *My Turn*, p. 125.

[25] *Ibid*, p. 126.

CHAPTER 6

An Education in Politics

For eight years between 1954 and 1962, Ronald Reagan paid a weekly visit to Americans in their living rooms as host of "General Electric Theater."

"GE Theater" was good television. It presented a wide range of dramas—a Western version of Charles Dickens' *A Christmas Carol*, starring Jimmy Stewart, a political play about the brainwashing of POWs in Korea, a dramatization of *Rider on a Pale Horse*, and even some biblical stories. Through the early 1960s, "GE Theater" was television's highest-rated Sunday-night show.[1]

A new generation of Americans became acquainted with Ronald Reagan through "GE Theater"—a generation born after Reagan's Hollywood days. One young television viewer, Jim Kuhn, became one of Reagan's personal assistants in the White House.

> My first impression of Ronald Reagan was growing up as a young man on a farm in northwestern Ohio, watching him on Sunday evenings on the "General Electric Theater." And as a young boy, he had an impact on me. There was a certain appeal that reached out to you even at a very youthful age. And you found yourself almost looking forward to each Sunday night so that you could watch Ronald Reagan on television.[2]

"If you believe, as Ronnie does, that everything happens for a purpose, then there was certainly a hidden purpose in Ronnie's job with General Electric," Nancy later wrote.[3] That hidden purpose, perhaps, was the clause in Reagan's contract which stipulated that he spend ten weeks a year touring General Electric offices and factories across the country as a celebrity spokesman and morale-booster. In the process, Reagan got a political education few could even dream of.

> GE was perfect for him. And the reason it was is that he was able to get out on the road and talk to people at a long distance from anybody else—speeches that were rarely covered, and if covered at all, were covered in the town newspaper. No national coverage. And he was free to make mistakes. It was a kind of apprenticeship that isn't there for most people, and he made the most of it.[4]

By his own account, Reagan visited all 135 GE plants and met 250,000 employees. "At one plant I distributed 10,000 photos, and in two days I signed all of them. In another they had a reception and I stood in the receiving line and shook 2,000 hands. At Appliance Park in Louisville, Kentucky, there were forty-six miles of assembly line. I walked all of them. Twice. . . . No barnstorming politician ever met the people on quite such a common footing. Sometimes I had an awesome feeling that America was making a personal appearance for me."[5]

"More than any President since Jackson," wrote Reagan speechwriter Peggy Noonan, "he spent the years before power with the people, the normal people of this country. At a time [when] most leaders of the eighties were joining government and learning its language, he was going from plant to plant for GE, shooting the breeze with the workers in the cafeteria, talking to the owners, the guys telling him what they thought."[6]

All tours followed the same format. Reagan would meet the top people at the plant, then show up at an assembly with the workers, where he shook hands, signed autographs and listened to their thoughts. In the evening, he would deliver a speech at a banquet arranged through some local civic group, such as the Chamber of Commerce.

At first, his speeches mostly promoted Hollywood as a wholesome place, where the crime and divorce rates were lower than the national average. He also told anecdotes of his fight against Communists in the 1940s. But as time went on, his speeches began to reflect what he was discovering were the chief concerns of management and workers at General Electric.

> GE was at that time the embodiment of modern progressive capitalists. And these modern progressive capitalists are worried about all the restrictions that are coming on them out of Washington. Most of the workers identified with the middle class, and a lot of them identified with the concerns of management that there were too many restrictions on them.[7]

"The Hollywood portion of the talk shortened and disappeared," Reagan later wrote. "I went out of my way to point out the problems of centralizing power in Washington with the subsequent loss of freedom at the local level."[8]

By 1959, after five years on the GE circuit, the rudiments of the philosophy Ronald Reagan would take to Washington two decades later had taken shape. Already an avowed anti-Communist, Reagan had come to believe that even America's democratic government was encroaching steadily on individual freedom and initiative. His speeches, entitled "Encroaching Control" and "Our Eroding Freedom," delivered in messianic, almost apocalyptic tones, warned against "the rising tide of collectivism which threatens to inundate what remains of our free economy."[9]

Reagan, who had rescued 77 people from drowning at Lowell Park, countless others in his roles as movie hero, and rescued SAG from Communist influence, now had a new cause: to rescue everyday Americans from big government.

"We are told that taxes can't be reduced until spending is cut," Reagan would repeatedly tell his audiences. "No government in history has ever voluntarily reduced itself in size. Government does not tax to get the money they *need*—government will always *find* a need for the money it gets." Quoting Supreme Court Justice Oliver Wendell Holmes, he would exhort them to "strike for the jugular. Reduce taxes and spending. Keep government poor and remain free."[10]

Reagan was becoming a much sought-after speaker by business groups such as the National Association of Manufacturers. By the late 1950s, he ranked as the second most demanded public speaker in the country behind President Dwight D. Eisenhower. He had successfully parlayed his acting skills into a promising career on the podium.

Whether consciously or not, Reagan had evolved into a favorite spokesman for the political right. He attacked the "socialized medicine" of the Veteran's Administration hospitals system, rising social security taxes, and rising income taxes, which by 1960 were taking 31 cents out of every dollar on the average.[11] But he was becoming too controversial for GE's progressive corporate image. When he attacked the Tennessee Valley Authority—a combined government/private enterprise giant that brought GE $50 million worth of business a year—as an example of government waste and expansionism, GE threatened to cancel his contract. Though he dropped the references to the TVA from his speeches, he'd already crossed the line of acceptability at GE. In 1962, the company cancelled

"GE Theater." Reagan was relieved of his duties as host and as corporate spokesperson. By then he was so popular that his bookings for GE-sponsored speaking tours had to be cancelled as far ahead as 1966.[12]

Reagan had gotten as much out of his GE years as he could possibly have hoped for: public exposure, a political education, a reputation as a speaker, and money.

GE had not only paid Reagan handsomely, but had also furnished the Reagan's Pacific Palisades home with every conceivable electric comfort and gadget GE manufactured. An ocean view, a backyard swimming pool, and a ranch on the Malibu Hills completed the Reagan family's California dream life.

The memories of those years remain deeply engraved in Reagan's children as playful and magical times. Home movies depict a happy family life. There were Sundays spent around the swimming pool, trips to the beach just down the hill, horseback rides at the ranch. "I have a lot of happy memories of my father when I was younger," Patti Davis told *The American Experience*.

> I tried to keep up with him athletically, because it was something I loved—but it was also a way to spend time with him. Both my brother and I learned to swim probably before we could walk. My father, having been a lifeguard, believed that you just learn to swim and you are not ever gonna get into trouble.[13]

What Ronald Prescott Reagan remembered most was the ranch in Malibu. "That would probably be the place where all of us probably spent the most time with him," he told *The American Experience*.

> We used to go out horseback riding, of course. He made sure we all had horses at a relatively early age. We

would go out ground squirrel hunting. There were ground squirrels all over, and they would dig holes in the pastures where the horses were, and he had a worry that the horses would step in the holes and break their legs—which was not an unfounded worry. And so . . . one of our sort of father–son things to do would be to go out with a little .22 rifle, and we would sit and wait by a ground squirrel hole, and eventually they'd pop their little heads out. And . . . you'd shoot them. But of course you had to be perfectly still and perfectly quiet for this to happen, so there wasn't a lot of conversation. The conversation was limited to, "There he is, is it your shot or mine?"[14]

But the magical moments, all the Reagan children agree, were few and far between, and never emotionally satisfying. Reagan was not only absent from home a lot of the time, he was also emotionally absent, absorbed in his work and in his wife. The Reagans' close marital relationship, which worked so well for Nancy and Ron, not only excluded the rest of the world, but also their children:

Maureen: They have a self-contained, very insular relationship. They don't . . . need a lot of outsiders. There was so much there, and it didn't really require us.[15]

Patti: As a child I suppose I felt sort of left out by that. I felt that it was so complete that I was almost superfluous.[16]

Ron: We were conscious, I think, growing up—all of us, I know I was—that there were really two sets of peo-

ple, two definite and distinct sets of people involved in
the family. There was my mother and father, and there
was everybody else. And that we were all part of the
family. [But], when push came to shove there was a dis-
tinction to be made. It really wasn't like, you know, be
seen and not heard, but it was, you know, we were
expected to put ourselves in second place. . . . I don't
think in my life that I've ever had a real conversation
with him. . . . I don't think we've ever just sort of sat
around and you know, just talked—ever.[17]

The impact of Reagan's emotional distance was compounded
by the contentious relationship between Nancy and her daughter Patti. The difficulties between mother and daughter, exposed
by Patti in a 1986 book, irreparably damaged family life.

If one is to believe her account, published in a novel and an
autobiography in the mid-1980s, the Reagan household was a
battlefield. As she told *The American Experience*,

For most of my life, my relationship with my mother
was one of conflict. And, the effect of that was very
powerful in our family. I don't think any sort of healing
could take place in our family until my mother and I
repaired our relationship. A mother-and-daughter relationship is a very, powerful one, and I think it sort of
resonates with everybody, probably within a five-mile
radius! Certainly with everyone in the family. And it
was a constant source of pain for my father. I think it
was an open wound for him, and I don't think I was terribly sympathetic to that because I had a lot of anger.[18]

Like many of her generation, Patti would later use politics as a
form of rebellion against her father. But that would be later. Ron

was merely five and Patti eleven, when family life all but ended for the Reagans. For the next twenty-five years, Ronald and Nancy would be completely absorbed in the political career that was taking off with dizzying speed. By the time that career ended, it would be almost too late for the family to repair the damage.

Reagan's ascent as a political figure is inseparable from the rise of Conservatism. "He saw the wave," wrote Lou Cannon, "and rode it to the top."

The birth of the modern incarnation of American conservatism has been dated to the founding of William Buckley's *National Review* in 1955 and to the publication of Whittaker Chambers' *Witness*. Conservatism entered national politics in the early 1960s in the person of Barry Goldwater, who spoke for a growing number of mostly white, middle-class Americans who rejected the prevailing consensus that government intervention could right America's wrongs—including ending segregation.

Reagan had first met Barry Goldwater at the Phoenix home of Nancy's parents, Loyal and Edith Davis, and had been impressed by him. Goldwater's 1960 book, *The Conscience of a Conservative*, argued that Eisenhower had perpetuated Franklin Roosevelt's New Deal, and that a dangerous erosion in state's rights, "the cornerstone of America's freedom . . . is fast disappearing under the piling sands of statism."[19] Goldwater's phrases, "big government" and "encroachment on individual freedom," sounded familiar to Reagan, who had been preaching against the evils of big government for quite some time.

By the time Reagan joined Goldwater, the era of "big government" was in full swing. President Lyndon Johnson had just launched his Great Society program, which, Reagan felt, "made most of the tax-and-spend Democrats [before him] seem miserly by comparison. . . . I thought we sorely needed Goldwater to reverse that trend."[20]

Reagan became co-chairman of the Goldwater for President

campaign in California, and on October 27, 1964, he spoke on national television on behalf of the Republican candidate. He called his speech "A Time for Choosing." It later became known among conservatives simply as "The Speech."

> . . . We have come to a time for choosing. Either we accept responsibility for our own destiny, or we abandon the American revolution and confess that a far distant capitol can plan our lives for ourselves. Already the hour is late. Government has laid its hands on health, housing, farming, industry, commerce, education.

> . . . No nation in history has ever survived a tax burden that reached a third of its national income. Today thirty-seven cents out of every dollar earned in this country is the tax collector's share, and yet our government continues to spend $17 million a day more than the government takes in.

> . . . Government programs take on weight and momentum. We approach a point of no-return when government becomes so huge and entrenched that we fear the consequences of upheaval and just go along with it.

> . . . You and I have a rendezvous with destiny. We will preserve for our children this, the last best hope of man on earth, or we will sentence them to take the last step into a thousand years of darkness.[21]

"The Speech" was, according to Edmund Morris, "the culmination, the quintessence of all his speeches honed on the GE circuit. All of the catch phrases that he'd found worked well, all the ideology that he'd polished during his years as a GE corporate spokesman and emerging political orator—it all came together at this moment."[22]

Lyn Nofzinger, who heard the speech that night, explained its appeal:

> I think probably what impressed the American people was that they'd been listening to these two politicians out there, Barry Goldwater and Lyndon Johnson, and all of a sudden, here's a man who is saying some things that they believed, or a lot of them believed, [and he] was saying them in a very reasonable manner. He wasn't shouting, he wasn't demanding or anything, and of course, he was well known: Ronald Reagan, the actor and the movie star.[23]

Reagan's "A Time For Choosing" was an instant success. *Time* magazine called it "the one bright spot in an otherwise dismal campaign." While it could not save Barry Goldwater's candidacy (he was trounced by Lyndon Johnson in November), it did raise more than $8 million dollars for Goldwater and the Republican Party, and it catapulted Reagan into the political spotlight. "Of course I didn't know it then, but that speech was one of the most important milestones in my life," Reagan later wrote.[24] As Barry Goldwater receded into political obscurity, Ronald Reagan took his place as the spokesperson of the Conservative movement. His style, as George Will explained, turned Conservatism into a much more palatable philosophy.

> Ronald Reagan put a smile on the face of conservatism. Barry Goldwater was the nicest man alive, but he tended to come across as sandpapery, to put it politely. You know, kind of . . . cranky and angry.

Ronald Reagan understood that. Conservatism had seemed to be scowling and a kind of root-canal kind of conservatism (to use Jack Kemp's phrase)—stern, dour, Calvinist. Ronald Reagan was sunnier.[25]

"Reagan translated conservatism into a doctrine or a set of political and philosophical beliefs that made sense to the average American," Edwin Meese, Reagan's close aide and himself a political conservative observed.

When he talked about limited government, when he talked about individual liberty, when he talked about free-market capitalism, when he talked about strong national defense, when he talked about traditional American values—these things which are the substance of modern conservatism—he was able to explain what they meant in practical terms.[26]

One year after "The Speech," as Californian Republicans cast about to find a suitable candidate to oppose liberal Democratic Governor Edmund Brown, who had defeated Richard Nixon in 1962, they found a depleted field.[27] A group of conservative California millionaires looked outside the Republican Party for an alternative. They approached Reagan, the former actor, television host, corporate spokesperson, and sudden political star, with the proposition that he run for governor in 1966.[28]

The names Holmes Tuttle, Henry Salvatori and Cy Rubel entered political folklore as Reagan's "kitchen cabinet." For the rest of his political life, Ronald Reagan would have to contend with allegations that he was little more than a mouthpiece for a group of conservative millionaires; an allegation vehemently denied by those who knew Reagan at the time. "There's no truth in that at all," said Stu Spencer in an interview with *The American Experience*:

> . . . Ronald Reagan has his own value system. He had it then. He had his own goals, the things that he wanted to accomplish if he was in public life. Some of those coincided with what those gentlemen believed in too, and a lot of other people in America, but no . . . . Ronald Reagan was his own man in every aspect. They were a big help to him, but on policy matters, no, they were not important.[29]

At first, Reagan rejected the suggestion that he run for governor. "I'd never given a thought to running for office and I had no interest in it whatsoever," he wrote in his memoirs.[30] But soon thereafter, he agreed to test the waters, embarking on a six-month speaking tour to see if there was any interest among voters in his candidacy. Three months later, Reagan reports telling Nancy, ". . . at the end of every speech, . . . all these people tell me that I ought to run for governor."[31]

Both Edmund Morris and Lou Cannon believe Reagan's reluctance might have been feigned. "Reagan," Cannon told *The American Experience*, had gotten the political "bug" while campaigning for Barry Goldwater and "thought he could do well."[32] "He knew he could lead, he wanted to lead," Morris concurred. "From October 1964 on, I think he was 'spoiled.'"[33]

But Reagan, who had risen in politics by railing against government, could never admit that he had chosen politics as a career. After two terms in Sacramento and two terms in Washington, he still maintained he'd entered politics because he could not say "no to all of those people."[34]

On January 4, 1966, he announced his candidacy for governor of California.

I've come to a decision that even a short time ago I
would have thought impossible for me to make. And
yet I make it with no lingering doubts or hesitation. As
of now, I am a candidate seeking the Republican nomination for governor.

In the year Ronald Reagan launched his gubernatorial campaign, California was going through tumultuous times. The
prosperous, safe, white, middle-class world Californians had
enjoyed in the 1940s and 1950s was coming apart. Property
taxes were increasing. Welfare rolls were growing out of control.
Crime was on the rise. University students were growing restless.
Watts exploded in the worst race riots in the nation's history.

He runs in 1966, as a staunch Goldwater conservative. He is someone who is coming to their rescue from
big government, from taxes, from disorder in the society. He's very comfortable in that role, and people find
him comfortable in it. And they see him as an honest
man, they see him as an honest politician, as someone
who speaks his mind, who's playing the role of hero—
and people like it.[35]

In what would become a common—and fatal—mistake
among Reagan adversaries, Governor Brown underestimated
the man he was up against. In campaign ads and in speeches,
he sought to remind voters of Reagan's inexperience, and of
Reagan's Hollywood career.

"What have my opponent's contributions been to this growing, thriving state of ours?" Brown asked rhetorically,

. . . He's divided his time between propaganda pictures against everything from Medicare to the Ten-

nessee Valley Authority. And starring in such unforget-
table screen epics as "Bedtime for Bonzo."

"Pat was a nice man, really, but a traditional old politician,"
Lyn Nofziger recounted in an interview with *The American
Experience*. "[His campaign] looked at Ronald Reagan, 'that
dumb actor,' and they said, 'Oh man, this is the guy we want to
run against. He has no political experience, he's not going to be
able to handle himself well.'"

Aware of their candidate's vulnerability, Reagan's "kitchen
cabinet" hired a public relations firm, Spencer and Roberts,
which had run Nelson Rockefeller's campaign for the Republican nomination in 1964. Their mission was to design a campaign strategy and to prepare Reagan for the job of governor.
Their first task was to transform Reagan's weaknesses into
strengths. Reagan was inexperienced in government? No problem. He would be promoted as a citizen politician.

"I am an ordinary citizen with a deep-seated belief that much
of what troubles us has been brought about by politicians; and
it's high time that more ordinary citizens brought the fresh air
of common-sense thinking to bear on these problems,"[36] Reagan repeated in speech after speech.

But the biggest challenge Spencer and Roberts faced was to
convince voters that Reagan was not the empty actor portrayed
by Brown's campaign.

> So we devised a technique where he would give his
> twenty-minute speech—and incidentally, Ronald Rea-
> gan wrote all his own speeches when he ran for gover-
> nor in 1966—he'd give the twenty-minute speech and
> we'd open it to twenty minutes of Q and A for people
> there at the meeting, or the press, and if he could han-
> dle those questions, we felt we could get over the hump

of "here's an empty person who doesn't know anything about government or doesn't have any real ideas."[37]

"From the beginning," attests Nofziger, "[Reagan] was supremely confident that he could handle himself in the political arena. In his mind, party politics could not possibly be as tough as the union politics he'd been involved in as president of the Screen Actors Guild [when] the Communist party was attempting to dominate the film industry."[38]

Lou Cannon, a reporter for the *San Jose Mercury* at the time of the 1966 campaign, witnessed an early Reagan performance at one of the press conferences devised by Stu Spencer.

> Reagan's challenge was to show that he wasn't just an actor reciting lines, and once he got over that hurdle, I think he was home free as far as the election was concerned. . . . [I was] in Sacramento for the San Jose paper, and my editor called and said, "This Reagan's in town. Do you want to go over and see what you think of him?" And I did. And here Reagan is. He's answering questions. Now, he doesn't know a lot, but he doesn't do too bad. He doesn't mishandle any questions and if he doesn't know something he says, "I don't know." And I came back and I called my editor, and he said, "What did you think of him?" And I said, "I don't know why anybody would want to run against this guy. Why would you want to run against somebody who everybody knows and likes and who's friendly and popular?"[39]

Reagan reached out to his audience. His Hollywood celebrity drew large crowds seeking his autograph, hoping for a handshake. As his exposure grew, his aides began to consider how they could convert the dapper Hollywood actor and corporate spokesman who lived in Pacific Palisades into someone with true populist appeal. Lynn Nofziger, Reagan's press secretary, stumbled on what turned out to be a brilliant idea.

A political reporter for KPIX [television] in San Francisco said, "I want to do an interview with Reagan on horseback." And I said, "That's a great idea, that really humanizes him." And of course, he'd made a lot of Western movies when he was an actor. And so, he had a ranch out in Malibu Canyon, about twenty-five miles from downtown Los Angeles. So, we went out there and he came out wearing jodhpurs. And I said, "What in the hell are you doing in those jodhpurs?" "Well," he said, "that's how I always ride around here," very huffily. And I said, "Ron, we're trying to win an election here, you know. People in California, as they see you in those jodhpurs, are going to think you're an Eastern sissy." He says, "Well, this is what you wear when you're jumping horses." I said, "We're not jumping horses, we're going for a ride. She [the KPIX reporter] wants you to be a cowboy. I want you to be a cowboy, because that's what the people here will identify with." So, he said, "Well, all right." So, he went back in and changed into jeans and boots . . . . And they went riding off on the trail with the [film] crew following her in a jeep, and it was beautiful—it was just beautiful.[40]

The image that would play such a large role in Reagan's political career had been born. For most Americans, he would come to embody the great myth of the American West—the independent cowboy standing tall, willing to take on any challenge that came his way, the hero coming to the rescue. As much else in Reagan's career this was a mixture of reality and fiction. Reagan, the fictional cowboy of Western films, was coming to the people's rescue, much as the real lifeguard of Lowell Park had done.

But if his aides defined his image, it was Reagan who discovered the most important issue of his campaign. In a series of speaking tours across the state he began to notice growing public concern about the restlessness on the campuses of California's universities.

> There was a great deal of campus unrest, particularly at Berkeley, and it was making the papers. Not front-page stories, but it was making the papers. He was very upset about it. He had very strong personal feelings about campus unrest. If you're gonna protest, there are other ways to protest . . . in every speech he talked about it, and one night in Fresno, Visalia, someplace, I said, "Ron, you know it doesn't even show up in our polling data, the campus unrest." He said, "What are you saying?" I said, "Well, why are you talking about it? It doesn't even show up." "Well, I believe it," he says, "and I'm gonna keep talking about it." I says, "Okay." I don't know, four or five, six weeks went by, and all of a sudden, it started showing up in our polling data, and I've always maintained that the issue was out there, but he created [the idea] that something should be done about it. He had a very great skill of reading his audiences and of reading the public.[41]

Reagan stuck to his principal message: the "mess" at Berkeley, the fiscal condition of California, and Brown's lack of leadership. His standard concluding line, delivered in Spanish, simply said *"Ya Basta!"* meaning, "Enough Already!" Brown continued to campaign against "the actor," Ronald Reagan. Maureen recalls one particular campaign commercial:

> I'll never forget this. They did a campaign film. It was a thirty-minute film. It was like an infomercial kind of thing. And it started out with Pat Brown sitting back in a sweater in a . . . kind of like a lounge chair, with a . . . a remote control and flicking the channels of a television set, and every time he flicked the channel there was a young cavalry officer. There was a lawman with a badge and a gun. There was . . . a baseball player, and they were all shots from my father's films. . . . And in the middle of this film there is the governor of California in an elementary school surrounded by a group of African-American little boys and girls, and [Brown] turns to one of them and says, "You know, I'm running against an actor. It was an actor who shot Lincoln."[42]

Lyn Nofzinger later marvelled at Reagan's reaction to Brown's attack.

> Reagan was making a speech at the Commonwealth Club in San Francisco when this [ad] first came out, and somebody came up and told me about it, and so I went and got Reagan, who was at the head table, and I said, "Now, you know, this is what's happened, and I think we ought to play it real cool and not react to it." He said, "Don't worry—don't worry." So, he leaves after he makes his speech, and the press grabs him, and somebody asks him about this [ad], and he says, "Oh, I can't believe Pat Brown would say anything like that, and I wouldn't really want to comment on that until after we've seen just what he said, because he just wouldn't

say anything like that." So we walked away, and I said, "Man, that was an Academy Award performance." He says, "Hush, they may be listening."[43]

The commercial backfired on the Brown campaign, particularly in the Hollywood community. Stu Spencer believes this is the point when the Reagan campaign broke through in Hollywood, "and we got Frank Sinatra and several other Hollywood types who were basically Democrats for years."[44]

Ultimately, Reagan beat Brown because he promised to stand against the growing challenges to the traditional values, institutions and way of life of California's white middle class. "The electorate of California had been radicalized," concluded Richard Norton Smith,

> . . . there was a sense that traditional values, traditional institutions, were being challenged, were breaking down—whether it was on the campuses or elsewhere. So people took a chance, and voted on a Hollywood star, against an established and relatively popular incumbent governor.[45]

In November, Reagan not only beat Brown, he beat him by one million votes. The governor had underestimated Reagan's challenge. He would not be the last to pay the price for that mistake.

NOTES

[1] Lou Cannon, *Reagan*, p. 94.
[2] Jim Kuhn, Interview with Josh Clark.
[3] Nancy Reagan, *My Turn*, p. 267.
[4] Lou Cannon, Interview with Austin Hoyt.
[5] Ronald Reagan, *Where's the Rest of Me*, p. 261. By Nancy's estimate, Reagan spent two of his eight years at GE on the road.

[6] Peggy Noonan, *What I Saw at the Revolution: A Political Life in the Reagan Era* (New York: Ivy Books, 1990), p. 174.

[7] Lou Cannon. Interview with Austin Hoyt. Though at the time GE was the beneficiary of many defense contracts, some of the anti-government sentiment Ronald Reagan was picking up at General Electric might have been the result of an anti-trust suit the Justice Department was mounting against GE.

[8] Ronald Reagan, *Where's the Rest of Me*, p. 267. Reagan was predisposed to take up the issue of government interference. In the late 1940s, for a short period of time, his $1 million seven-year salary with Warner Brothers had been taxed at 91 percent.

[9] Ronald Reagan, *Where's the Rest of Me*. p. 266.

[10] "Encroaching Control," presented at the Annual Meeting of the Phoenix Chamber of Commerce, March 30, 1961.

[11] *Ibid*.

[12] Ronald Reagan, *Where's the Rest of Me*. p. 267.

[13] Patti Reagan, Interview with Austin Hoyt.

[14] Ronald Prescott Reagan, Interview with Austin Hoyt.

[15] Maureen Reagan, Interview with Author.

[16] Patti Davis, Interview with Austin Hoyt.

[17] Ronald Prescott Reagan, Interview with Austin Hoyt.

[18] Patti Davis, Interview with Austin Hoyt.

[19] Barry Goldwater, *The Conscience of a Conservative* (Hillman, 1960), pp. 26–27.

[20] Ronald Reagan, *An American Life*, p. 139.

[21] For a full text of "A Time For Choosing" refer to Ronald Reagan, *Speaking My Mind*, Simon and Schuster, NY, 1989. pp. 22–36.

[22] Edmund Morris, Interview with Author.

[23] Lyn Nofziger, Interview with Author.

[24] Ronald Reagan, *An American Life*, p. 143.

[25] George Will, Interview with Author.

[26] Edwin Meese, Interview with Author.

[27] The Republican primary pitting Nelson Rockefeller versus Barry Goldwater had been so bloody that it nearly ruptured the Republican Party.

[28] Tuttle was an old friend from the 1940s. He'd been the one to suggest that Reagan's "Time For Choosing" speech be broadcast.

[29] Stuart Spencer, Interview with Author.

[30] Ronald Reagan, *An American Life*, p. 145.

[31] *Ibid*, p. 147.

[32] Lou Cannon, Interview with Austin Hoyt.

[33] Edmund Morris, Interview with Author.

[34] Ronald Reagan, *An American Life*, p. 147.

[35] Robert Dallek, Interview with Author.

[36] Lou Cannon, *Reagan*, p. 108.

[37] Stuart Spencer, Interview with Author.

[38] Lyn Nofziger, *Nofziger* (Washington: Regnery Gateway, 1992), p. 44.

[39] Lou Cannon, Interview with Austin Hoyt.

[40] Lyn Nofziger, Interview with Author.
[41] Stuart Spencer, Interview with Author.
[42] Maureen Reagan, Interview with Author.
[43] Lyn Nofziger, Interview with Author.
[44] Stuart Spencer, Interview with Author.
[45] William Norton Smith, Interview with Author.

CHAPTER 7

California Here He Comes

One minute after midnight, January 3, 1967, with Nancy gazing lovingly at him, Ronald Reagan was sworn in as governor of the State of California.

The timing of Reagan's swearing-in ceremony caused a great deal of speculation. The choice of the midnight hour, it was rumored, had been advised by an astrologer. But in her memoirs Nancy denies this vehemently. "It had nothing to do with astrology," she wrote. And she might have a point. Reagan, in fact, was in a hurry to take over the office of governor, to prevent the outgoing Brown Administration from continuing to fill judicial posts—since election time, Governor Brown had appointed, on the average, eight to ten judges per day.[1]

The Reagan family was divided in their feelings about Reagan's new job. Maureen was delighted, and told *The American Experience* she had felt her father would make a great governor because of his common sense and his ability to listen to people.[2] Patti, on the other hand, confided she had been "hysterical."

> The Vietnam War was going on. Berkeley was going on. The one place I wanted to be—if I hadn't been 14-years-old and at a boarding school in Arizona—was on the streets of Haight-Ashbury, braiding flowers into my hair. I mean, this was my goal in life. And now my father was governor of California. So this was, I just didn't think it was a good image for me, you know?[3]

With no prior experience in government, Reagan faced the task of running the state of California, the most populous state in the nation and the sixth largest economy in the world.[4] When reporter Lou Cannon asked what kind of a governor he would make, he quipped, "I don't know. I never played governor."

> He faced an enormous challenge, because Reagan really didn't know anything about politics or government, and he had a lot of people around him who arguably knew even less. I remember Lyn Nofziger once said, "You know, we weren't just amateurs. We were *novice* amateurs."[5]

"As soon as Reagan won, we had a team up in Sacramento, and we began immediately to put together a Cabinet and that sort of thing," Lyn Nofziger recalled. "So when we got up there . . . at least we had the things in place with which to start doing—as soon as we figured out what we were supposed to do."[6]

"He was not really totally prepared for governing," admitted Stuart Spencer,

> We had helped him through the period of the campaign . . . talking about how you introduce a bill, how you do this; you know, where the bathroom is in Sacramento and these sort of things, and he listened and he learned from it, but he wasn't well-versed as most politicians are by the time they reach the governorship.[7]

From the beginning, Reagan proved a "hands-off" governor, relying heavily on the help and advice of a core of close advisors, many of whom would remain with him through his first years at the White House. They proudly announced that the new Administration would be "government by committee." "While the staff had its share of strong personalities," wrote Edwin Meese, Reagan's Attorney General in Sacramento, "there was also a high level of *esprit de corps*, a willingness to work together as a team."[8]

Reagan would be kept informed of the issues through a device invented by his Cabinet Secretary William P. Clark, the "mini memo." It simplified issues into three or four easily digestible paragraphs.

The first issue the new administration had to confront was state finances. Reagan had inherited a $200-million deficit which Governor Brown had accumulated in his last year in office and concealed through budget maneuvers. Required by law to submit a balanced budget, Reagan faced a tough choice: to raise taxes or cut expenses. Rejecting a tax increase, Reagan promised to "cut, squeeze and trim" to bring the budget under control. But then, in a blunt move which betrayed his unfamiliarity with government, he simply ordered a 10-percent cut across the board. "It was a disaster," recalls reporter Gary Wills. "He cut equally into bare-subsistence programs, efficiently run ones and padded ones. Like rain falling on the just and the unjust, it punished the needed and the unnecessary."[9] Reagan himself later admitted, "I was learning that it was one thing to preach a sermon about reducing the size of government, and another to put it into action. . . . I made a lot of mistakes because of inexperience."[10]

One of the most controversial cuts fell on California's mental health system, already stretched beyond capacity. Another fell on the University of California. In addition to the across-the-board 10-percent cut, Reagan suggested that students pay tuition for the first time in the university's history. On February 9, students staged an orderly demonstration in front of the state capitol, protesting tuition payment and budget cuts. Two days later, a much louder group marched, carrying signs which read "Tax the Rich." The politics of fairness—the debate about who should bear the burden of the state's and the nation's financial health—was now on the agenda. The battle line between Reagan and his political opponents for years to come, was first drawn that day in Sacramento.

Other precedents were set in Sacramento. It was there that Nancy Reagan first became a lightning rod for bad press. It all began rather innocently when she called the old governor's mansion in Sacramento "a firetrap," and announced she would be moving her family to a new home. Though she protested that her decision had been based on concerns for the safety of eight-year-old Ron, northern Californians, who valued the governor's mansion as a part of their heritage, felt slighted.

Reporter Joan Didion, later a famous essayist, led the charge. Didion savaged Nancy in an article for *The Saturday Evening Post* which she titled "Pretty Nancy." After a morning at home with California's First Lady, Didion reported she had found everything about Nancy a "put on," calling her smile "a study in frozen insincerity," and concluded that Nancy had the "beginning actress's habit of investing even the most casual lines with a good deal more dramatic expression than is ordinarily called for on a Tuesday morning on 45th Street in Sacramento."[11]

Even 45th Street, the address of the Reagan's new home, became an issue. The plush Tudor in an exclusive Sacramento suburb, bought by friends of Reagan and rented to the governor, was seen as evidence that the Reagans were beholden to the rich and preferred to live among them.

Nancy was devastated by the bad press. Nothing had prepared her for the world of politics. "After a while," Reagan later recalled, "when I'd get home from the capitol I'd know exactly where Nancy was—in the bathtub, having imaginary conversations. . . . She'd just talk to the walls to get it off her chest."[12]

Nancy talked to the walls; Reagan talked to God.

Michael Deaver remembered walking into Reagan's office one day and finding the governor drinking out of a bottle of Maalox, which he had pulled from his briefcase sitting on the credenza behind his desk:

> He put the lid back on the bottle and put it back in his briefcase, and I said, "What are you doing?" And he said, "Oh, my stomach's bothering me." I saw this two or three times. And maybe a month or two later, I went in and he was doing fine, and I said, "What happened to the bottle of [Maalox]?" He said, "Well, I finally figured out what the problem was." I said, "What's that?" He said, "I was always turning around behind me to look for the answer, [when] I should have been looking up."[13]

By the end of his first term, Reagan needed all the help he could get. The student unrest that had begun with the Free Speech Movement at Berkeley in 1964 was escalating into open rebellion. San Francisco Mayor Willie Brown, at the time a young Assemblyman, described the circumstances.

> The Vietnam War had energized lots of people to be campus activists. The environmental movement was beginning to grow. The whole business of ethnic identification and ethnic pride was very much a part of the college campuses, with the concept of the Black Panthers and others, and there was a quest for academic freedom by a faculty basically hostile to anything Ronald Reagan was about.[14]

Reagan's tough campaign rhetoric, his budget cuts, and his vocal support of the Vietnam war, had made him a villain in the eyes of many students and even faculty members at the University of California. The students, in the words of Brown, became a "vocal and identifiable anti-Reagan force."[15] Reagan too stoked the fires of discontent. For the first two years of his governorship, he had missed few opportunities to express his contempt for the student radicals. "Their signs say 'make love not war' but they don't look like they could do much of either," he told a crowd. He said of a demonstrator "he had a haircut like Tarzan, walked like Jane and smelled like Cheetah." Lyn Nofziger, who accompanied Reagan on many a controversial visit to university campuses, explained Reagan's strong feelings:

> He thought [the campus unrest] was outrageous because those kids were getting a good education at a very low price and he felt that they were clear out of line, and he wanted to put an end to it. . . . It just went against his grain, you go to school to learn something, you don't go to school to demonstrate.[16]

The inevitable confrontation between governor and students came early in 1969, at Berkeley. In February, the campus was paralyzed by a strike called by the Third Liberation Movement. It was joined by thousands of students, members of the Black Panther Party, and some professors.

From Sacramento, Reagan watched the situation with growing concern. He interpreted the uprising as an effort by a radical minority to deny a majority their legitimate rights. He blamed much of the problem on a minority of "left wing" radicals.

> There was a spellbinding moment when he was governor, confronting a bunch of Berkeley university profs

. . . in the spring of 1969. Reagan, confronting these angry profs, suddenly recognizes in their midst a radical from his Hollywood days, his name was, I think, "Popski." And he said, "You, Popski. I know you, and I know what you stand for." Lost his cool. There was a direct connection there—the anarchy that prevailed on the Berkeley campus in 1969 with the anarchy that he saw immediately after World War II outside the gates of Warner Brothers.[17]

When the Berkeley police were sent in to break the strike, violence erupted. Reagan sent in the Alameda County Sheriff's Deputies and the California Highway Patrol. "The state had the responsibility to establish rules of behavior," Reagan later wrote, ". . . and as Governor, it was my job to enforce them."[18]

But the heightened police presence only exacerbated tensions. Riots broke out on campus and on the streets of Berkeley. One student, James Rector, was killed by a deputy. Outnumbered, the law enforcement officers called for help. Earlier, Reagan had gone on television to issue a warning: "I believe that when any group's rights are being imposed upon or any individual's rights by any others, it is the obligation of government to protect those constitutional rights at the point of bayonet if necessary."

Now he made good on his threat. At his request, the National Guard descended on Berkeley with bayonets fixed. They occupied the city for seventeen days.

Reagan succeeded in pacifying Berkeley, and 80 percent of Californians applauded his determined stand. But there were those who felt deeply that the governor had grossly over-reacted at Berkeley, and that he had shown his true self as a trigger-happy extremist. The events at Berkeley later became cause for anxiety among those who feared Reagan's finger on the nuclear trigger.

With the university at peace, Ronald Reagan prepared to run for a second term as governor, on a record which Lou Cannon later described as "responsible but undistinguished."

In his first campaign, he had promised to lower taxes, and to control expenditures by reducing government waste. In fact, income and corporate taxes had risen during his governorship, and the California state budget increased.[19] Even at the state level government had proved a tough beast to starve through cutbacks in "fraud waste and abuse."

Reagan had lost some of his luster. In 1966 he had beaten Brown by one million votes. When he ran for a second term in 1970, against former Assembly Speaker Jesse Unruh, his margin of victory was halved.

Following his election, Reagan immediately turned his attention to the issue of government growth. In his first term, he had naively believed he could reduce the size of government through "cut, squeeze and trim" and had implemented a 10-percent across-the-board cut. A more experienced man, he now focused his attention on a single program. "Welfare," he told Californians in the first address of his second term, "is the biggest single outlay of public funds at three different levels of government: federal, state and county. And welfare is adrift without rudder or compass."

Between 1963 and 1970, the number of Californians receiving assistance under the Aid to Families with Dependent Children program (AFDC) had almost quadrupled, with the caseload continuing to grow at a rate of 40,000 per month.[20] The "welfare monster," as Reagan called, it was "the big villain that kept all of our savings from being returned to the people."[21] California had earned a reputation as the "welfare capital of the nation" and Reagan was determined to change that perception.

Reagan's Welfare Reform Bill, the first ever in the country, became the centerpiece of his second term. Taking rhetorical aim at "welfare cheats," Reagan told Californians "public assistance should go to the needy and not the greedy."

> The Republicans would argue that [welfare reform] was in fact needed. That the alarming rate and the number of people who were going on the rolls and that the evidence of abuse was so rampant that welfare needed to be reformed. I think they're wrong on both scores. I don't think there was such rampant fraud that it should have constituted a motivation for reform. Was welfare reform needed for other reasons? Absolutely. We did not have at that stage of the game [enough] emphasis on putting people to work and that's what more than anything else should be the trust of any welfare reform effort. That was not what Reagan had in mind.[22]

Although Reagan's welfare proposal did include measures to put people back to work, its emphasis was on saving taxpayers money and on reducing the scope of government.

Reagan's proposal faced a tough battle in the Democrat-controlled State Assembly. Bob Moretti, Assembly Speaker, said, "They forget that behind those figures are real-life people. We need a more humane approach."

In his first term, Reagan governed through confrontation. Now he needed to collaborate with the Assembly if he wanted his welfare bill to pass. William Hauck, then Assistant to Speaker Bob Moretti, explained why the welfare bill was of paramount importance to Ronald Reagan.

> Reagan was beginning to think about his own legacy. He was beginning to think about the accomplishments

that would be looked back on when he left the governorship, and I'm sure people would argue that Reagan
was also beginning to build, or try to build, a record to
run for President.[23]

Reagan bargained and cajoled state legislators to get what he
wanted. He also used a political tactic he later perfected in the
White House. The administration organized a letter-writing
campaign to put pressure on the Assembly. Whether because of
this pressure, or because he too had political aspirations,
Moretti decided to meet Reagan half-way.

The agreement did not come overnight. For one week, in the
summer of 1971, Reagan and Moretti engaged in intense round-
the-clock negotiations, Reagan got to exercise the skills he had
first acquired in the 1950s as president of the Screen Actors
Guild. The governor and the speaker "negotiated . . . swore and
questioned each other's motivations,"[24] but in the end they hammered out a compromise which was passed by the State Assembly. The 1971 Welfare Reform Bill called for strengthened family
responsibility, increased grants for those "with nowhere else to
turn," and a requirement that those able to work take a job or
enroll in job training. Born from compromise, the 1971 bill,
Edwin Meese pointed out, nevertheless "embodied some of the
key themes of Ronald Reagan's conservative philosophy."[25]

"By almost any yardstick, liberal, conservative or manager-
ial," wrote Lou Cannon, "the welfare bill was a success." Partly
due to the tightening of eligibility requirements, the monthly
increase in welfare rolls declined from 40,000 to 8,000. Yet payments to those categorized as "the truly needy" increased by
nearly 40 percent.[26] Efforts to help people back to work were
less successful. By July 1975, when Reagan's "Work Experience
Program" was cancelled, only 9,600 former recipients of AFDC
had found jobs.[27]

Most important, Reagan was able to fulfill the promise he had made to voters in his first term, saving taxpayers $2 billion, and bringing the spiraling growth of state government under control.

The signing and implementation of the Welfare Reform Bill also showed how far Reagan had come since the confrontational style and indiscriminate budget-cutting strategy of his first term. By most accounts, it was in the process of getting his Welfare Reform Plan through the California Assembly that Ronald Reagan learned to govern.

> [It] showed him that he could make some changes, that he could not only talk about and move people to get things done, but he could actually move the mechanics of government to get things done. And I think that confidence that it gave Reagan, was more important than most people realize.[28]

If Reagan had gained confidence as a leader, Nancy was relieved to see her husband's political career coming, apparently, to an end.

"At the end of Ronnie's second term, I found myself sitting alone in an empty room after packing everything away," Nancy recalled wistfully, "I sat on the bed and looked at the garden, so lovely with all the camellias in bloom. . . . As it grew darker outside and I sat alone in that empty room, I thought to myself, 'So this is how it ends.' Our eight years in politics were over."[29]

NOTES

[1] Nancy Reagan, *My Turn*, p. 134.
[2] Maureen Reagan, Interview with Author.
[3] Patti Davis, Interview with Austin Hoyt.
[4] After the United States the Soviet Union, France, Germany and Japan.
[5] Lou Cannon, Interview with Austin Hoyt.
[6] Lyn Nofziger, Interview with Author.

[7] Stuart Spencer, Interview with Author.

[8] Edwin Meese III, *With Reagan: The Inside Story* (Washington: Regnery Gateway, 1992), p. 23. The team moved on with Reagan from California to the White House. Ed Meese would later serve as Counselor to the President, Bill Clark, as one of Reagan's six National Security Advisors, Michael Deaver, as Deputy Chief of Staff during Reagan's first presidential term, and Lyn Nofziger, who served as advisor to the President for two years. They were eventually joined by Caspar Weinberger, who became Reagan's Secretary of Defense between 1981 and 1987.

[9] Gary Wills, *Reagan's America*.

[10] Ronald Reagan, *An American Life*, p.166.

[11] Joan Didion, "Pretty Nancy," *The Saturday Evening Post*, June 1, 1968. quoted in Cannon, p. 143. Didion's portrait stuck. Nancy reports that when she met Kay Graham, owner of *The Washington Post* in 1981, Mrs. Graham commented "Just about the only thing we knew about you was that article by Joan Didion in *The Saturday Evening Post*." Nancy Reagan, *My Turn*, p. 35.

[12] Ronald Reagan, *An American Life*, p. 167

[13] Michael Deaver, Interview with Author. Deaver called it "stomach medicine," According to Reagan it was Maalox. *An American Life*, p. 168.

[14] Willie Brown, Interview with Author.

[15] Willie Brown, Interview with Author.

[16] Lyn Nofziger, Interview with Author.

[17] Edmund Morris, Interview with Author.

[18] Ronald Reagan, *An American Life*, p. 181.

[19] During his two terms, but mostly as a result of a 1967 tax bill, corporate taxes grew from 5.5 to 9 percent, and income taxes from 7 to 11 percent. Cannon, *Reagan*, p. 156.

[20] Ronald Reagan, *An American Life*, p. 188, Lou Cannon, *Reagan*, p. 178.

[21] Quoted in Cannon, *Reagan*, p. 177.

[22] Willie Brown, Interview with Author.

[23] William Hauck, Interview with Author.

[24] Lou Cannon, *Reagan*, p. 181.

[25] Edwin Meese, Interview with Author.

[26] *Ibid*, p. 182. Ronald Reagan, *An American Life*, p. 190.

[27] Lou Cannon, *Reagan*, p. 183.

[28] Michael Deaver, Interview with Author.

[29] Nancy Reagan, *My Turn*, p. 145.

CHAPTER 8

Candidate

R onald Reagan emerged from his eight years as governor of California with a national following and a staff committed to see the governor become a candidate for President. "I think Reagan felt that he was the heir apparent for the nomination of the Republican party in 1976."[1] But Watergate intervened. Richard Nixon resigned in favor of Gerald Ford. Two years later, Ford decided to seek the Republican nomination. Reagan faced a difficult choice.

He was 65 years old, and this might be his last shot at the Presidency. But it was a long shot. He would have to wrestle the nomination away from a sitting President with all the resources of an incumbent and the support of the Republican Party. Those around him urged him to take the risk. "We figured Reagan's time had come," said Reagan's friend and communications director, Lyn Nofziger, "and that's what politics is all about."[2]

Nofziger, along with Reagan's millionaire backers Tuttle, Salvatori and Rubel, the "kitchen cabinet," had their eye on the White House even before Reagan took office as governor of California. The governorships of New York and California were always considered stepping-stones to the Presidency. So when Reagan was elected, he joined Nelson Rockefeller, the governor of New York, as a possible candidate in 1968. But there was more to Nofziger's interest in Reagan than the customary Republican line of succession. Shortly after joining

Reagan, Nofziger became convinced that Reagan "might some-day" be elected President.[3]

> What got me when I began working for Reagan and traveling with Reagan was the fact that people out there were excited about him. There was something between him and the people he talked to—whether it was an individual or whether it was a group of people, it didn't make any difference—there was something there that attracted people to him. People wanted to be his friend, people wanted to talk to him. . . . He would finish this speech and people would come up and ask for his autograph and I would say, you know, Ron, we've got to get out of here. We've got to go. "Well, just a minute," and he would sign every darn autograph that people asked for. He was just an instinc-tually nice man who attracted people to him and he was articulate and he was a man of conviction. No, there was never anything phony about Ronald Reagan, and maybe that's what it was.[4]

In December 1966, Nofziger and the California millionaires called on governor-elect Reagan at his home to try to convince him to run for President in 1968. Reagan, in the words of Nofziger, was "not enthused by the idea." "My feeling was that to go straight from Hollywood to governor and one year after you were in the position [to say] 'I want to be President of the United States' [was not] credible."[5] Although Reagan refused to formally announce his candidacy, this did not prevent his backers from promoting it in 1968. With half a million dollars from the "kitchen cabinet," Nofizger launched a draft initia-tive. Reagan was billed as "the rising star in the West." Much as he had done while 'not running for governor' in 1965, Reagan missed few opportunities to speak at Republican events and fund-raisers.

The initiative gave many Americans their first glimpse of the governor of California, and many liked what they saw—a tough-talking candidate committed to standing up against the radicalism of the 1960s. When the Republicans gathered in Miami in 1968 to select a candidate, Reagan, after only eighteen months in elected office, had pulled 23 percent of the primary vote and was the clear favorite among Republican youth. Caught in the excitement of his success, he mounted the podium at the convention and announced he was candidate for the Republican nomination. But by then, former Vice President Richard Nixon already had a lock on the nomination. Reagan lost his half-hearted first bid for the presidency. But he was not upset. "I knew I wasn't ready to be President," he later wrote.[6]

Eight years later, with two terms as governor under his belt, Reagan felt ready. On Halloween night 1975, the family gathered at their home in Pacific Palisades. "In three weeks," Reagan told his children, "I'm going to announce that I'm entering the race. Otherwise I'd feel like the guy who always sat on the bench and never got into the game."[7]

The Reagan campaign targeted the Democrats and big government, not Gerald Ford. Reagan would later write: "My theme was familiar to anyone who had heard me speak over the years: scale back the size of the federal government, reduce taxes, balance the budget and return to the people the freedoms usurped by bureaucrats."[8] He ran as an outsider, stressing his California roots and the fact that he was not part of the Washington establishment. In the wake of Watergate, the scandal which had so badly eroded public confidence in politicians and government, running against government was a good strategy. It was, in fact, the same strategy Jimmy Carter was using in his bid for the Democratic nomination.

At first, the going was rough. Reagan lost to Ford in New Hampshire and again in Massachusetts, Vermont, Florida, and even Illinois, his native state. The North Carolina primary, in late March, was a must-win for Reagan, and polls showed he trailed Ford by ten points. Everyone, including Nancy, who feared her husband would be "embarrassed," urged him to quit.

"It was at this point that one really saw the essence of Reagan's character in its full flower," Martin Anderson, one of Reagan's closest advisors, told *The American Experience*, "the solid tempered steel bar beneath the silky exterior":

> The campaign was basically considered dead in the water. He had just lost five straight Presidential primaries to President Ford. He was regarded by many in his party as almost a traitor for running against an incumbent Republican President. Most leading Republicans were calling for him to get out of the race.[9] The newspaper editorials—the *L.A. Times* for example saying, it's not a matter of *if*, it's a question of *when* Reagan gets out of the race. Maybe most importantly, we were about $2 million in debt. And our plane we had we couldn't pay for, so they took it away. And we were forced to rent this little tiny plane. I remember it was painted bright yellow. We called it the Yellow Banana. And nobody would sell us anything unless we paid in advance, cash. We'd come into a campaign stop, and Michael Deaver, who later became Deputy Chief of Staff, would go out and find the local McDonald's or Kentucky Fried Chicken, and get one of those big buckets, and bring it back and put it in the aisle of the plane, and we would have lunch.[10]

The afternoon of March 23, facing imminent defeat, the

campaign staff met with Reagan in a hotel room to decide what to do next.

> All the top people in the campaign were in the room. And the consensus was, "certainly you have to quit." And Reagan was just sitting there listening to this.
>
> "I'm telling you right now," and he was looking at everybody in the room, "that I am going to run in every single primary from here to the convention even if I lose every single one." I'm thinking, "My God, you know, I'm on a kamikaze flight here. We're going to go into these primaries one after another, loss after loss, after loss." And he was dead serious.[11]

Reagan stumped North Carolina day and night trying to re-ignite his campaign. Up until that point, his main foreign policy issue had been to oppose the ongoing negotiations to hand the government of Panama control of the Panama Canal. But in North Carolina, Reagan "took off the gloves." He abandoned his strategy of not attacking Ford, and savaged the President and his Secretary of State Henry Kissinger with a dramatic—even apocalyptic—speech on the failure of détente:

> Ladies and gentlemen, I'm deeply concerned about our defense posture. Despite the assurances of Dr. Kissinger and Mr. Ford, the United States is no longer the first military power on earth. The Soviet army is now twice the size of ours. Russia's annual investment in weapons, in strategic and conventional, now runs some 50 percent ahead of ours. Under Kissinger and Ford, this nation's become number two in military power in a world where it's dangerous—if not fatal—to be second best.

Instead of the defeat that polls had predicted, Reagan beat Ford in North Carolina by ten points. The anti-détente speech, broadcast nationwide, rallied conservatives behind Reagan, raised a desperately needed $1.5 million and set his campaign back on track.[12]

Geography now favored Reagan. His message appealed to voters in the more conservative West and South. In quick succession, he won Texas, Alabama, Georgia, Indiana, Nebraska, and not surprisingly, California. It was a hopeful Ronald Reagan who arrived in Kansas City on August 18 after fighting, as he had said he would, every campaign all the way to the convention. "I believe that there is a very great possibility—if not probability—that I could go to the convention with enough delegates in advance to win on the first ballot," he told reporters. On the convention floor his supporters carried a banner promising that Reagan would "make peanut butter" out of the Democratic nominee, former Georgia governor and peanut-grower Jimmy Carter.

Reagan got 47.4 percent of the delegates and lost the nomination to Gerald Ford. But when the voting was over something new and strange took place. Those who watched the Republican convention on August 19, 1976, witnessed Ronald Reagan work his magic on the American people. Reagan's son, Ron, who accompanied his parents to the convention, described the moment:

> Ford had given his acceptance speech, and he then turned to the skybox where we were, where my father was, and sort of beckoned my father to come down. He wanted to have him come down, and they could sort of throw their arms around each other and you know, bring the party together. My father was very reluctant, because he thought it was Ford's day, and he should

have it, he should have the podium to himself. But Ford kept motioning, and the crowd kept cheering.[13]

"The response of those delegates was something unbelievable," recalled Nancy Reagan, "just unbelievable. There we were in this box way back in the back, and he stood and kept motioning to them to sit down. They never would sit down. They wouldn't stop yelling and yelling for him, and, "Speech! Speech!"[14]

After basking in the audience's adulation for close to twenty minutes, Reagan heeded Ford's request. He slowly wound his way through the crowd as the applause built to near frenzy. "This is theater of the purest kind, as he well understood," noted a biographer.

Reagan appeared on the stage looking tall, vibrant, magnificent. His eyes shining with emotion, he uttered a few graceful remarks thanking Ford and the delegates. And then, after a moment's hesitation, he launched into a speech, the same speech, some say, he would have given had he won the nomination.

If I could just take a moment. I had an assignment the other day. Someone asked me to write a letter for a time capsule that is going to be opened in Los Angeles one hundred years from now. We live in a world in which the great powers have poised and aimed at each other horrible missiles of destruction, nuclear weapons that can in a matter of minutes arrive at each other's country and destroy virtually the civilized world we live in. And suddenly it dawned on me, those who would read this letter one hundred years from now will know whether those missiles were fired. They will know whether we met our challenge. Whether they have the freedoms that we have known up until now, will depend on what we do here.

The hall fell into complete silence. "You could hear a pin drop," Nancy later recalled.[15] As cameras panned the crowd, there were tears streaming down many faces.

> They were mesmerized. You go to anyone who was at that convention, and they'll say it was one of the greatest speeches they ever heard. And you'll say, well, what did he say, and they can't quite remember. And it's fascinating, because under that kind of pressure, what kind of squirted out in its essence was, 'Look, I'll tell you, in my mind, the most important thing we have to face is, how do we save the world from Armageddon? How do we do something about this threat of nuclear war?[16]

"Those delegates had gotten a glimpse into Reagan's soul," Michael Deaver later wrote. "It was his first [major] defeat and in losing he won. He had made the turn toward becoming a credible figure on the national stage."[17] Nancy Reagan later called the 1976 Republican Primary "a glorious defeat."[18]

The day after the convention, choked with emotion, Reagan bid farewell to his campaign staff. Her back turned to the audience, Nancy wept uncontrollably.

> Sure, there's a disappointment in what happened, but the cause, the cause goes on. Don't get cynical. Don't get cynical because look at yourselves and what you were willing to do. And recognize that there are millions of people out there that want what you want, that want it to be that way, want it to be a shining city on a hill.

On their way to the airport, the Reagans passed a sign which read: "Republicans, you picked the wrong guy."

The Reagans went home to California physically and emo-

tionally exhausted. On the return flight, Reagan read while
Nancy slept, her head on her husband's lap. Reagan's daughter,
Maureen, sat right behind.

> I was watching the back of his head, and I kept try-
> ing to think what he must be thinking looking out the
> window of that plane, when just a few days ago we'd
> come in with such high hopes, and now we were going
> home and would this ever happen?[19]

Martin Anderson approached Reagan and asked him to sign
his convention ticket to keep as a souvenir.

> And what he wrote was, 'We fought, we dreamed,
> and the dream is still with us." And looking back at it
> now, he never gave up, just kept right on going. It was
> an incredible, crushing defeat. And it didn't crush him.
> He just came back up, shook his head, and said, "OK,
> what's next?" And that began the campaign for the year
> 1980.[20]

For the next four years Reagan would keep his candidacy
alive doing radio commentary, writing a weekly newspaper col-
umn and giving speeches. Lyn Nofziger organized funds and
support through a Political Action Committee (PAC) called
Citizens for the Republic.

In his "wilderness years," Reagan found time to work at his new
Santa Barbara ranch, "Rancho del Cielo" and to bone up on his
reading. By the time he became President, chief speech writer
Anthony Dolan told *The American Experience*, Reagan was quite
familiar with the seminal works of conservatism: Friedrich Hayek
and Frederic Bastiat on the virtues of market capitalism, and
Whitaker Chambers on the evil of Communism.[21]

Reagan was the recognized leader of the conservative movement at time when a tide of conservatism was surging in America. In California, a highly publicized tax revolt known as Proposition 13 succeeded in drastically cutting back property taxes, capturing headlines and the nation's imagination. Reagan's conservative gospel—less government, less taxes and anti-Communism—was gaining more adherents every day. "There was a rebellion out there," he later observed, "and it was growing like wildfire."[22]

The rebellion was fueled by a growing sense of insecurity. The late 1970s were a tough time for many Americans. Inflation spiraled to 14 percent, mortgage rates pushed 20 percent. Many could not afford a home. Hard-earned savings were being eaten up by inflation. Unemployment was on the rise. Gasoline prices more than doubled, and long gas lines tested drivers' patience.

Americans were also seeing an erosion of U.S. influence abroad. An emboldened Soviet Union, exploiting U.S. paralysis in the wake of Vietnam, had grown increasingly aggressive, expanding its influence from Africa to Central America, even invading its neighbor Afghanistan.[23] In Iran, radical muslims deposed the U.S.-backed Shah Rehza Pavlevi and the Ayatollah Khomeini now headed a regime which regarded the United States as "the devil." In 1979, radical students overran the U.S. embassy in Teheran, taking fifty U.S. diplomats hostage. The Iran hostage crisis, headlined night after night on the evening news, was a daily reminder of America's impotence.

A beleaguered President Carter went on television to warn Americans of a "crisis that strikes at the very soul and spirit of our national will" and had cautioned Americans to lower their expectations for their own and their country's future.[24]

It was in this context that Ronald Reagan, once again, announced his candidacy for President. He was 69 years old, but he had the look and the energy of a much younger man. His presidential bid—his third and, as he said, his last—began inauspiciously. He lost the Iowa caucus to George Bush. But in New Hampshire he won 51 percent of the vote in a crowded field featuring prominent Republicans—Senators Howard Baker and Robert Dole and former CIA director George Bush among them. From then on he was the clear front-runner. The trend was unmistakable, Republican voters had shifted to the right.

By the time the Republican Party convened in Detroit to select a candidate, Reagan—having won 29 out of 35 primaries—was the sure nominee. The only thing left on the agenda was the choice of Reagan's running mate. After rejecting Gerald Ford on the grounds that having a former President in the White House could give the appearance of a "joint presidency," Reagan chose George Bush.

In his acceptance speech, Reagan issued the first of many appeals to America's sense of optimism, drawing a sharp contrast between his vision of the future and Jimmy Carter's.

> They say that the United States has had its day in the sun, that our nation has passed its zenith. They expect you to tell your children that the American people no longer have the will to cope with their problems, that the future will be one of sacrifice and few opportunities. My fellow citizens, I utterly reject that view.[25]

His daughter Maureen told *The American Experience:*

> He was so unhappy about what was happening to the country. The fact that people didn't believe in themselves. They didn't believe that they could make things better. That America was a nation in decline. All of those things, and he knew in his heart those things

were not true and he believed that as President he could make the American people look inside themselves and recreate what they needed to have their own American dream.[26]

His official biographer Edmund Morris explained:

> I think he felt sincerely in his heart that he was rescuing the United States from a period of poisonous self-doubt, loss of direction, loss of belief in itself. I think he felt in the late 1970s that he could rescue Jimmy Carter's America and carry her back to the shore and make her alive again.[27]

Reagan relished this great new opportunity to be a hero. It was a role he had first learned to love as lifeguard in Lowell Park, and played again as an actor in Hollywood and as governor of California—only this time the stakes were enormous, as were the possibilities.

He kicked off his campaign on Labor Day at Liberty Park in New Jersey, against the backdrop of the Statue of Liberty, her torch dark and her facade tarnished from years of neglect. In shirt sleeves, his hair tussled by the wind, a youthful-looking and vigorous Ronald Reagan addressed a blue-collar, mostly European ethnic audience, appealing to their patriotism and their pocketbooks.

> Let it show on the record that when the American people cried out for economic help Jimmy Carter took refuge behind a dictionary. Well, if it's a definition he wants, I'll give him one. A recession is when your neighbor loses his job. A depression is when you lose yours. And recovery is when Jimmy Carter loses his.

From the New Jersey waterfront, to a street in the Bronx, and a steel mill in Ohio, Reagan reached out to new constituencies—ethnic minorities working hard to "make it" in America, Catholics who supported his anti-abortion platform, and, most important, blue-collar workers—who had traditionally voted Democrat. "Our message was that the Republican party of traditional values and economic growth offered them a better prospect of effective government than did the crumbling New Deal coalition," wrote campaign strategist Edwin Meese.[28] In their effort to get voters to "cross over," the Republicans had their best weapon in the candidate who tirelessly preached how he himself had made the transition from New Deal Democrat to conservative Republican.

Carter was slow to recognize the danger of Reagan's assault. Much like Governor Brown in the 1966 California governor's race, he believed Ronald Reagan was not a worthy contender. "The Carter people were delighted to have Ronald Reagan as Jimmy Carter's opponent," recalls correspondent Sam Donaldson, who covered the Carter campaign. "They salivated over it. They thought their re-election was guaranteed."[29]

Reagan's early campaign performance validated Carter's optimism. The press kept calling attention to Reagan's "gaffes"—hastily spoken misstatements or factual errors which suggested that the President lacked depth and lacked true command of the issues. Reagan's biographer Edmund Morris explained that Reagan's photographic memory was to blame. "He tended to believe everything he read, and he would read books of spurious quotations, phony Abraham Lincoln quotes, statistics that were patently wrong, and he would repeat them."[30]

One of Reagan's most famous "gaffes" took place in Ohio, when he told an audience that trees contributed to pollution by emitting hydrocarbons. The press had a field day. At a campaign appearance at Claremont College in California a reporter hung a sign on a tree that read, "Chop Me Down Before I Kill Again." Lou Cannon, who covered Reagan in 1980, explained why the press devoted so much attention to the issue. "He had his share of gaffes. A lot of people that I have covered made huge gaffes, but when Reagan did it we saw it as evidence that he was a dummy because that's the way he was typecast."[31]

The reports hurt Ronald Reagan. By early October opinion polls showed that he trailed Carter by 10 points.

But as the season wore on, Reagan's campaign tightened its focus. The candidate kept his comments to handful of issues: He promised to cut taxes by 30 percent, to balance the budget, and to reduce government regulations. He also advocated a military buildup to counter the growing aggressiveness of the Soviet Union. He called his program "peace through strength." But mostly, he hammered away at Carter's failures.

Reagan attacked Carter for what he called the President's "lack of resolve," which had exposed America to attacks by "adversaries large and small." He questioned Carter's diagnosis of a national "malaise," which he contrasted with his own optimistic vision of the future. But most damagingly, Reagan focused his campaign on the economy—on the frustration caused by inflation, high interest rates and recession, coining a phrase, "the misery index," to summarize the country's economic situation. His assault on Carter's domestic policies boiled down to a single question: "Are you better off than you were four years ago?"

Aware of the President's vulnerability, the Carter campaign searched for a strategy which did not depend on his record. They targeted Ronald Reagan.

"We knew the voters had doubts about Reagan," Carter's pollster Patrick Caddell admitted, "that he was old, that he was not very smart, that maybe he was irresponsible and even somewhat dangerous. The most important thing for us to do was to make people think of whether they actually wanted a person like that to occupy the Oval Office."[32]

Carter's attack on Reagan became increasingly personal. Campaign ads depicted Reagan as a dangerous man, likely to start a nuclear war, and as a divisive ideologue. "Ronald Reagan," Carter told an audience in Los Angeles "would divide North from South, Christian from Jew, and rural from urban, black from white."

Reagan continued his assault on the Carter presidency: "The Carter record is a litany of despair, of broken promises, of sacred trusts abandoned or forgotten . . . I challenge Mr. Carter to defend his record of making Americans worse off economically than they were when he took office."[33]

He also blamed Carter for the fate of the American hostages in Iran, now in captivity for nearly one year: "I believe this Administration's foreign policy helped create the entire situation which made their kidnap possible and I think the fact that they've been there that long is a humiliation and a disgrace to this country," he told reporters.[34]

By late October the election was a dead heat.

The face-to-face showdown took place on October 28, when Republican candidate Ronald Reagan debated President Jimmy Carter in front of 100 million television viewers—the largest television audience in American political history.

"It was the 'Iceman' versus the 'Gipper'," recalls Michael Deaver. "Reagan was well-prepared and very relaxed. I even allowed him to drink a small glass of red wine to help him relax further and put a little rose color on his cheeks."[35]

"We had tried to paint Reagan as an extremist, a dangerous person," says Carter's pollster Patrick Caddell. "But he looked more like somebody's grandfather than a nut who would push the red button."[36]

The Reagan campaign team had carefully prepared their candidate in expectation of a personal attack from Jimmy Carter.[37]

> [They] prepared for Ronald Reagan a paragraph of stern rhetoric that he could lay on Jimmy Carter when as they expected during the debate Carter was mean. So the paragraph was written. You're lowering the tone of the campaign and engaging in rhetoric unworthy of a President, etc., etc., harumph, frump, frump. Perfectly unlike Ronald Reagan. And Reagan took it, put it in his briefcase.[38]

Midpoint into the debate, Carter accused Reagan of opposing Medicare. Reagan shook his head in disbelief and said, "there you go again. . . ."

With a single memorable phrase, Reagan had demolished Carter's strategy. As George Will later explained, "He was saying gently you're caricaturing me. Everything you people have heard about me is a caricature and here they go again."[39]

The next day *Washington Post* columnist David Broder wrote, "Carter has accomplished almost every objective, except a most important one: The destruction of Reagan's credibility as President."

Carter's fate was sealed.

On November 8, 1980, the Reagans voted at the home of friends in Pacific Palisades. At 5:15 P.M. Pacific time, with only 5 percent of the votes in, and the polls in California and other western states still open, Jimmy Carter conceded.

That night, the Reagans, with friends and supporters, celebrated in the ballroom of the Los Angeles Century City Hotel.

Reagan had optimistic view of America. "It is time to realize we are too great a nation to limit ourselves to small dreams. We're not, as some would have us believe, doomed to an inevitable decline. I do not believe in a fate that will fall on us no matter what we do . . . so with all the creative energy at our command let us renew our determination, our courage, and our strength."

The President would concentrate on the key issues of his Administration and on selling his program to Congress and to the people. From the day he took office the weight of his presidency would fall on three men—White House Counselor Edwin Meese, Deputy Chief of Staff Michael Deaver, and Chief of Staff James Baker. Collectively known as "the troika," they would serve as "deputy presidents." To them, Reagan delegated unprecedented authority.

Chief of Staff James Baker III was intelligent, suave, and deft at playing the Washington political game. Deaver had a background in public relations, a good rapport with Reagan, and the rare and complete trust of the First Lady. Edwin Meese III had a sharp and uncluttered legal mind, finely tuned to Reagan's thinking. His job was to "conceptualize" policy and advise the President.

"I am speaking to you tonight to give you a report on the state of our nation's economy. I regret to say that we're in the worst economic mess since the great depression. . . .Over the past decades we've talked about curtailing government spending so that we can then lower the tax burden. . . . But there were always those who told us taxes couldn't be cut until spending was reduced. Well, you know, we can lecture our children about extravagance until we run out of voice and breath. Or we can cure their extravagance by simply reducing their allowance."

Charlie Hatcher - D	Albany, Georgia (southwestern part of State), 2nd District, 1st term. Serves on the Agriculture Committee and the Small Business Committee. Recently joined the House Conservative Democratic Forum, but did not attend the President's March 5 breakfast meeting with Forum members. Reported to be undecided on the bipartisan substitute, leaning in favor of it.
We can count on his vote. Says the people of So. Ga. are 90% with us	
Dan Mica - D	West Palm Beach and Boca Raton, Florida, 11th District, 2nd term. Serves on Foreign Affairs and Veterans' Affairs Committees. He is a member of the Conservative Democratic Forum. In a recent discussion with him (Legislative Affairs Staff), he said that generally a majority of his constituents favor the President's program, but those opposed are the elderly and poor and that they are "scared" and "bitter." He indicated that he wants to support the President but that he remains undecided, because Jones has asked to see him upon his return to Washington and because he has not seen comparative analysis of budget proposals.
Sounds very supportive but has promised to listen to Jones pitch. He believes he'll end up with Gramm-Latta but hopes it can be fine tuned to reassure those Sr. citizens who are frightened and think they are going to be cut.	

Early in his Administration, Reagan, against popular perception, did not "watch television and go to bed." He took volumes of homework upstairs and obsessively went through every single bit of paper making extensive notes in the margins in preparation for the next day. As he became more detached from the job later in his Presidency, these notes would be replaced by simple checkmarks.

Reagan's chief domestic adversary, Speaker of the House Tip O'Neill opposed his conservative economic package, calling it a "soak the poor" program.

An unusually stern Reagan listens as budget director David Stockman, proponent of "supply-side economics," delivers a report on the growing deficit.

"He had written a check to some woman who was on welfare. And the next month he got his bank statement. Well, you know, the bank statement had these checks and her check wasn't in it. So, he called her on the phone and said you know, "You haven't cashed that check." She said, "Oh no, I framed it." He said, "Well my God I sent you that money so you'd have some money to eat. I'll send you another check, you keep that one framed and cash this one."

—Interview with Michael Deaver

A Reagan family portrait at Christmas in the White House.

As the nation plunged into recession in 1982, Reagan Reagan worried that "Our projections are out the window . . . We [are looking] at $200-billion deficits if we can't pull off some miracles."

The image of the President as rancher and rugged outdoorsman projected the values of freedom and individualism which his Administration advocated.

After the attempted assassination Reagan would never again mingle with his constituents. Here he "works the crowd" from the safety of his limo.

Mother Theresa visited with Reagan at the White House shortly after Hinkley's assassination attempt. She confirmed his belief that God had spared him for a reason.

The President writing at his desk in the White House living quarters.

Reagan visiting with staunch Solidarity supporter Pope John Paul II in the Vatican, June 1982. Both had just survived assassination attempts.

Rancho del Cielo was Reagan's refuge. There he could renew and rejuvenate himself.

Ron and Nancy relaxing over a casual dinner in the living quarters of the White House.

"There was nothing he enjoyed more as President than saluting. As Commander in Chief, he would do that little extra flip to the salute, which you hardly ever see in the Armed Services anyway, it was a real Hollywood salute. But it meant a great deal to him."
—Interview with Edmund Morris

The President and Nancy mourn the space shuttle *Challenger* disaster.

Reagan had beaten Carter by 10 points, carrying 44 out of 50 states. Riding on his coattails, the Republicans had taken control of the Senate and added 30 seats to their numbers in the House. The Reagan camp was elated. "Republicans," commented Maureen Reagan, "did not win these kind of elections the way we did."[40]

It was a spectacular victory, not only a triumph for the Conservative movement but also a vote against Jimmy Carter. Reagan's conservative followers, the "true believers," had paved his way to the presidency. But he would never have gotten there without the "cross-over" vote of Democrats, particularly the blue-collar workers fed up with the Carter years.

Reagan's political strategist and pollster, Richard Wirthlin, and his chief domestic advisor, Martin Anderson, concur that the 1980 victory resulted from a combination of Ronald Reagan the man, his message, and the times.

> The only way Ronald Reagan won in 1980 was reaching out and both by message and by who he was to bring in the blue-collar, middle-class, Catholic ethnic vote which I think he did not so much appealing to the issues but more articulating the values of patriotism, of self-esteem, of accomplishment, to a sense of security, [and] that served him very well.[41]

> Ronald Reagan's message in terms of optimism, economic growth, national security had not changed [since the 1970s]. What had changed was that the country had gone through a couple of very bad years. If times had been good it would have been very difficult for him to get elected. But the times were bad and [voters] said, OK, what is the alternative?[42]

NOTES

[1] Stuart Spencer, Interview with Author.

[2] Lyn Nofziger, Interview with Author.

[3] Lynn Nofziger, *Nofziger*, p. 42.

[4] Lynn Nofziger, Interview with Author.

[5] Reagan, Interview with Lou Cannon, July 30, 1981, quoted in Lou Cannon, *Reagan*, p. 159.

[6] Ronald Reagan, *An American Life*, p. 178.

[7] Nancy Reagan, *My Turn*, p. 181.

[8] Ronald Reagan, *An American Life*, p. 201.

[9] Eleven of the twelve former Republican chairmen, the National Republican Conference of Mayors, and Republican governors called on Reagan to withdraw. Even Barry Goldwater, a friend of the Davis's, had endorsed Ford.

[10] Martin Anderson, Interview with Author.

[11] Martin Anderson, Interview with Author. Anderson was not alone in experiencing Reagan's determination at his own expense. Reagan's son, Ron, told us an anecdote which took place at Rancho del Cielo, the Reagans' ranch, while he helped his father collect flagstone for a patio he was building around this time:

> We went out to retrieve a lot of these big heavy stones and load them into a little trailer that would be then hauled behind this ancient old original Jeep. I mean this was just like the proto-Jeep that he still had, because he'd never throw anything away. And so we'd, you know, spend a few hours hauling these big heavy rocks and we'd load them into the little trailer, It's now piled high. It must weigh tons. Climb back into the Jeep and head up this slope that's steep. I mean this is steep. And on one side you've got a sheer drop to the Santa Ynez Valley, you know, 2,000 feet below, and on the other side a gully full of rocks. And we're hauling this huge mass of sandstone behind us. Now this Jeep, this poor thing, it's . . . it's not going to make it. And about three-quarters of the way up this steep hill, it starts to give out. And it's mmm-mmm-mmm, and it becomes apparent that we're not going to crest the hill. And now we're actually going backwards. We're not hauling the rocks, the rocks are hauling us. And I'm ready to get out. Not him. He's—handling it. He's going to back this thing down, by God. And he does . . . and we make it down . . . the rocks haul us back down the hill, but we manage to stay on the road. Now I'm thinking, well, OK, so now we're going to turn around and go some other way, because there's no way we're going up, we're not going to try that again. Oh no, no, we're going to go up that hill. You know, by God, we're going up that hill. I . . . it must have taken us three or four tries, of getting almost up the hill and being hauled back down, and each time I'm thinking OK, you know, which way do I jump. [LAUGHS] He's cool as a cucumber. Didn't bother him at all.

[12] Reagan's candidacy in North Carolina was helped by the campaign spot

against detente, but also by his commitment not to give away the Panama Canal and by the political organization of North Carolina Senator Jesse Helms, himself a staunch conservative.

[13] Ronald Prescott Reagan, Interview with Austin Hoyt.

[14] Nancy Reagan, Interview with Austin Hoyt.

[15] Nancy Reagan, Interview with Austin Hoyt.

[16] Martin Anderson, Interview with Author.

[17] Michael Deaver, *Behind the Scenes*, p.72.

[18] Nancy Reagan, *My Turn*, p. 178

[19] Maureen Reagan, Interview with Author.

[20] Martin Anderson, Interview with Author.

[21] Anthony Dolan, Interview with Author.

[22] Ronald Reagan, *An American Life*, p.

[23] Between 1974 and 1980 ten countries fell under the Soviet orbit: South Vietnam, Cambodia, Laos, South Yemen, Angola, Mozambique, Ethiopia, Grenada and Nicaragua.

[24] James Carter, Address to the Nation, July 15, 1979.

[25] Ronald Reagan, Address to the Republican Convention.

[26] Maureen Reagan, Interview with Author.

[27] Edmund Morris, Interview with Author.

[28] Edwin Meese III, *With Reagan*, pp. 45–46.

[29] Sam Donaldson, Interview with Author.

[30] Edmund Morris, Interview with Author.

[31] Lou Cannon, Interview with Author.

[32] Patrick Cadell, Carter Administration's Oral History.

[33] Address before the International Business Council, Chicago.

[34] Remarks at Pensacola Airport, Florida.

[35] Michael Deaver, *Behind the Scenes* (New York; William Morrow & Company, 1988).

[36] Patrick Cadell, Oral History, Carter Presidential Library.

[37] The Reagan team had illegally obtained a copy of Carter's brief which they used in mock debates with Reagan.

[38] George Will, Interview with Author.

[39] *Ibid.*

[40] Maureen Reagan, Interview with Author.

[41] Richard Wirthlin, Interview with Author.

[42] Martin Anderson, Interview with Author.

CHAPTER 9

Happy Days Are Here Again

On January 21, 1980, Ronald Wilson Reagan placed his right hand on his mother's Bible and took the oath of office as the fortieth President of the United States. With his back to the Capitol, Reagan faced away from Washington—away from government. His address that morning was an exhortation to Americans to seek inspiration from the distant past to regain the promise of a bright new future.

> Standing here, one faces a magnificent vista, opening up on this city's special beauty and history. At the end of this open mall are those shrines to the giants on whose shoulders we stand. Directly in front of me the monument to a monumental man, George Washington, father of our country . . .[1]

Beyond the monuments to Washington, Jefferson and Lincoln, Reagan saw a troubled America—besieged by economic problems, losing ground to an expansionist Soviet Union, suffering from a loss of confidence in itself and even in the very office he had just assumed.

Every American presidency of the last twenty years had ended in failure. Kennedy was assassinated, Johnson led America into Vietnam, Nixon resigned under threat of impeachment, Ford failed to get elected. Carter mired the nation in self-doubt. At a time when the American economy was in shambles and the Cold War was intensifying, many wondered if anyone could master the presidency, least of all a former Hollywood "B" movie actor. But Reagan shared none of these misgivings. Like Franklin Delano Roosevelt fifty years before him, he felt that what America needed most was a shot of self-confidence, "a spiritual revival."[2]

> It is time to realize we are too great a nation to limit ourselves to small dreams. We're not, as some would have us believe, doomed to an inevitable decline. I do not believe in a fate that will fall on us no matter what we do . . . so with all the creative energy at our command let us renew our determination, our courage, and our strength.[3]

Unlike the Carters, who had come to town as outsiders and remained outsiders to the end, the Reagans made every effort, in the words of the President, "to serve notice that we are new residents." They attended and hosted dinners with "establishment" Republicans and Democrats, demonstrating that they possessed the requisite social graces for Washington society and that the new Administration meant to be inclusive.

Reagan's inaugural festivities were intended to convey a mood of renewal and optimism. At an estimated cost of $8 million, the three-day extravaganza began with a $800,000 fireworks display at the Lincoln Memorial followed by two nights of show-business performances including Frank Sinatra, Jimmy Stewart, Rich Little and Johnny Carson. Three tons of jelly beans—Reagan's favorite candy—were flown in. At $2,000 per night limousines had to be brought in from as far away as Atlanta, to ferry around the movie stars, millionaire Californians and conservative midwesterners who had descended on the capital to celebrate in style. It was, in the words of critic Gary Wills, "Hollywood on the Potomac."[4]

The party culminated in ten inaugural balls, an ostentatious display of wealth not seen in Washington in decades, if ever. From Almaden Vineyards came 14,400 bottles of champagne, from the Society of American florists $13,000 in flowers, from Ridgewell's caterers 400,000 hors d'oeuvres. "In Jimmy Carter's day we served a lot of shrimp salad," noted a happy caterer looking forward to a booming business in the Reagan years. "Now it's all shrimp."[5]

The President and the First Lady danced their way through the evening. Nancy sparkled in a white beaded Galanos gown. The President wore white tie and the assurance of a man perfectly at ease. He had been preparing for this role for fifteen years, and was coming to Washington with a script well in hand. "I had come to Washington with my mind set on a program and was anxious to get started on it," he later wrote.[6]

The dirty little secret of American democracy is that lots of Presidents go to Washington without the slightest idea of what they want to do, as President. They want to be President—it would be very nice to live in the White House for eight years, but they don't have much of an agenda when they get there. Reagan had an agenda to a degree that's almost unique, certainly in recent American history. But, along with that agenda, Reagan had a philosophy, if you will, about the executive office, which runs totally counter to the conventional one that we've been given the last 50 years. Reagan believed that a President was there to accomplish two or three overriding things, and basically, the rest of the government could fend for itself.[7]

During his years in public life, Ronald Reagan had distilled his ideology to a few simple principles: government was too big and taxed too much, and the Soviet Union was getting away with murder internationally.[8] His answers were as simple as his formulations: reduce the size and scope of government, revive the flagging economy, and strengthen the nation's defenses.

Even prior to his election, the Reagan team had transformed his agenda into concrete policy proposals. And from election day on, in what has been called the most efficient transition in presidential history, Reagan's staff holed up in hotels and make-shift offices, screening applicants for every job, drafting policy initiatives, and in their own words, "indoctrinating" future members of the Administration on the President's policies. On the day Reagan moved into the White House every position in his Administration was filled, every important policymaker committed to the President's agenda, and every policy detailed in a notebook they facetiously referred to as "the black book."

Martin Anderson, Reagan's chief domestic advisor, remembers:

> We knew what we were going to try to do. We weren't sure how well it was going to work completely because you can't always forecast what policy changes will do. But we knew what we wanted to do, in economic policy, in national defense policy, in welfare. You name the policy, we knew.[9]

The first job was to set priorities. "Everybody wanted an issue they wanted addressed," recalls Chief of Staff James Baker.

> Secretary of State Al Haig wanted Central America made a priority. The 'Moral Majority' wanted us to take on social issues like S and school prayer. But we understood very early on that our success depended on our ability to husband our resources and the President's

energies to what I facetiously called "the three main issues": the economy, the economy and the economy.[10]

The morning after the inauguration, at the first Cabinet meeting, the Reagan team was ready to begin implementing the plan.

> . . . There was a sense of urgency because we realized that after any spectacular election here is a honeymoon period, which we figured to be about 180 days. So we had a 180-day strategic plan from Inauguration Day on the 20th of January, till about the middle of August when Congress took their recess. And we figured in that time to make major progress on the two primary objectives: the revitalization of the economy and the rebuilding of our national defenses.[11]

The Administration's economic plan faithfully mirrored Reagan's conservative philosophy. It called for a large tax cut, reductions in government expenditures, and a balanced budget. But Reagan also wanted a military buildup as a first and essential step in the pursuit of his Soviet policy. With less taxes and huge increases in defense, balancing the budget would require a balancing act.

"Everything depended on everything else. If we cut tax rates, we would have less money to spend on defense. If we increased defense spending, it would be more difficult to balance the budget. If we could slow the decrease in domestic spending it would make it easier to increase defense expenditure without increasing the deficit."[12] Two critical factors would determine the success of Reagan's program: identifying enough budget items to cut, and the validity of a controversial economic theory, "supply-side economics."

"Supply-side economics" was put forward by Arthur Laffer and a few other young economists. They argued that the tax rate in the United States had become so high that it was curtailing productivity, and that if one reduced that rate, "there would follow an economic expansion that would increase the tax base to a degree where the revenues lost to the initial tax cut would be recovered."[13] One prominent supply-side proponent was Republican Congressman Jack Kemp, who is credited with bringing it to Reagan's attention during the 1980 presidential campaign.

Many prominent economists shared the supply-sider's belief that high taxes were choking the U.S. economy and that a tax cut was necessary to fuel economic growth. But not all agreed with the premise that the economic expansion would generate enough revenues to cover the shortfall created by the initial cut.

During the 1980 campaign, Independent presidential candidate John Anderson had dismissed Reagan's economic plan as "smoke and mirrors"; candidate George Bush had referred to it as "voodoo economics"; and the Senate Majority Leader, Tennessee Republican Howard Baker, had called it "a riverboat gamble."[14] Even Reagan's Budget Director David Stockman, himself a proponent of "supply-side," privately worried that a tax cut, if not accompanied by massive reductions in spending, could result in deficits as high as $100 billion per year.

The President, however, harbored no doubts about his economic program or about the assumptions on which it was based. Like many of his convictions, Reagan's faith in the stimulating effect of a tax cut was based on his own experience. "I needed no convincing on the matter of a tax cut," he wrote. "As an actor, I had been on the 90-percent marginal tax bracket. When I reached a certain point, I stopped working . . . . Some people call it 'supply-side,' I call it common sense."[15]

Reagan's commitment to a tax cut was a matter of deep conviction, as was his commitment to budget cuts. "Although he showed a keen interest in spending controls, he did not offer any grand vision of program elimination, or restructuring or privatization or devolution of responsibility to the states," recalled Presidential aide Richard Darman.[16] Reagan believed substantial budget savings could be achieved by getting rid of government waste, fraud and abuse. Budget Director David Stockman would have to identify the necessary budget reductions, with little direction from the President, whose one recommendation was a report on the efficient operation of the motor pool.[17]

Reagan would rely on Stockman to identify budget cuts. But the weight of his presidency at large would fall on three men— White House Counselor Edwin Meese, Deputy Chief of Staff Michael Deaver, and Chief of Staff James Baker.

Born into one of Texas's most prominent families, James Baker III had come into the Reagan Administration through his close association to his fellow Texan, Vice-President George Bush. Known as "Mr. Cautious," he was intelligent, suave, and deft at playing the Washington political game. As Chief of Staff he was responsible for imposing discipline and he always kept an eye on politics. He would lead the Congressional lobbying effort. A seasoned Washington insider, Baker shared the epicenter of Reagan's White House with two of Reagan's long-time California aides, Michael Deaver and Edwin Meese.

Deaver hailed from a modest background in central California. He had spent most of his adult life in the service of the Reagans. He had a background in public relations, a good rapport with Reagan, and the rare and complete trust of the First Lady. As Deputy Chief of Staff, much of his time was spent on the President's schedule."

Edwin Meese III was from San Francisco, and like James Baker came from a prominent family. He had taught law and served Reagan as chief of staff in California. His sharp and uncluttered legal mind was finely tuned to Reagan's thinking. His job would be to "conceptualize" Administration policy and advise the President. The three men, Baker, Deaver and Meese, collectively known as "the troika," would serve as "deputy presidents." To them, Reagan delegated unprecedented authority.

> In some ways he governed like a Turkish pasha. I've never seen anyone else like him. Most politicians I've been associated with, people in the academic world and business, the leaders drive, they instruct, they tell you what to do, they plot, they give orders. Ronald Reagan never gave orders. He assembled people around him, brought people in, talked to them, and they said, look, here are all the options. Here's this thing, here are the facts. But then he always made the final decision. Made it clear to them what he wanted to do, and then he just assumed that these things would be done. A consequence of this unusual management style was that [it made Reagan] very dependent upon his personal advisors.[18]

Reagan's second term would expose the weaknesses of Reagan's passivity and his tendency to over-delegate. But for now Ronald Reagan had a loyal staff who knew and understood him and Washington well. They would capably handle the details of government, allowing the President to concentrate on the key issues of his Administration and on what he did best: inspiring Americans and selling his program to Congress and to the people.

On February 5, Reagan issued the first of many appeals on behalf of his economic program. "That morning he came into the office visibly disturbed in a way that Reagan rarely was and it turned out that he had the speech text. It had been prepared and he didn't like it. It just didn't feel right so he spent the day writing his own speech and putting it on 4 x 6 cards."[19]

There would be many more addresses to the American people, but on this evening of his presidential television debut, Reagan pulled all the stops. Using coins and dollars to illustrate the meaning of inflation, he spoke in simple, homespun ways.

> I am speaking to you tonight to give you a report on the state of our nation's economy. I regret to say that we're in the worst economic mess since the great depression. . . .
>
> Over the past decades we've talked about curtailing government spending so that we can then lower the tax burden. Sometimes we've even taken a run at doing that. But there always are those who told us taxes couldn't be cut until spending was reduced. Well, you know, we can lecture our children about extravagance until we run out of voice and breath. Or we can cure their extravagance by simply reducing their allowance.[20]

Since Franklin Roosevelt's New Deal, Washington had played a growing role in the effort to solve the nation's economic and social ills. Ronald Reagan believed that in the years after FDR's New Deal, government had grown so big as to become an impediment to the nation's creative and productive energies. "I believed the policies of the federal government reaching back for decades were mostly responsible for the problems. . . . I wanted to begin reversing those mistakes."[21]

On February 18 less than one month after his inauguration, Reagan unveiled the details of his program to a joint session of Congress. There would be a large increase in the defense budget. There would be reductions in Medicare payments, child nutrition, public service jobs, college education benefits and unemployment compensation. One million food stamp recipients were to be struck from the rolls. The immensely popular bedrock New Deal entitlement programs like Social Security were left largely untouched.[22]

Reagan wrote in his diary: "The press is trying to paint me as trying to undo the New Deal. I remind them that I voted for FDR four times. I am trying to undo LBJ's Great Society. It was his War on Poverty that got us into this mess."[23]

"He never really challenged the New Deal," observed conservative columnist George Will. "What offended him were later developments in American liberalism. The fundamental New Deal arrangement I don't think bothered him."[24]

In addition to the cuts in anti-poverty programs, Reagan also asked for a 30-percent tax cut phased in over three years. All Americans would benefit, but the wealthy would benefit most. The tax rate of America's richest would be halved from 70 percent to 35 percent.[25] Even assuming additional revenues due to the supply-side effects at the estimated 5.2 percent economic growth rates, the budget Reagan presented to Congress that day showed a $50-billion deficit. Reagan, who in his campaign had vowed to balance the budget, promised to find those savings. He still believed that his staff could find the missing $50 billion by tightening up on waste, fraud and abuse. But as Richard Darman noted, "to achieve such savings would require far more draconian measures."[26]

At the end of Reagan's speech, the American people were

shown to favor the President's program two to one. But in Congress opposition was stiff. The Congressional Black Caucus accused the Administration of planning to make the poor "hungrier, colder and sicker."[27] "Reagan's program," the powerful Speaker of the House Thomas "Tip" O'Neill said, "amounts to soaking the poor to subsidize the rich."[28]

A "Great Society" Liberal, Tip O'Neill would become Reagan's nemesis until his own retirement from politics in 1986. As Christopher Matthews said to *The American Experience*, in their views on government the President and the Speaker were at opposite ends of the philosophical spectrum.

> O'Neill's view of government was very simple. It was people need help, the government's going to give them help and the wealthier people are going to pay for it— as simple as that. Tip O'Neill was one of the kids who use to cut the lawn on his knees at Harvard Yard. Ronald Reagan, who didn't grow up in great circumstances, went out to Hollywood, had a screen test, was found to be physically what they were looking for. I'm sure the Speaker saw him benefiting from what God gave him—great looks—and going on to believing that everybody would get breaks like that. And, I think he probably figured that Ronald Reagan looked upon life as if everybody was going through this similar experience when in fact, he had been immensely lucky, fortunate to be born with a with a face and a voice.[29]

O'Neill vowed to fight: "We're not going to let them tear asunder programs we've built over the years," he said.

The 1980 landslide had given Reagan the gift of a Republican Senate. But the House belonged to the Democrats led by the formidable O'Neill. Reagan's greatest success in Sacramento, his Welfare Reform Bill, had been achieved by engaging the Democratic-dominated State Assembly. Now his success as President depended on his ability to reach across the aisle and convince twenty-six of Tip O'Neill's Democrats to break rank and vote for his economic package.

The lobbying effort, wrote *Washington Post* correspondent Lou Cannon, had the atmosphere of a sales pitch. There were presidential cufflinks, voodoo rings, David Stockman knives.[30] But there was also hardball politics, and plenty of "pork." Reagan's Chief of Staff James Baker, in charge of Reagan's Congressional strategy, identified Southern Democrats as a crucial voting bloc, and Reagan lobbied them hard. Four Louisiana Democrats agreed to go along with the President's bill in exchange for the Administration's reviving an expensive sugar support program. Then the ultimate carrot: Reagan's lobbying team promised moderate southern Democrats that in exchange for their vote, Reagan would not campaign against them in the upcoming 1982 mid-term Congressional elections. (This provoked an outcry among dyed-in-the-wool conservatives, who expected a political realignment in the South in 1982.)

Before he finished lobbying for his plan, Reagan would hold 69 meetings and would speak personally to 467 Congressmen. Once, from his suite at the Century Plaza Hotel in Los Angeles, Reagan called twenty-five members of Congress in one single night. Some House members said that they saw more of Ronald Reagan during his first four months in office than they had seen of Jimmy Carter in four years.

He was going to go up to the Hill to visit Congress personally, say hi. Well, they didn't quite know what to do. Once he went up there and he went into a meeting room and the Democrats were, I think fair to say, hostile, waiting for him, appalled that he had been

elected President of the United States. And he came
in this room where they had just hung a huge portrait
of Senator Mike Mansfield, who was revered I think
by every Democratic Congressman. Reagan came in to
speak to them in this room. and he pointed to the portrait and smiled and said, "I just thought I'd let you
guys know that tomorrow I'm going to appoint former
Senator Mike Mansfield as the Ambassador to Japan."
And they were stunned. I mean this was obviously a
great thing to do. They were looking up at Mike's picture, they were in his room. Now this Republican was
going to appoint him to be Ambassador to Japan and
honor him, so what could they do but cheer and
applaud. They'd been had.[31]

During his second term, Ronald Reagan would become pro-
gressively disengaged from the day-to-day workings of his
office. But the Reagan of the early days, as recalled by his close
aides, was "an extraordinarily hard worker who never once
moaned about making a Congressional call"[32]—a President
who, against popular perception, did not "watch television and
go to bed," but took volumes of homework upstairs and obsessively went through every single bit of paper making notes on
the margins in preparation for the next day. So diligent was the
President, that the First Lady complained early on that Reagan's staff was giving her husband too much work and keeping
him up too late.[33]

Reagan's opportune charm, dedication and hard work were
great assets to the lobbying effort, but the Administration's best
weapon was Ronald Reagan's skill as the "Great Communicator." The strategy was simple. Reagan would try to convince
individual Representatives of the merits of his economic package. But he would also incite their constituents into pressuring

them to go along with it. "I knew that we were going to get it passed. It wouldn't be enough to make Congress see the light; I had to make 'em feel the heat."[34]

> Many of you have asked, what can you do to help make America strong again. I urge you again to contact your Senators and Congressmen. Tell them of your support for this bipartisan proposal. Tell them you believe this is an unequaled opportunity to help return America to prosperity and make government again the servant of the people.

Reagan, who liked to quote Theodore Roosevelt's definition of the Presidency as a "bully pulpit" for mobilizing public sentiment, loved to go on television in front of the American people to get his message out, "and he would and repeat it and repeat it and repeat it so people knew where he stood."[35] It was a message that appealed to a nation thirsting to recapture the national spirit—their sense of optimism and exceptionalism.

> All you wanted to do is fix the camera on his head and let him talk. You didn't need him to walk around the desk or sit on the corner and do all of those things that people have to do to make politicians interesting. He was interesting because he was able to speak in ways that the American people believed and in a language that they understood and agreed with. I mean, he vocalized their frustrations and hopes and fears and gave them a vision. He said, you know, there really is a shining city on a hill. And they wanted to believe it.[36]

Reagan's inter-connect with the American people went far beyond words. "His communication was also empathetic, and that's really what established that special link between Ronald Reagan and the American public."[37] As Reagan's daughter Maureen explained, this "empathetic" link with the American people was a direct result of his long career in Hollywood and in television.

> When you're in politics and you want to get a message across to people you have to be able to project out to those people. That's what actors do. They make *you* feel happy or sad. They make *you* laugh and cry. They make *you* feel all of the emotions.[38]

> And Ronald Reagan understood that. So that when he was talking, when he was speaking, he wasn't just happy the way the words came out of his mouth. He was happy in the way that the words affected other people and the response that it evoked from them.[39]

In the heady atmosphere of the early days of an Administration fighting for what they thought was a "revolution" in the role of government, the formidable Ronald Reagan was a man to reckon with.

> We had a President who was able to go to the American people and leverage the Congress. He would make a speech a televised national address and say, call your Congressman, call your Senator, help me out. And boy, the calls would flood the Congressional switchboards. It was very very effective.[40]

One after another, Congressmen began to line up behind the President's economic program.

The Administration's lobbying effort was proving so successful that even Tip O'Neill would later admit that Reagan was "great at fighting for his policies" and that his 1981 team was the "best run political operating unit [he'd] ever seen."[41]

> The legislative team was very good. And they exploited very well the defection of the southern Democrats who did not want to stand up to Reagan, because they were afraid if they did it was going to cost them their seats. And once you had that momentum going, once it became clear that you couldn't block Reagan's programs, if you were an ordinary Democrat from anywhere in the House you wanted to be able to go home to the people and say I voted for tax cuts. I voted to cut the budget.[42]

The mood in the White House was jubilant. The Reagan presidency, wrote Lou Cannon, "possessed an aura of invincibility."[43]

The afternoon of March 30, 1981, seventy days into his presidency, Ronald Reagan delivered yet another pitch in support of his program, this time to an AFL-CIO convention at the Washington Hilton Hotel. At 2:25, he left the meeting and approached his limousine for the short ride to the White House. Reagan raised his arm to wave to reporters gathered outside just as a deranged lone gunman, John Hinkley, Jr., fired six bullets from a .22-caliber gun.

NOTES

[1] Ronald Reagan's Inaugural Address, January 20, 1981. Reagan, *Speaking My Mind*. pp. 59–66

[2] Ronald Reagan, *An American Life*, p. 219.

[3] Ronald Reagan, *Speaking My Mind* (New York: Siomon &Schuster, 1989), pp. 59–66.

[4] Gary Wills, *Reagan's America*, p. 237.

[5] Nicholaus Mills, *Culture in an Age of Money*, Edited by Nicholaus Mills. (Chicago: Ivan R. Dee, 1990), pp. 16–18

[6] Ronald Reagan, *An American Life*, p. 229.

[7] Richard Norton-Smith, Interview with Author.

[8] George Will, Interview with Author.

[9] Interview with Author.

[10] James Baker, Interview with Author.

[11] Edwin Meese, Interview with Author.

[12] Martin Anderson, *Revolution*.

[13] David Stockman, from "The Education of David Stockman," by William Greider, *The Atlantic*, December 1981.

[14] "It was a gamble on whether it would stimulate the economy or not. It was a gamble on whether or not the Congress would go along with the cuts, the savings that he asked for." Senator Howard Baker, Interview with Author.

[15] Ronald Reagan, *An American Life*, p. 231.

[16] Richard Darman, *Who's In Control?* (New York: Simon and Schuster, 1996), p. 43.

[17] *Ibid* Reagan was following the same approached he used as governor of California, "cut, squeeze and trim."

[18] Martin Anderson, Interview with Author, and *Revolution*, p. 291.

[19] William Norton Smith, Director, Reagan Library. Interview with Author.

[20] Television Address to the Nation, February 5, 1981.

[21] Ronald Reagan, *An American Life*, p. 230.

[22] To this day, Lou Cannon argues that Reagan missed an historic opportunity to bring social security under control early in his Administration. In February 1981, New Mexico Republican Senator Pete V. Domenici, head of the Senate Budget Committee, approached Reagan with a bipartisan proposal to save the Administration $10 billion in 1981 and as much as $25 billion in 1986 by adopting a freeze in the cost of living adjustments. Reagan rejected it. He had made a commitment not to cut Social Security in his 1980 campaign, and going back on that commitment as he reportedly put it "could cause me real problems. I don't want to go back on my word."

[23] Ronald Reagan, *An American Life*, p. 316. There were other, contradictory references in *An American Life*. On p. 205, Reagan wrote, "After half a century that had given them the New Deal and The Great Society, people were just fed up." On p. 233, "I had come to Washington to dismantle everything [Tip O'Neill] believed in . . . starting with the New Deal." The contradiction is perhaps resolved by arguing, as Reagan did when he took on the Aid to Dependent Families program in his California Welfare Reform initiative, that FDR's New Deal had been necessary, but that it had been expanded beyond, and maintained in existence longer than, FDR had intended.

[24] George Will, Interview with Author.

[25] A few months later, this was negotiated down to 25 percent. Mathematically, the tax cut Reagan initially proposed was actually a 27.5-percent cut because it

would have been spread out into three 10-percent cuts over three years. Anderson, *Revolution*, pp. 242–243.

[26] Richard Darman, *Who's In Control*, p. 77.

[27] Lou Cannon, *Role of a Lifetime*, p. 240.

[28] Tip O'Neill, *Man of the House*, (New York: Random House, 1987) p. 343.

[29] Christopher Matthews, Interview with Author.

[30] Lou Cannon, *Role of a Lifetime*, pp. 333–334.

[31] Martin Anderson, Interview with Author.

[32] James Baker III, Interview with Author.

[33] Richard Darman, Interview with Author. Darman recalls an instance when the "too late" was actually 2:30 in the morning, which brought him a stiff reprimand from the First Lady.

[34] Reagan, *An American Life*, p. 287.

[35] Kenneth Duberstein, Interview with Author.

[36] Michael Deaver, Interview with Author.

[37] James Baker III, Interview with Author.

[38] Maureen Reagan, Interview with Author.

[39] Edwin Meese III, Interview with Author.

[40] James Baker, Interview with Author.

[41] Tip O'Neill, *Man of the House*.

[42] Lou Cannon, Interview with Austin Hoyt.

[43] Lou Cannon, *Role of a Lifetime*, p. 115.

CHAPTER 10

John Hinkley's Bullet

The day after the attempt on Reagan's life, April 1, Johnny Carson introduced the "Oscars" in Los Angeles. The ceremonies, scheduled for the night before, had been postponed.

> Ladies and gentleman . . . Because of the incredible events of yesterday, that old adage 'the show must go on' seemed relatively unimportant. The Academy . . . and all of us connected with the show felt because of the uncertain outcome as of this time yesterday, it would have been inappropriate to stage a celebration.
>
> But the news today is very good. . . .The President is in excellent condition . . . he has been conducting business. And he happens to be in good spirits. . . . So tonight the show does go on. Now two weeks ago President Reagan videotaped a opening greeting for this occasion . . . Ladies and gentlemen . . . here is the President of the United States.[1]

From an oversized video screen, the President saluted his old Hollywood friends, his words drowned out by thundering applause.

Like most of America, neither the audience nor Johnny Carson knew that the robust man whose recorded image they had just cheered was in critical condition after only narrowly escaping death.

Years later, in his autobiography, Reagan would recollect the harrowing details of the afternoon of March 30 when he and three other people were shot as they walked out the side entrance of the Washington Hilton Hotel.[2]

"I was almost to the car when I heard what sounded like two or three firecrackers over to my left—just a small fluttering sound . . . *pop pop pop.* I turned and said, "What the hell's that?"

All around, people scrambled to the ground as Jerry Parr, the head of Reagan's Secret Service unit, shoved the President into the limousine and slammed his body on top of his.

"As we landed I felt a pain in my upper back which was unbelievable. It was the most excruciating pain I ever felt. 'Jerry,' I said, 'Jerry get off, I think you've broken one of my ribs.' . . . I tried to sit up . . . and was almost paralyzed by pain. As I was straightening up I had to cough hard and saw that the palm of my hand was brimming with blood."[3]

Deputy Chief of Staff Michael Deaver, who had scrambled into the limousine behind the President's car, could see the back of Reagan's head leaning against the seat.

> I thought we were going to the White House. We started going over dividers on Connecticut Avenue and realized when we came into the portiere of the George Washington Hospital that we were going there. I jumped out of the car and Reagan's getting out of the car, and he always had this thing where he would pull his pants up to be sure they were just right, button his coat again, which he did when he got out of the limousine, and I thought, he's fine. Walked into the hospital—the minute he hit the door, he went down.[4]

When Reagan arrived at the hospital, one of his doctors recalled, "he was right on the margin."

At first they thought he'd suffered a heart attack. His chest hurt and he was having trouble breathing. No one knew what was wrong. "All they knew was that the President was dying in front of their eyes."[5]

As the trauma team struggled around the President, Deaver called Chief of Staff James Baker and Counselor Edwin Meese to ask them to come to the hospital and to persuade the First Lady to wait at the White House. But by then she was already on her way.

"I didn't know he'd been shot," recalled the First Lady in an interview with *The American Experience*, still fighting back tears even after fifteen years:

> I had just returned to the White House from a luncheon and was in the third-floor solarium when the head of my Secret Service detail waved me to come down the ramp toward him. "There's been a shooting at the hotel. Some people were wounded, but your husband wasn't hit." . . . I started moving at the word "shooting." "George," I said, "I'm going to that hospital. If you don't get me a car I'm going to walk." A White House limousine pulled up to the Diplomatic Entrance and we got in. . . . It was not until I arrived at the emergency entrance that Michael Deaver told me he'd been shot."[6]

By the time Nancy reached the George Washington University Hospital, the doctors had discovered a small hole under Reagan's left arm. One of John Hinckley's bullets had ricocheted off the side of the President's limousine, pierced his left side and ripped through his left lung, missing his heart by a quarter of an inch. There was no exit wound, and Reagan would have to undergo surgery to extract the bullet.

Nancy, who had made Reagan her life, waited anxiously in

the chaos of the emergency room where doctors and nurses worked frantically around the President, his Press Secretary Jim Brady, who had suffered a serious head wound, and Secret Service agent Tim McCarthy, who had been shot in the chest.

The news on Reagan was alarming. His left lung had collapsed and he had lost more than half his blood. Twice, the nurses couldn't find his pulse and were afraid he would go into shock. "I knew that if that happened, we might lose him," Nancy later wrote.[7] She told *The American Experience:*

> I insisted they let me see my husband, but they were afraid I would be traumatized by what I saw. And they were right. Ronnie looked so pale, I've never seen anyone look so pale, and his lips were caked with dried blood. He saw me, pulled off his oxygen mask and whispered, "Honey, I forgot to duck."[8]

Even as he was being wheeled into the operating room, Reagan managed a quip. He turned to the team of doctors and nurses surrounding him and said, "Please, tell me you are all Republicans."

Five hours after the shooting the President was delivered into the recovery room. His operating team had found the bullet. Barring complications, the prognosis was good.

That night, frightened and unable to speak because of a respirator tube inserted in his throat, Reagan asked for a pad of paper and penned W.C. Fields's famous line: "All in all I'd rather be in Philadelphia." In another note, he quoted Winston Churchill, "There is no more exhilarating feeling than being shot at without result."[9]

Humor had always been Reagan's stock in trade. He used it to defuse tension, to deflect issues, to make his audience feel comfortable, and even to convey ideas. At a time when his life was threatened, his humor served to reassure the nation, and conveyed to the American public that the actor who had so often played the hero in Hollywood was, in fact, the real thing.

Washington Post columnist David Broder wrote, "During his sixty-nine days in office President Reagan had shown wit and grace. When he displayed that same wit and grace in the hours after his own life was threatened, he elevated those appealing human qualities to the level of a legend."[10]

> I think that was that moment when we really saw inside the man. We really saw what he was made of. To have that grace and that humor at that particular time was very comforting to Americans and . . . people couldn't believe that somebody who'd been shot would be that at peace, that controlled, and I think it was a moment when things changed and were never the same as far as the public's attitude about Ronald Reagan.[11]

> I believe that Presidents are defined more in their moments of crisis than they are in their moments of success . . . and that crisis enabled people to see Ronald Reagan as those of us who were more intimately connected with him [did]. Americans got a glimpse of Ronald Reagan that I don't think they would have probably ever had, had he not faced an assassin's bullet, and that courage as Hemingway defined it: Grace under fire.[12]

The assassination attempt brought the Reagan family together. Maureen, Ron and Patti flew to Washington the moment they heard their father had been shot. As they recounted to *The American Experience* their visit with their father, their admiration was unmistakable:

"I wanted to get my hands on this Hinkley character," remembered Ron. "That's what I was thinking about, you know. Just let him go. Just let him out on the street, that's all I want. But by that time my father had already forgiven him. He'd . . . had his sort of communion with his maker and assumed that it was some poor troubled character and that he deserved pity more than revenge."[13]

"He believed that if he did not forgive the person that did this to him that he was not going to get well, and so that was one of the first things he did," recalled Maureen. "But I do remember when I went to see him the first day, and he had been wearing a brand new suit the day it happened (which of course had been cut off him by the doctors), he said, "I understand this young man has a very wealthy family. Do you think they'd buy me a new suit?"[14]

"The biggest lesson in what true spirituality is and, and actually true Christianity as distinguished from what passes as Christianity today, was my father's willingness to forgive Hinkley," said Patti. "It was a very effortless comment and a very effortless state of mind for him. And I think I said something like, 'You're the best Christian around.'"[15]

Reagan returned home twelve days after the shooting. He wore a red cardigan sweater above a bulletproof vest. His cheeks looked ruddy as he cheerfully waved to the crowds with a smile on his face. But those who saw him up close could tell that the President was a long way from the full recovery his staff sought to convey. "I was shocked by his appearance," recalls Richard Darman, who saw Reagan the next day. "He was obviously uncomfortable walking and his face looked deathly pale . . . his distinctive smooth voice was lost. In its place was a low, raspy substitute."[16]

It would be years before anyone outside Reagan's innermost circle learned how close to death the President had been.

Though the consequences of the assassination attempt were not immediately apparent, John Hinkley's bullet would later prove to have been a crucial turning point. Two decades later, its significant is just becoming fully appreciated.

Reagan's strategist and pollster Richard Wirthlin, a devout Mormon, went to the White House two days after the President returned home.

> I visited with him in his bathrobe and we reviewed that in fairly personal and intimate terms. The thing that he told me was that he felt that very close to passing through that that portal of death and that he was spared, if you will, because "there was something," in his words, "the Lord wanted him to accomplish," and that event for him had rededicated his vision, his view as not simply trying to serve the Republican Party or even serving the people of the United States, but serving in a larger sense all people.[17]

"I owe my life to God and will try to serve him in anyway I can," Reagan wrote in his diary shortly after coming home.[18]

Reagan's mother Nelle and her Disciples of Christ Church had instilled in young Reagan a deep faith in God, and a strong belief in destiny. Now, at age seventy, his near-death experience deepened the meaning of these lessons from childhood. As William Norton Smith observed,

> I think it confirmed everything he'd ever been taught, beginning [with] his mother about God's plan for him as an individual. I think Reagan emerged from that whole period of his life more convinced than ever that he was doing God's work in trying to end the arms race and in trying to prevent Armageddon.[19]

In time, the President recovered physically from the ordeal, even lifting weights to add a few inches to his arms and chest. But Edmund Morris and Reagan's son Ron agree that his recovery was never as complete as his physical appearance suggested:

> It did slow him down. You have to remember this was a 70-year-old man and he was nearly killed. So, yes, I think it's fair to say that physically he was never really the same after that. I've seen footage of him, just before, and of course, I know what he was like just after, and thereafter. And there was a certain bounce that was taken out of his step.[20]

> He really changed after the assassination attempt. He became gentler, and slower, and this was partly a physical thing. Because that assassination attempt really knocked it out of him physically. His thoughts became slower, his speech became slower, he deliberated more, he hesitated more when he spoke. He lost his quickness. And for the rest of the Presidency it was a very, very slow and steady mental and physical decline.[21]

Lou Cannon believes that the Reagan presidency might have followed a different course had John Hinkley not fired his near-fatal bullet.

> The assassination attempt did two things. It gave him instant mythic status. After that, nobody could really stand in his way. . . . Inside it did something that I think was serious and deserves more attention than it's gotten. . . . He could work very little at first. [And] for months he didn't do very much except approve the papers that his top aides brought him, and make certain

ceremonial appearances, all of which he did spectacu-
larly, with this flare for the drama that he always had.
But his education stopped.[22]

Cannon summed up the effect of the assassination attempt
on Reagan in a revealing passage: "It aborted the inner life of
the Presidency, put the Reagan presidency on this track where
Reagan was more distanced than he should have been from
decision-making. I think it's clear he would have been a more
involved President if that assassination attempt had not
occurred."[23]

However profound the consequences of the assassination
attempt were on Ronald Reagan, for Nancy they were devastating. Since their marriage in 1952 she had made it her duty
to protect her husband; now her concerns bordered on obsession. "I continued to be haunted by what happened as well as
by what had almost happened," she later wrote.[24]

Nancy's fear took her beyond the rational and into the
superstitious. At the time of Reagan's election, someone had
written about a pattern in presidential history. Every president
elected on or re-elected in a year ending in zero had died in
office. Four—Abraham Lincoln (1860), Garfield (1880),
McKinley (1900) and John F. Kennedy (1960)—had been
assassinated.

Now that my own husband was President and an
attempt had been made on his life, the historical pattern became terrifying to me. Was the shooting in
March 1981 merely an omen, an early warning that
something even worse might lie ahead? Night after
night, I lay beside my husband and tried to drive these
gruesome thoughts from my mind. Ronnie slept, I could
not. I had no appetite for food. When I came to Wash-

ington I weighed 112 pounds, after the shooting I slipped below 100.[25]

It was then that Nancy Reagan, according to her own account, heard from her friend, Merv Griffin, that a San Francisco astrologer, Joan Quigley, could have prevented the events of March 30. "I could see from my charts that this was going to be a very dangerous day for him," Quigley had told Griffin. Nancy called Quigley without hesitation. "'I am so scared,' I told her. 'I am scared every time he leaves the house. . . . I cringe every time we step out of a car or leave the building.'" From that moment on Nancy, by her own admission, spoke to Quigley once or twice a month. With the President's schedule in front of her, she would ask Quigley which days were dangerous and which days were safe. She would then ask Deputy Chief of Staff Michael Deaver to adjust the President's schedule accordingly.[26]

> My attitude was, "If that makes you feel better, if that keeps Ronald Reagan alive, I'll do whatever you want me to do," and so I did. She might have said, "I wouldn't fly on that date or I wouldn't do a public appearance on that date," so we'd change it. And, it was always you know three to six months out. So, it was not something that you would have to make all kinds of arrangements for and excuses about. It was quietly done and taken care of.[27]

Years later, the nation would be riveted by the revelation that Nancy Reagan consulted an astrologer and by speculations about Quigley's influence on the Reagan White House. But Reagans' White House aides rank Quigley's interference between a logistics nightmare and a harmless annoyance.

More damage was done by the security measures instituted by Deputy Chief of Staff Michael Deaver partially in response to the First Lady. "In the day after the assassination I decided to be involved in seeing that my husband was protected in every possible way."[28]

"We resolved to do what we could to protect the President from crowds," Michael Deaver later wrote:

> I would not forget . . . that he had been hit while turning in the direction of reporter's question. . . . From then on I liked it better when the President did not stop for them. Which may explain all those TV clips of Reagan striding briskly from his helicopter to his car, signaling with his hand that he couldn't hear over the noise of the blades.[29]

"He never again saw average citizens," observed ABC White House correspondent Sam Donaldson, who made a reputation out of yelling questions at Ronald Reagan.

> He never again walked across an airport tarmac. He never worked a fence line. He never got out of his limousine on a public sidewalk. [And] it began to close down the Presidency even more from the standpoint of access to the average citizen, the average voter in this country.[30]

This isolation would in time, damage Reagan's ability to read the public mood, which since Sacramento had been one of his greatest political assets. But as his Administration redoubled its effort to get the President's economic package through Congress, Reagan's growing distance and detachment were obscured by the near-mythic standing he now enjoyed.

Even while he struggled to recover at the White House, Reagan's staff wasted no time in making political capital out of his immense popularity. Before the assassination attempt, Reagan's Congressional strategy had succeeded in making inroads among "boll weevil" Democrats in the South, but had failed to break into the Midwest and the Northeast. "If he could do that, that might break the back [of the Democrats] and open up the flood gates," recalls Kenneth Duberstein, a key player in the lobbying effort.

> The President was recuperating from his assassination attempt when we came up with a Congressman who had expressed some interest to me and other members of our staff that he might be willing to vote for what President Reagan wanted. His district had been carried by President Reagan by 60 percent or so and I called the Congressman, and the Congressman said he wanted to help but wouldn't commit to me. But I suggested—based on the conversation—that here was a possible phone call for Ronald Reagan to make. Ronald Reagan called him and the White House switchboard tracked the Congressman down. He was in the middle of a live radio call-in show back home in Pennsylvania. And the next voice you heard [on the airwaves] was the voice of Ronald Reagan and the Congressman was flustered. [All] the networks carried a tape of the conversation, 'cause it was the first time the American people had heard President Reagan's voice after the assassination attempt. This Congressman had no wiggle room. He was committed and that gave Ronald Reagan the opportunity to say, "See, we've broken into the Northeast and the Midwest."[31]

On April 28, four weeks after the attempt on his life, a barely recovered Reagan appeared before a joint session of Congress. He was greeted with a standing ovation of a sort rarely seen on Capitol Hill. The first words out of his mouth were a breathless quip: "You wouldn't want to talk me into an encore," he said. But Reagan had not come to Capitol Hill simply to bask in the adulation of Congress. He was there on business:

> I have come to speak to you tonight about our economic recovery program and why I believe it's essential that Congress approve this package.

Christopher Matthews, aide to the Speaker of the House Tip O'Neill, remembers the occasion with a measure of admiration for Reagan's courage, and for the political acumen he displayed.

> There he was, standing almost Lazarus-like before the Congress. Here's a guy who had survived a very deadly shot of an assassin and to come back with such élan and to ask for support was big stuff. I mean, you're talking about Hollywood drama here and he played it for all it was worth and he should have.[32]

It was at that point, Matthews believes, that Ronald Reagan ran his vote over the top. On June 25, 1981, Congress passed Reagan's budget bill. On July 29, his tax bill was approved. He had needed 26 Democrats to break rank. He got 40.

Reagan rejoiced in what he called "the greatest political win in half a century." After decades of scandal and ineffectual government, a President finally demonstrated that leadership mattered, that government could get things done.

Reagan was soon presented with a new opportunity to exercise his leadership when on August 3, 13,000 members of the Professional Air Traffic Controllers Organization (PATCO)— one of the few labor unions which had backed Reagan in the 1980 campaign—walked off their jobs when the federal government refused them a salary increase. The walkout left the airport control towers and radar centers responsible for the safety of the nation's skies unattended.

Another President might have hesitated. In February 1981, Reagan's pollster, Richard Wirthlin, had conducted a poll on how people felt about public employees and specifically their right to strike. "What I found in that study was that people favored giving public employees the right to strike in a ratio of about two to one. Now the President was aware of that when the air traffic controllers went on strike."[33]

But polls never mattered much to Ronald Reagan, who objected to the strike as a matter of principle. He gave the striking air controllers forty-eight hours to return to their posts. The ones who didn't, he simply fired. As he later wrote, "No President could tolerate an illegal strike by federal employees . . . and every union member had signed a sworn affidavit agreeing not to strike. . . . I agreed with Calvin Coolidge, who said, 'There is no right to strike against the public safety by anybody, anywhere, at anytime.'"[34]

Although it would take two years to train and replace all the controllers Reagan fired that day, the decision would be looked upon as a turning point in the Reagan presidency.

> All of a sudden, a kind of shock therapy had been administered to the American electorate, that—wait a second—this guy isn't necessarily what we thought he was. Here's someone who is willing to take a stand.[35]

Much as the American electorate, Reagan's domestic and

foreign adversaries also took notice of Reagan's toughness and determination.

> That was the moment when Tip O'Neill and the world learned that this guy was different—that he wasn't [just] a nice guy. He could be very, very tough. He didn't have a meeting. He didn't have a cooling-off period. He didn't negotiate like Jimmy Carter or like Gerald Ford [would have]. He broke them. Tip had contacts in the Soviet Union. I think [it was] Dwayne Andreas, a business guy who had been going back and forth there, who heard that the Russians were very impressed, that [this] American President was like a Czar.[36]

NOTES

[1] Johnny Carson, Proceedings, XX Academy Awards, April 1, 1981.

[2] The other three victims were Press Secretary Jim Brady, Secret Service agent Tim McCarthy and policeman Tom Delehanty. McCarthy and Delehanty recovered, Jim Brady, shot in the head, would never be the same.

[3] Ronald Reagan, *An American Life*, p. 259–260.

[4] Michael Deaver, Interview with Author.

[5] Nancy Reagan, *My Turn*, p. 5.

[6] Nancy Reagan, Interview with Austin Hoyt, and *My Turn*, pp. 3–7.

[7] Nancy Reagan, *My Turn*, p. 5.

[8] Nancy Reagan, Interview with Author. The line was allegedly said by Jack Dempsey to his wife the night he was beaten by Gene Tunney for the heavyweight championship.

[9] Nancy Reagan, *My Turn*, p. 11.

[10] David Broder, *The Washington Post*. April 1, 1981.

[11] Ronald Prescott Reagan, Interview with Austin Hoyt.

[12] Richard Wirthlin, Interview with Author.

[13] Ronald Prescott Reagan, Interview with Austin Hoyt.

[14] Maureen Reagan, Interview with Author.

[15] Patti Davis, Interview with Author.

[16] Richard Darman, *Who's in Control*.

[17] Richard Wirthlin, Interview with Author.

[18] Ronald Reagan, *An American Life*, p. 263.

[19] William Norton Smith, Interview with Author.

[20] Ronald Prescott Reagan, Interview with Austin Hoyt.

[21] Edmund Morris, Interview with Author.

[22] Lou Cannon. Interview with Austin Hoyt.

[23] Lou Cannon, Interview with Austin Hoyt.

[24] Nancy Reagan, *My Turn*, p. 45.

[25] *Ibid.*

[26] Nancy Reagan, *My Turn*, pp. 46–47.

[27] Michael Deaver, Interview with Author.

[28] Nancy Reagan, *My Turn*, p. 17

[29] Michael Deaver, *Behind the Scenes*, p. 28.

[30] Sam Donaldson, Interview with Author.

[31] Kenneth Duberstein, Interview with Author.

[32] Christopher Matthews, Interview with Author. According to George Will, "Christopher Matthews studied Ronald Reagan with the attention that any pedestrian would give to a semitrailer that made a habit of running over his instep." George F. Will, *The New Season* (New York: Simon and Schuster, 1988), p. 32.

[33] Richard Wirthlin, Interview with Author.

[34] Ronald Reagan, *An American Life*, p. 282.

[35] Richard Norton Smith, Interview with Author.

[36] Christopher Matthews, Interview with Author.

CHAPTER 11

The Ranch in the Sky

In August 1981, the Reagan Administration and the White House Press Corps drove north from Santa Barbara, along U.S. Highway 1. After turning off the coastal highway, they climbed seven miles of twists and turns all the way to the top of the Santa Ynez mountains. They arrived at Rancho del Cielo—the Ranch in the Sky—Reagan's 688-acre retreat. They were there to witness Ronald Reagan sign his Economic Recovery Program into law.

Rising 2,250 feet above the Pacific Ocean, Reagan's ranch evoked the spirit of the Old West, with rugged terrain and trail markers made by 19th-century pioneers. Dusty and windy, searingly hot by day and chillingly cold at night, with 2,000-foot drops straight into the valley below, the landscape is not for the faint of heart. Yet it is easy to see why Ronald Reagan fell in love with the spectacular vistas of his ranch in the sky.

To the west, one can see all the way out to the horizon, where the sun sets on the blue Pacific Ocean. To the east, the Santa Ynez valley stretches out for miles, as far as the eye can see. "Rancho del Cielo," Reagan later wrote, "could make you feel as if you are on a cloud looking down at the world."[1]

Rancho del Cielo was Reagan's refuge. "It was a place where he could renew himself and rejuvenate himself. He would disappear into the hills for hours, with a chain saw, or just on horseback, he was happy as a clam doing his ranch thing."[2]

In his eight years as President, Reagan managed to spend 345 days—almost a full year—at Rancho del Cielo. Visits to the ranch, as Deputy Chief of Staff Michael Deaver discovered early in the Reagan presidency, were non-negotiable.

> One morning, when we had only been in the White House about six months, he called me in, and he had nothing on his desk except this schedule. And he said, "Mike, I've been looking at this schedule, and I don't see any ranch time." And I said, "Well that's right, sir. Every time you've gone out to that ranch, the press have made a big deal about you being away from Washington, and the cost to the taxpayers of you traveling out to your ranch, and so forth and so on." And he put his hand up. He said, "Let me just tell you something, Mike. You can tell me a lot of things to do, and I'll do them, but you're not going to tell me when to go to the ranch. I'm convinced that the more often I get out to that ranch, the longer I'm going to live, and I'm going to the ranch. So, you might as well put it in right now."[3]

"He just loved it up here, just loved it. He would just take a big sigh when he got on a horse," recalled Secret Service agent John Barletta, who had the difficult job of protecting Ronald Reagan while he was at Rancho del Cielo.

> The problem was, the President was such a good rider that you had to make sure that you knew what you were doing. And sometimes the [Secret Service] agents, we had . . . problems trying to control our own horses to get where we were going to protect him. But after a short period of time that all blended in very nicely. Actually, the President was kind enough to stop jumping fences and going too fast for us when he went out for rides.[4]

Reagan bought Rancho del Cielo, then known as "Tip Top Ranch," just as his second term in Sacramento was coming to a close. Between 1975 and 1980, with the help of Dennis LeBlanc, a young man who had been assigned to protect Reagan, and Barney Barnett, a former California highway patrolman, Reagan transformed the neglected wreck that was "Tip Top" into a picture-perfect spot, a ranch any Hollywood studio could have used as a set.

The three men rebuilt the dilapidated ranch house into a modest yet comfortable and appealing home, with adobe walls and a red tile roof. They defined each stretch of property with fences made out of telephone poles, starting first around the house, then the pasture, and then the orchard. The fences which extend into the distance in perfect symmetry are indeed a beautiful sight. They also built a flagstone patio and even dug in a pond, complete with dock and canoe. Throughout, Reagan worked side-by-side with Barnett and LeBlanc.

> Everything that we did up at the ranch here, he would never ask myself or Barney Barnett to do something that he wouldn't do also. There were some times—especially when he was President—when we were up here during the month of August, hotter than heck, and one of the things he wouldn't want to do would be to cut wood in the heat. We knew that we would have to . . . and it needed to be done. He never backed away from it. And we would come back just completely soaked and tired. But he said, "OK, if that's what you fellows want to do, we'll do it."[5]

There was always work to do at Rancho del Cielo. Nearly every day, Reagan, Barnett and LeBlanc set out, chain and pole saw in hand, to open vistas, cut branches and clear brush so Reagan could ride beneath the trees along the horse trails.

> Figure him sitting on a horse and then add another five or six feet to it. So we were trimming maybe about ten feet up. Once the trees were up, the brush also had to go. And so we ended up making it look like a park.[6]

Rancho del Cielo, and Reagan's genuine love for his Western retreat, had provided a bonanza for the Administration's image-makers. Reagan the Western cowboy, first created by Lyn Nofziger in 1966 to appeal to California voters, had proved an enduring icon. Though Reagan still preferred to wear jodhpurs and ride English saddle, the image of the President dressed in cowboy hat and boots at his rugged Ranch in the Sky projected the values of freedom and individualism which his Administration advocated.

Rancho del Cielo was thus the perfect place to sign into law Reagan's program of less government and stronger defense. "It was perfect for the imagery of the Western, romantic, American tradition," remarked Richard Darman years later. "Symbolically, an ideal place to start the ratification of Step One of the Reagan Revolution. And so, it was a well chosen set."[7]

But on the actual day of the signing, a thick fog rolled in over the ranch. "You could hardly see the President when he came out to sign the bill," recalls Darman. "The thought crossed my mind that maybe *we* were all doing something in a fog—that is, without as clear a vision as we should have had of what we were up to."[8]

Darman's brief moment of doubt in the fog would prove prescient.

When Ronald Reagan first introduced his Economic Recovery Program in February 1981, he asked Congress to approve a

30-percent tax cut, and Congress had agreed to cut taxes by 25 percent. He had also promised to find additional cuts to make up a $50-billion deficit. But instead, by the time Reagan signed the 1,000-page bill at Rancho del Cielo on that foggy August day, so many cuts were not achieved, and so many "incentives" had been granted members of Congress in exchange for their votes, that the projected deficit had grown to $80 billion—the largest deficit in U.S. history.[9] Even as he signed his bill, Reagan promised that further cuts were still to come.

Budget Director David Stockman, conscious of the significance of an early legislative victory to create political momentum, had gone along grudgingly with the deficit, all the while planning a "fall offensive" to make additional cuts.

Stockman, however, had already cut into every discretionary budget category. The only two remaining possibilities for cuts were Social Security and defense. Reagan had long advocated reforms in Social Security, and had once been intrigued with the idea of voluntary contributions. But just that May, he had been burned by vociferous opposition to an Administration proposal to phase out early retirement.[10] Reagan was not about to touch Social Security again.

By the fall of 1981, Stockman knew that the success of his "fall offensive" depended largely on his ability to convince the President to scale back the projected increase in defense expenditures. Stockman, Secretary of Defense Caspar Weinberger and President Reagan agreed to meet on September 9 at the Oval Office to settle the defense question once and for all. "The meeting was billed as a shootout," Richard Darman later recalled, "but it was really no contest at all."[11]

During the meeting, Stockman warned that even at high growth rates *and* assuming the tax revenues resulting from supply-side effects, the budget deficit could rise as high as $100 billion. He pleaded with the President to reduce the 9-percent defense increase currently included in the budget to the 5–7-percent increase the President had originally promised in his campaign.

But Weinberger argued that Reagan's defense buildup was needed to restore America's strength. He presented the President with a chart depicting three cartoon characters representing three different budgets. The first was a tiny soldier without a rifle, labeled "Carter's Budget." The second was a bespectacled soldier holding a wooden rifle; this represented Stockman's budget. The third was a square-jaw, fully-armed GI Joe. This was to represent the 9 percent increase Weinberger wanted, and he presented it as "Reagan's Budget."

Though Stockman later ridiculed Weinberger's chart as a deliberate play on Reagan's intellectual naiveté, what the Secretary of Defense showed the President that day was in line with standard Pentagon briefing procedure. Weinberger's chief advantages were his relationship with the President, which went back to the Sacramento days, his reputation as a fiscal conservative (which in his days as Richard Nixon's Budget Director had earned him the nickname "Cap the Knife"), and most importantly, Reagan's own commitment to the strongest possible defense.[12] As Weinberger told *The American Experience* about Reagan:

> He said frequently during those first years, that he [would like] to balance the budget, to get government expenses down. But if it were a question—and he always phrased it this way—"if it were a question of balancing the budget or regaining strong military capabilities," he'd always opt for the latter. And he never never wavered in that. . . . That was his first priority.[13]

The President's decision to go for the highest defense budget made it more difficult for Stockman and his "budget cutters" to convince Congress to cut deeper into domestic spending. Further compounding the budget dilemma, Reagan would not consider rescinding any portion of his tax cut.

By November, the President was ready to accept that the deficit might exceed $100 billion. Darman recalls a November 2 meeting in which Reagan admitted, "We're not going to achieve our deficit goals," and then added, "but the time comes, if inflation is down, business is up, jobs are up—even if the deficit is bigger—the man on the street will say, 'Okay, things are better.'"[14]

Reagan's prediction would prove remarkably prescient. But before it came true, the "man on the street" would live through some of the hardest economic times since the days of the Great Depression.

NOTES

[1] Ronald Reagan, *An American Life*, p. 195

[2] Ronald Prescott Reagan, Interview with Austin Hoyt.

[3] Michael Deaver, Interview with Author.

[4] John Barletta, Interview with Austin Hoyt.

[5] *Ibid.*

[6] Dennis LeBlanc, Interview with Austin Hoyt.

[7] Richard Darman, Interview with Author.

[8] *Ibid.*

[9] True in dollars, but not in percentage of GNP (the deficit was 30.3 percent of the GNP in 1943). U.S. Historical Statistics.

[10] Tip O'Neill called the proposal "despicable." David Broder of *The Washington Post* wrote: Reagan did what no other American President has ever dared do—urge Congress to take a major slice from the most cherished and widely supported benefits program on the books. Quoted in Cannon, *Role of A Lifetime*, p. 251.

[11] *Richard* Darman, *Who's In Control*, p. 95.

[12] The President had given his Secretary of Defense what amounted to a "carte blanche." "Order what we need," he said, "and don't worry about the money."

[13] Caspar Weinberger, Interview with Austin Hoyt.

[14] Richard Darman, *Who's in Control*, p. 101.

CHAPTER 12

Staying the Course

Reagan's Economic Recovery Program, signed at the Ranch in the Sky in August, was based on the assumption of an expanding economy. His economic team had estimated growth rates as high as 5.2 percent. But in 1982, instead of growing, the economy shrank by 1.5 percent.[1]

The recession was not of Reagan's making. Paul Volker—appointed by President Carter to head the Federal Reserve Board, an agency charged with controlling interest rates and the money supply and invested with the power to operate independently from the White House—firmly believed that inflation, which had reached 14 percent in the Carter years, was the nation's number-one economic ill. Volker's cure was to tighten the money supply and to maintain high interest rates. Recession was the inevitable result.

The Reagan Administration nevertheless bears responsibility for its own overly optimistic economic forecasts, which led to outlandish predictions of balanced budgets by 1984.[2] Stockman later admitted these forecasts had been based on little more than faith.[3] The "rosy scenarios" may have weakened the Administration's determination to cut into popular middle-class entitlement programs such as Social Security and Medicare, which could have helped balance Reagan's defense budget increases and his tax cut. It is doubtful, however, that a more sober assessment of the future would have moderated Reagan's commitment to his two chief convictions—a stronger defense and lower taxes. In September, when Reagan approved the largest of the defense budgets presented by Caspar Wein-berger over the objections of David Stockman, he was already aware that signs pointed to a recession in the months ahead.

Though history would record the Reagan era as one of the most prosperous in America and the 1980s as a decade of wealth and excess, between the fall of 1981 and the spring of 1983, Volker's harsh anti-inflationary medicine sank the country into its deepest recession since the Great Depression. "While Ronald Reagan did not want to be an inflicter of pain," George Will commented, "he was President while the country was put through a terrific ringer."[4]

> It was very, very hard on the people at the bottom of the pile and some of the people in the middle of the pile, as those things always are. I suppose you could say that Reagan was at fault because he was President and went along with [Volker's] program.[5]

Set against the growing economic hardship, public outcry over Reagan's cuts into poverty relief programs acquired new resonance.[6]

> They did some things that were clearly harmful, like cutting child nutrition programs. I don't think that's a defensible cut. [But] a lot of the stuff they did was . . . stuff on the margin . . . and some of it backfired on them, like the classifying of catsup as food [vegetable] and that sort of thing, which really didn't have much impact on anything. But it enabled the critics of the Reagan Administration to say Reagan is heartless.[7]

In April 1982 a PBS television documentary entitled "People Like Us," by journalist Bill Moyers, dramatized the plight of

American's poorest. Moyers presented heart-rending stories of hardship and destitution: An Ohio man with cerebral palsy dropped from the Social Security rolls; a Hispanic woman in New Jersey, cut from Welfare and Medicaid who could not afford preventative cancer surgery for her thirteen-year-old son; a Milwaukee Church providing food for the downtrodden overwhelmed by requests for aid.

"These are the people who slip through the safety net and are falling away," an impassioned Moyers told viewers. "In the great outcry about spending, some helpless people are getting hurt."

Airing nine days after the President returned from Barbados, where he had vacationed in the luxurious home of actress Claudete Colbert, Moyers' documentary crystallized growing concerns about the Administration's disregard for the poor. "Reagan," wrote *Washington Post* television critic Tom Shales, "splashed . . . in the lap of luxury, while Americans go hungry."[8]

Reagan's critics jumped on "the fairness issue," drawing a stark contrast between the extravagance of the early Reagan White House and the plight of America's poorest. Much of the criticism was directed at the First Lady. Nancy's lavish entertaining, her millionaire friends, her designer dresses, her remodeling of the White House, and her alleged purchase of new china at a cost of more than $200,000, provided daily fodder for those who argued the First Couple disdained and disregarded the poor.[9] Though Nancy admits she might have been naive about how her actions would be perceived, she had felt it was her public duty to restore some lost dignity to the seat of the American presidency. She was devastated by a reporter's accusation that "she was using her position to improve the quality of life for those in the White House."[10]

By the end of 1981, Nancy had the highest disapproval rating of any other First Lady in modern times.[11]

Reagan's image-makers tried hard to reverse the perception of the First Couple's insensitivity. Michael Deaver, who had by then unofficially taken charge of White House public relations, remembers "spending a lot of time to get the other side of Reagan across":

> That meant associating with common people, doing things with the average guy. . . . One time we stopped at a pub in Boston and Reagan hoisted a schooner of beer with some working guys . . . and the picture of that went across the country.[12]

But no matter how hard Michael Deaver tried to associate Reagan with the"average guy" or how often Reagan repeated that the recession had its roots in the Carter years and that it was necessary medicine against inflation, or how often the White House accused the liberal press of overplaying the plight of the poor, the perception of Reagan as "uncaring" stuck.

In February 1982, polls showed that 23 percent of Americans believed Reagan favored the wealthy. By September, that figure had climbed to 52 percent.

Reagan was deeply stung by the accusations of insensitivity. In the depths of the 1982 recession he told a reporter from *The Daily Oklahoman*, "I'm scrooge to a lot of people. And if they only knew it, I'm the softest touch they've had for a long time."[13]

Reagan's mother, Nelle, had devoted her life to charity. Her example and the teachings of her Disciples of Christ Church had fostered in Reagan a genuine benevolence. Michael Deaver revealed to *The American Experience* how the President practiced charity from the Oval Office:

> He would have three or four checks, personal checks, in the top drawer of his desk in the Oval Office and he

was always running out of those checks because he was writing checks to people. I went in there one time and he had written a check to some woman who was on welfare. And the next month he got his bank statement. Well, you know, the bank statement had these checks and her check wasn't in it. So, he called her on the phone and said, you know, "you haven't cashed that check." She said, "Oh no, I framed it." He said, "Well my God, I sent you that money so you'd have some money to eat. I'll send you another check, you keep that one framed and cash this one."[14]

But the President's "soft touch" coexisted with a harsher, determined side. "We've been on a binge for thirty years," Reagan would often tell his advisors. "This is the price you have to pay."[15]

Many were puzzled by what journalist Sam Donaldson called "the clash between Reagan's ideology and his instincts:"

> I used to say facetiously that if you were down on your luck and you got past the Secret Service into his office and said, "Mr. President, I'm down in my luck," he'd give you the shirt off his back and then, in his undershirt, he'd sit down at his desk and he'd sign legislation . . . throwing kids off the school lunch program, other people off welfare, all in the name of fiscal responsibility, as he sat there shivering because he had given you his shirt. He had a good heart, he has a good heart, but when it came to his ideology, his philosophy, [it was] "off with their heads."[16]

If you wanted something done by my father, if you wanted him to move a certain way on a certain policy, what you had to do was humanize it. Bring him a person that's afflicted by some problem or another, and all of a sudden it becomes very real to him.[17]

"He cares about people as individuals," explains Reagan's long-time aide, Lyn Nofziger. "I'm not sure that he ever looks upon the masses and says, 'I must go do something, there are my people.'"[18]

"He did not comprehend what poverty was. He thought he did," explained Edmund Morris:

> His invariable line when the subject of poverty and homelessness was raised was, "I know all about the Depression because I was out hitchhiking across the landscape looking for work in the depths of the Depression. I know about poverty." Actually it was just a matter of a couple of weeks. He got a job very quickly and from January 1933 onward never had to look anywhere for a salary check.[19]

"I don't think Reagan really fully understood that the luck of the draw didn't always go to everybody, the way it went to him," added Christopher Matthews:

> Ronald Reagan would fly around this country and see what he wanted to see which was the people that had made it. He lived in Bel Air. He certainly looked around him and said, everybody's doing pretty well here . . . Living that lifestyle . . . kept his vision open to the success stories of America.[20]

Through 1982, "like a runaway train that keeps hurtling along the tracks long after its locomotive has lost power,"

Reagan wrote, "the economy was racing deeper into a recession."[21]

The housing industry was working at its slowest pace since 1946. Automobile sales were at their lowest point in twenty years. Small businesses were failing by the thousand.[22] High interest rates were driving farmers off their land. Unemployment reached 11.6 percent—its highest level since the Great Depression. It was even higher in the industrial centers of the Northeast. In Milwaukee, in January 1983, 20,000 lined up in 20-degree weather to apply for 200 jobs at an auto frame factory.[23]

The poor had been the first to suffer the impact of hard times. But now, the brunt of the recession was being felt by blue-collar workers and hard-working farmers—"the man on the street"—the people whose votes had helped elect Ronald Reagan to office in 1980.

"I prayed a lot during this period," Reagan wrote, "not only for the country and people who were out of work, but for help and guidance in doing the right thing so I would be able to justify the faith Americans had placed in my hands the previous November."[24]

In his inaugural address Reagan had raised Americans' hopes with his promise of a "new beginning." But by mid-1982, Reagan's Economic Recovery Program—now derided as "Reaganomics"—had not only failed to produce growth, but was leading the nation into fiscal disaster.

"We are really in trouble," Reagan confided to his diary. "Our projections are out the window . . . We [are looking] at $200-billion deficits if we can't pull off some miracles."[25]

Pressure on Reagan to change course mounted.

Congress clamored for a relaxation of the money supply. Senate Majority Leader Howard Baker, worried about the upcoming Congressional elections in November 1982, said

"Volker's got his foot on our neck, he's got to take it off." Even Treasury Secretary Donald Regan openly attacked Volker for holding back economic recovery. But Reagan stuck by Volker and the harsh medicine of monetarism. "This Administration will always support the political independence of the Federal Reserve Board," he said.[26]

Congressional leaders—Republican and Democratic—urged the President to raise taxes and cut the defense budget. Republican governors called on him to cut back defense spending. Stockman, who had long advocated defense cuts, also joined the chorus of those urging the President to raise taxes.[27]

"Reagan," wrote syndicated columnists Evans and Novak, "was having to fight two thirds of his Administration to save his economic program."[28]

> There are very few conventional politicians who would have stuck it out as he did. But he came to office imbued with a conviction that less government and lower taxes would resolve the pervasive sickness of the American economy. And what he saw in 1982 was the fever that was about to break.[29]

> I think you can argue that those years were maybe his his finest years, in terms of maintaining a steady course in economic policy. I have yet to see a single economist stand up and say that in 1981 or 1982, what Ronald Reagan should have done to get us out of the recession is raise taxes, put back more regulations and increase government spending—not a single one. . . .What he did was to follow the best policy to get us out of a very difficult situation.[30]

Reagan made one concession. In September, he agreed to a

what was called a "revenue enhancing package" called the "Tax Equity and Responsibility Act of 1982," TEFRA, a tax increase, which was estimated to bring $98 billion into the budget over a three-year period. In exchange Congress agreed to match the new revenues three-fold with budget cuts.[31]

Reagan's "willful optimism" sustained him through the dark days of 1982. "I believed the economic recovery would work," he later wrote, "because I had faith in those tax cuts and faith in the American people."[32]

> [His] was not a false optimism. It wasn't an optimism based upon unrealistic expectations, but it was an optimism which was based upon the capabilities of the American people . . . on the values of our country. He really believed these things and, therefore, had an optimistic view of the future.[33]

In speeches and radio broadcasts, "The Great Communicator" tried to instill in Americans his own optimistic view. On the eve of the 1982 mid-term Congressional election in a televised address he said:

> I'm asking you to think carefully about what's at stake. We've begun to correct the problems and policies that did so much harm to groups like farmers, workers, housewives and small businessmen. We're doing the job that must be done. . . . Cast your vote for hope. Not despair.

In 1981 the American people had heeded Reagan's appeal to join him in "an unequaled opportunity to return America to prosperity and make government again the servant of the people." But in 1982, against the harsh economic realities of recession, with unemployment nearing 12 percent, his appeal rang hollow.

On November 2, Americans gave the President a vote of no confidence, throwing twenty-six Republicans out of the House. Though the Republicans retained control of the Senate, their losses in the House not only dashed their hopes of a conservative realignment, but strengthened the hand of the Democratic opposition and of its leader, Tip O'Neill.[34]

Reagan's commitment to "stay the course" was exacting a high political price. A *Wall Street Journal* poll showed a sharp decline in confidence among business executives. Another poll showed that only 20 percent of Americans believed the recovery was working. Trial heats showed Reagan losing to Democratic hopeful Walter Mondale by 12 points in 1984 and to Senator John Glenn, by even more.[35]

Pundits predicted Reagan's imminent demise. "The stench of failure hangs over Ronald Reagan's White House," wrote *The New York Times*.[36] "What we are witnessing is not the mid point of the Reagan presidency, but its phase out," echoed David Broder from *The Washington Post*.[37]

By January the President's public approval rating had dropped to 35 percent, the lowest in his presidency. Richard Wirthlin, Reagan's pollster, brought him the bad news:

> As I talked to him, I was sitting on the side of the desk . . . and he was very serious for a moment and then he smiled and he then reached over and patted me on the arm and said, "I know just what I can do about it." And I said, "What is that Mr. President?" He said,"I'll go out and get shot again."[38]

"Maybe it's true, as some people say, that it's always darkest before dawn," Reagan later wrote in his autobiography.[39] Though neither the President nor many economists yet realized it, the recovery had already begun the prior November. It was to be the longest sustained economic expansion during peacetime in U.S. history.

All along, Paul Volker had held the keys to Reaganomics. By 1982 his austerity program had succeeded in bringing inflation down from 14 percent to 5 percent. And in October, he released his chokehold on the money supply.[40]

The housing industry, most sensitive to interest rates, was first to rebound. Michael Deaver spared no effort to get the message across.

> After a year and a half trying to get the economy to turn around, somebody came into my office one morning and said, "Housing starts are going up." This was the first blip in two years. I said, "Somebody go out and find me the five cities in America where they're going up faster than any place else. And, I think it was Fort Worth, Texas, that we finally chose. We all flew out to Fort Worth, Texas, and on television that night, there's the President of the United States with a hard hat . . . with these carpenters and their bib overalls and a chart, talking about housing starts going up. Part of it was Reagan talking America into getting better . . . But part of it also was getting the visual so that people could take it in [through] the eyes as well as in the ears, that . . . things were getting better.[41]

"As the economy started to take off," Reagan later wrote, "I started joking around the Oval Office: Do you notice they're not calling it Reaganomics anymore?"[42]

The economic expansion lasted an unprecedented ninety consecutive months. Eighteen million jobs were created. George Will characterized it as "the equivalent of grafting onto our economy the economy of West Germany."[43] But Reagan failed to control the growth of government. Fueled by defense spending and rising social security costs, the federal budget grew at faster rate than tax revenues. Matching the direst predictions, deficits grew to $200 billion per year by the end of the Reagan Administration. The national debt, which surpassed $1 trillion in 1987, was just under that figure when Reagan left the White House.

Reagan saw the recovery as the fruit of his tax cut and the reduction of government interference in the economy.[44] But others saw it as boom fueled by an increase in consumption and by deficit spending.

But in 1983, even as Ronald Reagan basked in early success of his economic program, the President faced a new challenge. That year would be the worst year in Cold War history since 1962, when President John Kennedy and Premier Nikita Khrushchev matched wills in a dangerous nuclear stand-off over Soviet missiles in Cuba.

Just as he had through the dark days of the 1982 recession, as the Cold War intensified, Reagan determined to "stay the course."

NOTES

[1] Richard Darman, *Who's In Control*, p. 103.

[2] Reagan's economists underestimated the stubbornness of inflation, and Volker's commitment to bring it under control. Their enthusiasm and optimism also led them to interpret a brief rebound of the economy in late 1980–early 1981 as a long-term trend. This last point was made by Martin Anderson in a telephone conversation with the author.

[3] "None of us really understands what's going on with these numbers," Stockman admitted to William Grieder, "The Education of David Stockman," *Atlantic Monthly*, December 1981.

[4] George Will, Interview with Author.

[5] Lou Cannon, Interview with Austin Hoyt.

[6] Reagan supporters insist on distinguishing between "cuts" and "reductions in increases." The bottom line is that the programs which had been targeted had less money to spend than they had expected.

[7] Lou Cannon, Interview with Austin Hoyt.

[8] *Ibid*.

[9] The china, in fact, had been donated.

[10] Judy Mann, *The Washington Post*, quoted in Nancy Reagan, *My Turn*, p. 27.

[11] Nancy Reagan, *My Turn*, p. 39.

[12] Michael Deaver, Interview with Author.

[13] Lou Cannon, *Role of a Lifetime*, p. 266.

[14] Michael Deaver, Interview with Author.

[15] David Stockman, quoted in Lou Cannon, *Role of A Lifetime*.

[16] Sam Donaldson, Interview with Author.

[17] Ronald Prescott Reagan, Interview with Austin Hoyt.

[18] Lyn Nofziger, Interview with Author.

[19] Edmund Morris, Interview with Author.

[20] Christopher Matthews, Interview with Author.

[21] Reagan, *An American Life*, p. 306.

[22] 17,000 in 1981 alone, the second-highest number since the depression. Cannon, *The Role of a Lifetime*, p. 233.

[23] *Ibid.*

[24] Reagan, *An American Life*, p, 307.

[25] Reagan, *An American Life*, p. 323.

[26] Lou Canon, *The Role of a Lifetime*, p. 273.

[27] He had been arguing this for some time, but this is the time that he really focused on "revenue enhancers." Stockman, 393–395; Meese, *With Reagan*, p. 149.

[28] Paul Craig Roberts, *The Supply-Side Revolution*, (Cambridge: Harvard University Press, 1984), pp. 202–203.

[29] William Norton Smith, Interview with Author.

[30] Martin Anderson, Interview with the President.

[31] TEFRA called for increases in business an excise taxes. Reagan's Conservative supporters still regard TEFRA as the "Debacle of 1982"—the greatest domestic error of the Reagan Administration. It not only failed to reduce the growth of government spending, did not decrease the deficit, and divided the President from his most ardent supporters." Edwin Meese, *With Reagan*, p. 147.

[32] AL, 311.

[33] Edwin Meese, Interview with Author.

[34] The consequences of the larger Democratic majority became most evident in 1983 when the House voted in favor of a nuclear freeze, and in 1984 when the House passed the Boland Amendment, forbidding the Reagan Administration from aiding the Contra resistance in Sandinista Nicaragua.

[35] Lou Cannon, *Role of a Lifetime*, p. 274, and Richard Darman, *Who's in Control*, p. 115.

[36] "The Falling Presidency," *The New York Times*, January 8, 1983.

[37] Quoted in Darman, *Who's in Control*, p.115.

[38] Richard Wirthlin, Interview with Author.

[39] Reagan, *An American Life*, p. 324.

[40] The Mexican debt crisis of September 1982 scared Paul Volker into reversing his policies. His fear was that if he held on much longer, the repercussions of the Mexican collapse could create a ripple effect throughout the Third World, The

international baking system might not survive a chain of loan defaults and could come crashing down as it had in 1929.

[41] Michael Deaver, Interview with Author.

[42] Reagan, *An American Life*, p. 324.

[43] George Wills, Interview with Author.

[44] Others felt the growth was fueled by pent-up demand and Government spending in the defense industry. Only now are economists beginning to sort out the longer-term legacy of the Reagan economic recovery.

CHAPTER 13

Evil Empire

Ronald Reagan came to office with no experience in foreign policy, a spotty knowledge of history, and little interest in details, but with a strong sense America's mission, and his own.[1]

"He thought that America was sent here [by the Almighty] between two oceans for a very specific purpose . . . to be a beacon of freedom to the rest of the world," noted Lyn Nofziger.[2]

In the conduct of his foreign policy, Ronald Reagan appealed to America's patriotism and idealism. He spoke of the promotion of democracy and trusted in its ultimate triumph. Yet this American idealist faced geostrategic realities with the ease of a consummate practitioner of "realpolitik." Under his "Reagan Doctrine," he confronted Communism throughout the world, aiding dictators and democrats, Islamic fundamentalists and African warlords, faithful to the timeless maxim that "the enemy of my enemy is my friend."[3]

In 1976, as he challenged Gerald Ford for the candidacy of the Republican party, Ronald Reagan discovered the issue which ignited his 1976 primary campaign and would remain at the center of his Administration's foreign policy. Détente—the Soviet policy of three consecutive U.S. Administrations—he argued, was tantamount to appeasement: a safety blanket under which the Soviet Union had expanded its influence and improved its military standing while taking advantage of America's post-Vietnam paralysis.

The centerpiece of détente had always been arms control. Arms control served to guarantee the stability necessary for the condition known as Mutual Assured Destruction. That is, enough weapons in the arsenal of both superpowers should survive a first strike to be able to retaliate with enough force to destroy the attacker, thereby rendering the use of nuclear weapons suicidal.

> The enduring faith persisted that arms talks were the best way to manage if not quell altogether (superpower) differences . . . To those who believed in the process, arms control was a way of life . . . a tangible means by which the U.S. found a sense of stability in an uncertain and menacing world.[4]

But in the late 1970s, a group of American nuclear strategists and politicians who called themselves "The Committee on the Present Danger" began to question the basic assumptions of détente. The Soviet Union, the Committee maintained, had expanded and modernized its nuclear arsenal to a degree that it posed a threat to the deterrent forces of the United States.

The United States faced a so-called "window of vulnerability," which left it vulnerable to a first strike. In the event of an international crisis, they argued, the United States could be faced with the choice between surrender or annihilation.

Most mainstream nuclear strategists dismissed the scenario posed by the Committee on the Present Danger as alarmist, but another weakness of détente was becoming increasingly apparent. While the United States and the Soviet Union concluded arms control treaties, the Soviets were engaged in a relentless expansionist drive in those areas of the world geostrategic analysts called "the periphery."

In Asia, Vietnam, Cambodia and Laos had fallen under Communist rule. In Africa, Cuban soldiers and Soviet weapons had guaranteed Marxist victories in Angola and Ethiopia. In

Nicaragua, Cuban-backed insurgents, after overthrowing an unpopular dictator, were busily consolidating a Marxist regime. Leftist guerrillas also threatened to triumph in El Salvador. In the Caribbean island of Grenada, Maurice Bishop, a Marxist and friend of Fidel Castro, had assumed power. In December 1979, the Soviet Union, in a bold, aggressive move, had invaded neighboring Afghanistan, installing a puppet regime. Ronald Reagan came to office determined to arrest the relentless advance. "His goal," wrote Henry Kissinger, "was to bring home to the Soviets that they had overreached."[5]

Unlike his predecessors Richard Nixon, Gerald Ford and Jimmy Carter, Ronald Reagan saw the Soviet-American confrontation not as a competition to be managed, but as a moral struggle between good and evil. For him Soviet-American relations were a morality play—much like those his mother Nelle staged for her church when Reagan was a child.

"His hatred of Communism was visceral," Edmund Morris told *The American Experience*, "and that animus against this totalitarian system was about the only powerful negative emotion he had in his life."[6]

Reagan had nurtured his anti-Communism since his days in Hollywood in 1946, when he fought against what he saw as Moscow-directed Communist infiltration of the Screen Actors Guild and testified as a friendly witness in front of the House Un-American Activities Committee.

Once in the White House, Reagan showed an unflinching willingness to confront Communism in words and in deeds. On January 29, during his first press conference, Reagan shocked reporters and analysts with his response to a question by ABC correspondent Sam Donaldson:

> I know of no leader of the Soviet Union since the revolution, including the present leadership, that has

not more than once repeated at the various Communist conferences they hold their determination that their goal must be the promotion of world revolution and a one world and a socialist or Communist state. Now, as long as they reserve unto themselves the right to commit any crime, to lie, to cheat, in order to attain that. I think when you do business with them, even at a détente, you keep that in mind.

Reagan's response, though uttered in an unassuming, soft-spoken style, did not comport with the requirements of international diplomacy, and provoked quite a stir. "When the President uttered those words," recalls Richard Allen, Reagan's National Security Advisor, "there was a gasp in the East Room. The next day Reagan's remarks were headlined the world around. The reaction in Europe's capitals bordered on apoplexy."[7]

Alexander Bessmertnykh, Deputy Soviet Ambassador to the United States, recalled how he and other Soviet diplomats mobilized to soften the impact of Reagan's words in Moscow.

It was definitely shocking. [Those] of us sitting in Washington found ourselves in a very difficult position. We had to explain to Moscow what President Reagan meant, what he was all about. And [our] function was to smooth out the situation, just to kind of quiet down Moscow's official feelings about the President.[8]

That the Soviets might be offended mattered little to Ronald Reagan. He had no interest in doing business with the Russians unless it was from a position of strength. And he believed that in 1981, the United States was in a position of weakness. "The fiber of our military muscle was atrophied,"

Reagan later wrote; "fighter planes couldn't fly, and warships couldn't sail because there were no spare parts. Our strategic weapons hadn't been modernized in a decade, while the Soviet Union had created a war machine that was threatening to eclipse ours at every level."[9]

> He used to say "our opponents believe that the lion and the lamb can lie down together which is a very good idea if you have a fresh lamb to throw in every morning," and he believed when he went into office, that the only way that the United States could negotiate a reduction in arms with anybody and particularly with the Soviet Union was if we made it abundantly clear to them that it was an arms race that they could not win, so we needed to strengthen our military.[10]

Historians would later look back at the 1970s as the Soviet Union's last expansionist drive for what it was; the final gasp of a dying empire to extend its influence in ways which exceeded the resources of its economy and society. But at the time, the Soviet Union, with its huge armies and its awesome nuclear arsenal, still posed quite a threat. Reagan's greatest insight might have been his grasp of the great vulnerability behind the menacing facade.[11]

In June 1980, during a campaign visit to *The Washington Post*, Reagan surprised his audience of newspaper reporters and editors when he said: "I think there is every indication and every reason to believe that the Soviet Union cannot increase its production of arms. Right now we're hearing of strikes and labor disputes because people cannot get enough to eat. They've diverted so much to military spending, that they can't provide for their consumer's needs."[12]

"He had this overriding conviction that a strong military

face by the United States for a year or two would bring this hostile system to its knees,"[13] Edmund Morris said. Richard Allen concurred: "The message he wanted to convey to the Soviets was that we were willing to spend them into oblivion."[14] Reagan approved an across-the-board military buildup, the most massive ever in peacetime. He told his Secretary of Defense to order what was needed and not to worry about the budget.

Reagan restored many weapon systems cancelled by former President Carter and began new ones. He deployed the B-1 bomber to replace America's aging B-52s, began deployment of a new land-based missile system, the MX, and began a total overhaul and modernization of U.S. conventional and strategic forces. In mid-1981, Reagan approved every weapon system proposed by his Defense Department. In 1982, under Reagan's first defense budget, the Pentagon spent $21 million *per hour* to improve the U.S. arsenal, by 1989 that number had risen to $34.6 million per hour.

Most analysts regard Reagan's commitment to a military buildup as the keystone of his Soviet strategy, and as his single most important contribution to the Soviet Union's collapse. "Its scale and pace reinforced all the doubts in Soviet leadership about whether they could sustain the arms race economically and—most importantly—technologically," wrote Henry Kissinger.[15]

Alexander Bessmertnykh confirmed this when he told *The American Experience* that "the new Pentagon budget and the start of some new weapons programs was something that really concerned the Russian leadership."[16]

An arms buildup might have been the most effective weapon in Reagan's anti-Soviet arsenal, but it was not his only one.

Early in 1981, just days after becoming President, Reagan met with his CIA Director, William Casey. Casey, whose credentials as a spymaster went all the way back to WWII,[17] and whose anti-Communist convictions matched those of his boss, urged Reagan to wage a secret war on the Soviet Union.[18]

"Mr. President," Casey reportedly said to Reagan, "we have an historic opportunity. We can do serious damage to them."

Casey identified three weaknesses in the Soviet system: First, the Soviet economy was in deep trouble. Second, in "the periphery," anti-Communist insurgencies such as the 'Mujahedin' in Afghanistan were growing in numbers and intensity. Third, Poland, Solidarity, a labor union born on the docks and shipyards Gdansk, was challenging the Soviet empire in Eastern Europe.

Reagan, who "wondered how we as a nation could use these cracks in the Soviet system to accelerate the process of collapse,"[19] agreed in late January to a comprehensive strategy to exploit these vulnerabilities. Herbet Meyer, Special Assistant to Bill Casey, described it:

> The Casey and Reagan approach was, "Hey, my enemy is on his knees, it's a good time to break his head." These guys were not kidding around. They were not trying to slow down Communist expansion. They were trying to reverse Communist expansion. That had never been done before. . . . They decided . . . that they wanted to win the Cold War, and their definition of winning the Cold War was that the Soviet state would cease to exist.[20]

The Reagan strategy sought to apply direct economic pressure. The United States undertook—with little success—the daunting task of enlisting European support to deny the Soviets access to high technology, and to curtail their trade and access to foreign exchange.

The strategy also called for a commitment to aid anti-Soviet

insurgents, a policy which became the "Reagan Doctrine."
Under the "Reagan Doctrine," the CIA trained and assisted
anti-Communist insurgencies the world over: from Jonas Savimbi's UNITAS rebels fighting the Cuban-backed government
of Angola to the Islamic "Mujahedin" at war with the Soviets
in Afghanistan. The CIA also helped create and fund an insurgent group in Nicaragua to fight against the Soviet-Cuban
backed Sandinista regime. The Contras became one of Reagan's favorite causes. Reagan called them "the moral equal of
our Founding Fathers and the brave men and women of the
French Resistance," and vowed "not to turn away from
them."[21]

But these covert operations, as important as they were, were
wars on "the periphery." The opportunity to strike closer to the
heart of the Soviet empire came in 1981, in Poland, where
"Solidarity" had mounted a campaign to gain democratic freedoms.

"As seen from the Oval Office the events in Poland were
thrilling," Reagan wrote. "One of man's most fundamental
yearnings were stirring behind the iron curtain, the first break
in the totalitarian dike of Communism. . . . This is what we had
been waiting for since World War II. What was happening in
Poland might spread like contagion through Eastern Europe."[22]

However thrilled by the events in Poland, the Reagan
Administration weighed its options carefully. A Soviet invasion of Poland could not be ruled out, and Reagan did not want
a replay of the events of 1956 in Hungary, when a rebellion—
incited in part by the United States—had been brutally put
down by Soviet tanks.

Through 1981, the Reagan Administration kept a close
watch on events in Poland, as shipyard workers led by Lech
Walesa intensified their campaign. In December the Soviet
Union acted. Though it refrained from a full-scale invasion,

the Soviets pressured the Polish government to impose mar-
tial law. Solidarity leaders were arrested, and communications
with the rest of the world were shut off. Solidarity went
underground.

Reagan imposed sanctions against Poland and the Soviet
Union. He suspended negotiations on a long-term grain sale
agreement, banned flights by Aeroflot—the Soviet Union's
airline—into the United States and tried, unsuccessfully, to get
Europe to join the United States in boycotting construction of
an important European gas pipeline.

But most importantly, the Administration made a commitment to help Solidarity survive:

> The Reagan Administration made a fundamental
> decision to not let Solidarity die. The result was a num-
> ber of covert actions designed to help keep Solidarity
> alive and literally to keep its leaders alive, even though
> they were in jail for a while.[23]

The CIA, with the help of the Vatican under Pope John
Paul II, a Polish Catholic, supplied fax machines, printing
presses, paper and other communication equipment to Solidarity. It is also alleged that on one occasion, the CIA prevented
the Polish/Soviet regime from poisoning Lech Walesa while he
was in jail.

Reagan's actions in Poland, former Soviet officials told *The
American Experience*, "were very troubling."

> It was perceived as a design by Washington to acti-
> vate its policy in Eastern Europe as a whole, and Poland
> was a kind of testing ground. . . . The relationship that
> developed between the U.S. government and the Pol-
> ish opposition groups was very disturbing.[24]

The Soviets were not the only ones disturbed by Reagan's confrontational approach to East-West relations. Many in the United States worried that Reagan's arms buildup and his hot rhetoric were driving the world dangerously close to nuclear confrontation.

Reagan had predicated his arms buildup as a means to an end. That end, he said, was to reduce nuclear weapons. At the time, many dismissed as a propaganda ploy Reagan's claim that he was "building up in order to build down." "The deployments have been increasing," declared former Secretary of Defense Robert MacNamara, "more and more one hears of the necessity of developing plans for fighting and wining nuclear wars. Inconceivable to me. Madness." From the floor of the Senate, Massachusetts Senator Edward Kennedy said: "I reject the absurd theory that we can have fewer nuclear bombs tomorrow only if we build more nuclear bombs today."

Opposition to Reagan's buildup congealed into the Freeze Movement, which sought a Congressional resolution to force the Administration to "freeze" the number of nuclear weapons at existing levels. By spring 1982, the Freeze Movement had grown into one of the largest grass-roots movements in the history of America. Nearly one million people gathered in New York's Central Park on June 13, 1982, to rally support for a nuclear freeze.

Reagan's daughter, Patti, who had become an outspoken opponent of her father's foreign policy, had shared the stage with the leaders of the Freeze Movement. Fifteen years later, she would regret having played such a visible role:

> My motives were the same as everybody else's . . . I was out there with the intention of speaking . . . for world peace. But I wasn't like everybody else. My father was sitting in the White House . . . The best thing I

could have done for world peace . . . was to stay home. Because really all I was communicating was that I was at war with my father.[25]

Patti combined her public appearances with private pressures. She met Dr. Helen Caldicott, founder of Physicians for Social Responsibility, at a star-studded fund-raiser for the Freeze Movement at Hugh Heffner's Playboy mansion in Hollywood. She brought Dr. Caldicott to the White House hoping she would help convert her father. Dr. Caldicott related to us the details of her one-hour interview with Ronald Reagan in the Oval Office.

> To break the ice, I said to him, "You probably don't know who I am, do you?" And he said, "Yes, I do. You're an Australian, you read *On the Beach* when you were a young girl, and you're scared of nuclear war." And I said, "Yes, that's right." He said, "Well, I too am scared of nuclear war, but our ways to prevent it differ. I believe in building more bombs." After we'd been talking for about an hour, he reached into his inside pocket and pulled a piece of paper out. And he'd written in this backhand writing of his, "People who work for the nuclear weapons freeze are either KGB dupes or Soviet agents." And I said, "But that's from last month's *Reader's Digest*." And he said, "No, it's from my intelligence files."[26]

Dr. Caldicott recalled the meeting as "the most disconcerting" of her life. . . . "I left the White House hardly able to walk from shock and staggered back to my hotel." "I shared her fear about what the remaining years of my father's Administration would bring," Patti wrote. "I sat at the dinner table that night drinking too much wine. . . . I felt like I'd let down an entire movement."

Dr. Caldicott is "a nice, caring person," Reagan wrote in his diary. "But she is all steamed up. . . . I . . . couldn't get through her fixation. For that matter, I couldn't get through to Patti. I'm afraid our daughter has been taken over by that whole gang."[27]

Reagan dealt with the Freeze Movement as yet another political obstacle he needed to overcome. For months, he withstood pressure and criticism with a serenity which impressed his then Deputy National Security Advisor, Robert McFarlane.

> One of the very striking qualities of Reagan was that he could deal with criticism far better than any President I've worked with, because of his conviction and his comfort with himself that his place in history, his obligation to the people was secure—that he was right—and his sense of self-confidence about being right in opposing the Freeze Movement gave him a piece of mind that was quite unusual.[28]

A more difficult problem was presented by the growing opposition in Europe to the Administration's commitment to deploy a new class of ground-based missiles in Great Britain and on the continent. Unlike other missiles stationed in Europe, the Pershings could reach targets deep into the Soviet Union. The Soviets, who considered the Pershings IIs as strategic missiles, protested that their deployment violated the spirit of the SALT II agreement, which, though never ratified by the U.S. Senate was still treated by both superpowers as if it were binding.

The decision to deploy the Pershing IIs had been made by the Carter Administration in response to the Soviet deployment of a new medium-range missile, the SS-20. Reagan honored Carter's commitment. Beginning in November 1981, Soviet and American delegations began meeting in Geneva to discuss the problem of the Pershings and the SS-20s in Europe, but had failed to reach an agreement. By 1982, the decision to deploy the Pershing IIs had become so controversial that it threatened to split the NATO Alliance.

> Ronald Reagan found himself in the position of having to implement a decision he hadn't made, that was now opposed by many of the governments who had participated in the decision. And it was clear at once that this was a litmus test of the ability of the NATO Alliance to carry through on a tough decision. And he had the sense, we all did, that if we failed to carry out that plan, which we had all agreed upon and been announced to the world, it would have dealt NATO a devastating blow and probably one from which it couldn't recover.[29]

Though motivated by a genuine sense of insecurity, Europe's anti-nuclear movement became fertile ground for Soviet propaganda. Soviet involvement in the movement is now well-documented. Pavel Palazchenko, a former Soviet diplomat, told *The American Experience* in Moscow:

> At that time, we thought that . . . we'll somehow split Europe and the United States. It was always in the cards—this big game [to divide] major European countries and the United States, playing on their fears of nuclear war.[30]

> The Soviet objective was to neutralize Europe. Again, not to defeat Europe but to neutralize Europe.

So that Europe would break away from the United
States and supply the Soviet Union with the money
that it needed, the technology that it needed, the food
that it needed. We were fighting the Soviets for the
heart and soul of Europe. So that was one nasty fight.
The Soviets were up to their elbows in the political bat-
tles to stop the deployment of the intermediate-range
missiles, we knew that.[31]

The Reagan Administration countered the Soviet propaganda offensive with a proposal designed to deflect responsibility for the nuclearization of Europe from the United States
back to the Soviet Union. If the Soviets agreed to withdraw
their SS-20s and their older SS 4s and SS 5s, the United States
would not deploy the Pershing IIs. It was called the "Zero
Option," the first superpower proposal to reduce nuclear
weapons in the history of the arms race. It was, as expected,
immediately rejected by the Soviet negotiators, who saw it as a
"cunning plot" to get them to withdraw missiles already in
place in exchange for missiles not yet deployed. "It was [taken]
as a joke," recalled Soviet official Sergei Tarasenko. "Nobody
in his right mind thought of the possibility of a Zero Option."[32]

Reagan traveled to Europe in June 1982, to help his allies
resist the onslaught of public opinion. "I wanted to demonstrate that I wasn't flirting with doomsday," he later wrote, ". . .
that our military strength was a prerequisite to peace."

. . . But I wanted to accomplish something else beside
convincing the Europeans I wasn't determined to lead
the Western alliance into a nuclear war. . . . The
democracies, I suggested, like the Communists, should
adopt a policy of expansionism . . . and become worldwide evangelists for freedom.[33]

In a speech delivered before the British Parliament at Westminster, Reagan said:

> What I am describing now is a plan and a hope for
> the long term. The march of freedom and democracy
> which will leave Marxism and Leninism on the ash
> heap of history as it has left other tyrannies which have
> stifled the freedom and muzzled the self-expression of
> the people . . .

"We all recognized it as one of his great speeches," recalled
then British Prime Minister Margaret Thatcher:

> Ronald Reagan said it's not enough to contain Com-
> munism by our strength, we've got to carry the message
> of liberty, the battle of ideas, right into the heart of
> those who are suffering. We have a message, let's go out
> and preach the world over. Let other people hear it.
> Reagan's message was the message of liberty, justice,
> democracy, integrity. The fact was that it was individual
> enterprise working together that created the wealth to
> get people out of poverty.[34]

Though the Westminster speech probably did little to
assuage the anxiety of European demonstrators, it signaled the
beginning of a new rhetorical offensive against the Soviet
Union. The words were written by speechwriter Anthony
Dolan, but the ideas were Ronald Reagan's:

> Ronald Reagan understood the power of ideas. . . .
> He understood that in the end it's the great ideas in
> history that are moving forces. . . . Reagan understood
> that words have tremendous power [especially] at a

moment when everyone was wondering whether the
world was going to fall apart, or blow itself up, or sub-
mit to Soviet totalitarianism. He said "no." He said,
"man will endure because he has a soul and because he
believes in the great verities and the eternal truths."
And that was something that came out of the heart of
America. It came from his understanding of reality
which was essentially religious. He drove that Presidency with his ideas.[35]

Nine months later, on March 8, Reagan delivered what
would be his most controversial speech to a convention of
Evangelicals in Florida. The House of Representatives was
scheduled to vote on the freeze resolution the following week,
and Reagan used the occasion to state his philosophy on the
nature of the struggle between the Soviet Union and the
United States and to urge opposition to the nuclear freeze.

> . . . Let us be aware that while they preach the
> supremacy of the state, declare its omnipotence over
> individual man, and predict its eventual domination of
> all peoples on the earth, they are the focus of evil in the
> modern world. . . . So in your discussions of the nuclear
> freeze proposals, I urge you to beware the temptation of
> pride—the temptation of blithely declaring yourself
> above it all and label both sides equally at fault, to
> ignore the facts of history and the aggressive impulses of
> an evil empire, to simply call the arms race a giant mis-
> understanding and thereby remove yourself from the
> struggle between right and wrong and good and evil. . . .
> I believe we shall rise to the challenge. I believe that
> Communism is another sad, bizarre chapter in human
> history. . . . I believe this because the source of our

strength in the quest for human freedom is not material, but spiritual. And because it knows no limitations, it must terrify and ultimately triumph over those who would enslave their fellow man.

Tony Dolan explained the motivation behind what became known as the Evil Empire speech:

A great many of the opinion elite liked to take the position that . . . the Cold War was a giant misunderstanding. Maybe the Soviets had been a little worse than the West. . . . And sometimes it was worse than that. Sometimes there was what [UN Ambassador] Jeanne Kirkpatrick[36] called the "blame America first" phenomenon. What Reagan was saying in the Evil Empire speech was that moral equivalence between the Soviets and the West . . . was entirely invalid. That this was a government that was based on conquest, on oppression and the Devil.[37]

"He saw a lack of freedom. He saw social degradation. He hated what he saw," Edmund Morris explained. "He at least understood and was courageous enough to articulate to the rest of the world that what there is over there is despicable. It's evil. One of the oldest words in any language. Evil."[38]

Reagan's speech provoked outrage: "Primitive . . . and apocalyptic," cried *The New Republic*. "A fundamentalist reaction . . . with little to offer to a complex world," wrote Harvard Professor Stanley Hoffman.[39]

They saw him as something of a cowboy. They identified him with Barry Goldwater, who in the 1964 campaign says, we should think about "lobbing one into the men's room of the Kremlin." . . . In 1964, the Goldwater bumper sticker was "In Your Heart You Know He's Right." And the opponents said, "In Your Heart You Know He's Nuts," seeing him as a dangerous character who might provoke a nuclear war. Reagan was seen by many people as the heir of that rhetoric. And he frightens people.[40]

Even Nancy Reagan, worried about her husband's image, urged him to tone down his rhetoric.[41]

But the Kremlin did not get too concerned over Reagan's "war of words." Alexander Bessmertnykh:

> When he was talking about the evil empire . . . you felt that it was kind of expected and natural from him. Statements are important, but they can be lived through, I mean they are not really a tragic thing in diplomacy or foreign policy. But what was more important to us sitting on the other side of the barrier, was the arms race.[42]

But even that ground was shifting. Under Ronald Reagan, the arms race which so preoccupied the Soviets was about to take off into an unexpected new dimension: space.

NOTES

[1] In our interview, Lou Cannon recalled how journalists used to laugh at Reagan on the campaign trail. "When we would ask him about foreign policy, he used to list the foreign leaders he'd met and the countries he had visited."

[2] Lyn Nofziger, Interview with Author.

[3] Henry Kissinger, *Diplomacy*, p.774. In his chapter "The End of the Cold War," Kissinger provides a brilliant conceptual analysis of Reagan's foreign policy.

[4] Jay Winnik, *On the Brink*, (New York: Simon and Schuster, 1996), p.157

[5] Henry Kissinger, *Diplomacy*, p. 773.

[6] Edmund Morris, Interview with Author.

[7] Richard Allen, Interview with Austin Hoyt.

[8] Alexander Bessmertnykh. Interview with Austin Hoyt.

[9] Ronald Reagan, *An American Life*, p. 217.

[10] Maureen Reagan, Interview with Author.

[11] At the time, most "Sovietologists" dismissed the idea of vulnerability. Seweryn Bialer of Columbia University wrote in *Foreign Affairs*, "The Soviet Union is not now nor will it be in the throes of a true systemic crisis. His opinion was echoed widely well into the 1980s. Seweryn Bialer and Joan Afferica, "Reagan and Russia," *Foreign Affairs*, Winter 1982–83, p. 263.

[12] Cannon, *Role of a Lifetime*, p. 297. Reiterated in interview with Austin Hoyt.

[13] Edmund Morris, Interview with Author.

[14] Richard Allen, Interview with Austin Hoyt.

[15] Henry Kissinger, *Diplomacy*, p. 775.

[16] Alexander Bessmernytkh, Interview with Austin Hoyt.

[17] Casey had been an operative of the Office of Strategic Services, OSS, the precursor to the CIA. He had also managed Reagan's 1980 campaign after John Sears was fired in the wake of Reagan's first defeat at the Iowa caucus.

[18] This account of Reagan's "Secret War" draws on Peter Schweizer, *Victory* (New York: Atlantic Monthly Press, 1994), on Carl Bernstein in *Time*, February 24, 1992, and is confirmed by personal interviews with Meyer and by Reagan's National Security Advisor, Judge William Clark, who, though reluctant to unveil details about Reagan's policy, still confirmed Bernstein's account.

[19] Reagan, *An American Life*, p. 237–238.

[20] Herbert Meyer, Interview with Austin Hoyt.

[21] It was speechwriter Peggy Noonan who came up with the comparison, even though many Contra members were former "Somocistas" who had already been rejected by the Nicaraguan people. In time, however the Contra army attracted many peasants and members of the Nicaraguan middle class.

[22] Ronald Reagan, *An American Life*, p. 301.

[23] *Ibid,*

[24] Alexander Bessmernytkh, Interview with Austin Hoyt.

[25] Patti Davis, Interview with Austin Hoyt.

[26] Helen Caldicott, Interview With Austin Hoyt.

[27] Ronald Reagan, *An American Life*, p. 566.

[28] Robert McFarlane, Interview with Austin Hoyt.

[29] Richard Perle, Interview with Austin Hoyt.

[30] Pavel Palazchenko, Interview with Austin Hoyt. Through the history of the Cold War, "major European countries" was generally a euphemism for Germany. Germany had always been at the center of the superpower politics in Europe. The United States wanted Germany to remain strongly tied to NATO, while the Soviets wanted German to be neutral.

[31] Herbert Meyer, Interview with Austin Hoyt.

[32] Sergei Tarasenko, Interview with Austin Hoyt.

[33] Ronald Reagan, *An American Life*, pp. 554–555.

[34] Margaret Thatcher, Interview with Austin Hoyt.

[35] Tony Dolan, Interview with Author.

[36] Jeanne Kirkpatrick was Reagan's Ambassador to the United Nations and had authored a very influential book, *Dictatorships and Double Standards*, which was the intellectual justification for the "Reagan Doctrine."

[37] Anthony Dolan, Interview with Author.

[38] Edmund Morris, Interview with Austin Hoyt.

[39] Despite Reagan's appeal, the House of Representative voted in favor of the nuclear freeze resolution on May 4. The resolution, however never reached the Senate floor, as the Senate Relations Committee voted against it on September 20.

[40] Robert Dallek, Interview with Austin Hoyt.

[41] Reagan, *An American Life*, p. 570.

[42] Alexander Bessmertnykh, Interview with Austin Hoyt.

CHAPTER 15

Slouching Toward Armageddon

In July 1979, while campaigning for the presidency of the United States, candidate Ronald Reagan visited the North American Air Defense Command, NORAD, deep under the Cheyenne Mountains in Colorado. There he learned about hardened silos, pinpoint missile accuracy, flight times, throw-weights, survivability ratios, and all the other jargon of the nuclear priesthood. But when he asked, perhaps rhetorically, what protection there was in case of a nuclear attack, he was told there was no defense. Only the threat of retaliation.

Reagan's advisor Martin Anderson who accompanied the candidate on the trip to NORAD recalled the conversation that took place on the return trip from Colorado:

> On the plane coming home, I was discussing this with Reagan. He said, "Look, you know the President has two bad choices. If a nuclear missile is fired at the United States you can either do nothing, let the missile land and explode and kill a lot of people—or, you can retaliate. And, you're told the missile is coming in, you get ten, fifteen minutes before it hits. So, you'd push your own button and punish the aggressor—you know where the missile's coming from—and maybe set off a nuclear war between the United States and Soviet Union, and have an Armageddon, destroy most of our civilization." And he said, "Both choices are bad

choices. There has to be another way, and we need to really explore the whole question of missile defense."[1]

Reagan was not the first to find MAD, Mutually Assured Destruction, the most "maddening" and unsatisfying conundrum of the nuclear age. Land-based missile defense systems had been developed and tested in the 1960s, but they had proved technically unfeasible. It was hard enough to hit one incoming missile, but destroying thousands of warheads in a matter of minutes across the breadth of the United States proved to be an impossible objective. Besides, the incentive for both sides would be to build more and more offensive weapons to overwhelm any defense system, since it was cheaper to build more offensive missiles than it was to build the defense required to stop them.

To avoid a spiraling offense-defense arms race, the United States and the Soviet Union, in 1971, signed the Anti-Ballistic Missile (ABM) Treaty, agreeing to not pursue deployment of defense systems.

But by 1983, during Reagan's first term in office, the development of computer and satellite technology, as well as laser beams, had breathed new life into the dream of achieving a viable defense against nuclear weapons—this time, in space.

Two ardent proponents of such a defense, General Daniel Graham and Edward Teller, reassured the President that a future space-based defense was possible, if enough money and resources were devoted to its development.

On March 23, 1983, Reagan went on national television to announce the launching of a new defense program, the Strategic Defense Initiative:

Let me share with you a vision of the future which offers hope. It is that we embark on a program to

counter the awesome Soviet missile threat with measures that are defensive. I call upon the scientific community in our country, those who gave us nuclear
weapons, to turn their great talents now to the cause of
mankind and world peace, to give us the means of rendering these nuclear weapons impotent and obsolete.

For Reagan, the Strategic Defense Initiative, or SDI, was the
fulfillment of a long-held dream: a world in which America's
defense did not rely on the threat of mutual annihilation.

Reagan's abhorrence of Mutually Assured Destruction was
rooted in his belief in Armageddon, the biblical prophecy of
the end of the world. His interest in Armageddon, rooted in his
religious fundamentalist upbringing, had been stirred by Rev-
erend Billy Graham, who in 1968, while Reagan was Governor
of California, had told him that the end was near. One portent,
Reagan repeated widely in 1969, was the Communist takeover
of Libya. On more one occasion, Reagan's close aide Michael
Deaver recalled hearing the President talk about Armageddon:

I think that he believed in all of the prophecies in
Revelations, and when they talked about the metal
horses or the iron horses and so forth, he would refer to
those, as the tanks or the arms that we would be able to
develop. . . . In other words, he said, you could take those
descriptions of what was going to happen and show that
that was exactly what we were moving towards today
ourselves unless we did something about it.[2]

The phrase "unless we did something about it" revealed Reagan's unique interpretation of Armageddon. Ronald Reagan,
the optimist, the hero, the lifeguard, could not accept the idea
of Armageddon as an inevitable doom—the final apocalyptic

battle between good and evil. He felt it was an end from which he could rescue America and the world.

> More than once President Reagan in the Oval Office expressed how he felt about this balance of terror and I remember very well how each time he would be genuinely anguished and would physically withdraw and lean forward and with quiet passion explain his fear that Armageddon was at hand and that unless he tried to move us away from this incredible nuclear threat of each other, that it could happen in his lifetime and he was determined to do something about it. . . . That fear was what drove him so passionately to try to move us away from the strategy that relied on our ability to threaten the Soviet Union and toward a strategy that didn't rely so much on offense, but on defense.[3]

In 1983, SDI was only in the early stages of research. Most scientists and defense analysts regarded it as a dangerous pipe dream. SDI, they argued, was riddled with technical difficulties, some of which seemed insurmountable. A perfect defense was not only a practical impossibility, but any defense system was certain to destabilize the strategic nuclear balance and trigger a new arms race—on land, and in space.

But Reagan, the willful optimist who believed all things desirable were possible was undeterred by these arguments. He was convinced that American technological ingenuity would find a way to build a shield to protect Americans from nuclear holocaust.

> It goes back to Reagan's sense of optimism. I mean, this is man who's life spanned the 20th century, the American century, and as a boy, he saw automobiles—

By Liberty weekend, 1986, Reagan and the nation had much to celebrate. He boasted an approval rating of 68 percent and the country was experiencing an economic boom unrivaled in its recent history.

Early in Reagan's second term Don Regan would replace James Baker as his Chief of Staff. With the concurrent departure of Deaver and Meese, Regan alone would try to tackle all of the duties of the Troika.

Reagan broadcasting from Rancho del Cielo, his Santa Barbara ranch. "I'm pleased to tell you today that I've signed legislation that will outlaw Russia forever. We begin bombing in five minutes," he joked into a microphone that was inadvertently left open.

Reagan's daughter Patti at a celebrity Nuclear-Feeze gathering at Hugh Hefner's Playboy mansion. Years later she would regret having played such a visible role.

Secretary of State George Shultz lead the "moderates" who believed in using SDI as a bargaining chip in negotiations with the Soviets, while Secretary of Defense Caspar Weinberger headed the "hard liners" who were committed to its development.

Nancy and Ronald Reagan greet Soviet Foreign Minister Andrei Gromyko at the White House.

Reagan first met Gorbachev at the Geneva summit in November 1985. As they walked toward the boathouse on the shore of Lake Leman, the two men chatted about Reagan's movie career. It was their first opportunity to talk with each other as human beings.

"As we sat in stuffed chairs beside the hearth, I said, 'Mr. General Secretary, here we are, two men born in obscure rural hamlets, both poor and from humble beginnings. Now we are the leaders of our countries, and probably the only two men who can start WWIII, and possible the only two men . . . who can bring peace to the world. . . .'"

During the Geneva summit, the President stayed in the home of the Aga Khan, whose wife Sally asked that Reagan feed their son's goldfish while they were away. On rising one morning he discovered that one of the fish had died during the night. He made sure the boy's fish was replaced, and wrote this note in explanation and gratitude.

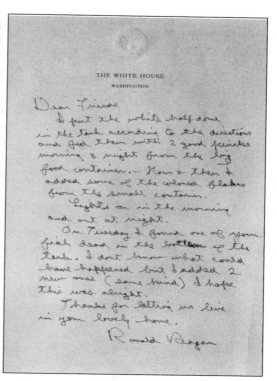

Reagan saw the Presidency as a position of moral leadership and took great care in editing his speeches, often rewriting them extensively, before delivering them.

"As the day went on, I felt something momentous was occurring. . . . As evening approached I said to myself 'Look what we have accomplished . . . the most massive weapons reduction in history.' . . . Then Gorbachev threw us a curve. With a smile on his face he said, 'This all depends, of course, on your giving up SDI.' I couldn't believe it."

—Ronald Reagan, commenting on the Reykjavik summit.

At the end of the Reykjavik summit, Reagan and Gorbachev both bear the look of disapointment at having come "so close" without reaching an agreement on arms reductions. Years after his departure from office, Gorbachev would declare this meeting the turning point that ultimately led to the end of the Cold War.

Reagan meets with National Security Advisor Robert McFarlane and Chief of Staff Donald Regan days after colon cancer surgery. During that meeting Reagan agreed to McFarlane's inititive to sell weapons to Iran.

Meeting with CIA Director Bill Casey in the Oval Office. Under the "Reagan Doctrine," Casey's CIA would support insurgencies around the world, one of which was the Contras in Nicaragua.

Reagan listens with dismay to the report of the Tower Commission's investigation into the Iran-Contra scandal. Although the commission never tied Reagan directly to the diversion of funds from the arms sales to Iran, it placed blame squarely upon his shoulders for failure to oversee the actions of his subordinates.

"First let me say I take full responsibility for my own actions and for those of my Administration. As angry as I may be about activities undertaken without my knowledge, I am still accountable for those activities. As disappointed as I may be in some who served me, I'm still the one who must answer to the American people for this behavior. . . . This happened on my watch. "
—Ronald Reagan, addressing the nation regarding the Tower Commission Report, March 4, 1987.

Reagan in the tack room at Rancho del Cielo near the end of his Presidency.

" In this two hundredth anniversary year of our Constitution, you and I stand on the shoulders of giants—men whose words and deeds put wind in the sails of freedom . . . We will be guided tonight by their acts, and we will be guided forever by their words."

—Ronald Reagan, 1987

And how stands the city on this winter night? More prosperous, more secure, and happier than it was eight years ago. But more than that; after two hundred years, two centuries, she still stands strong and true on the granite ridge, and her glow has held steady no matter what storm. And she's still a beacon, still a magnet for all who must have freedom, for all the pilgrims from all the lost places who are hurtling through the darkness toward home.

We've done our part. And as I walk off into the city streets, a final word to the men and women of the Reagan revolution, the men and women across America who for eight years did the work that brought America back. My friends: We did it. We weren't just marking time. We made a difference. We made the city stronger. We made the city freer, and we left her in good hands. All in all, not bad, not bad at all.

And so, goodbye, God bless you, and God bless the United States of America.

—Ronald Reagan,
from his farewell address to the nation,
January 11, 1989.

RONALD REAGAN

Nov. 5, 1994

My Fellow Americans,

I have recently been told that I am one of the millions of Americans who will be afflicted with Alzheimer's Disease.

Upon learning this news, Nancy & I had to decide whether as private citizens we would keep this a private matter or whether we would make this news known in a public way.

In the past Nancy suffered from breast cancer and I had my cancer surgeries. We found through our open disclosures we were able to raise public awareness. We were happy that as a result many more people underwent testing.

They were treated in early stages and able to return to normal, healthy lives.

So now, we feel it is important to share it with you. In opening our hearts, we hope this might promote greater awareness of this condition. Perhaps it will encourage a clearer understanding of the individuals and families who are affected by it.

At the moment I feel just fine. I intend to live the remainder of the years God gives me on this earth doing the things I have always done. I will continue to share life's journey with my beloved Nancy and my family. I plan to enjoy the great outdoors and stay in touch with my friends and supporters.

Unfortunately, as Alzheimer's Disease progresses, the family often bears a heavy burden. I only wish there was some way I could spare Nancy from this painful experience. When the time comes I am confident that with your help she will face it with faith and courage.

In closing let me thank you, the American people for giving me the great honor of allowing me to serve as your President. When the Lord calls me home, whenever that may be, I will leave with the greatest love for this country of ours and eternal optimism for its future.

I now begin the journey that will lead me into the sunset of my life. I know that for America there will always be a bright dawn ahead.

Thank you my friends. May God always bless you.

Sincerely,
Ronald Reagan

they were brand new. And as a teenager, he fell in love with radio, radio—what a miracle. Later on, the movies —my God, this is the American art form. And then television. Why shouldn't there be a way to shoot down these vehicles of nuclear destruction?[4]

He believed in this so strongly, that he began to think that SDI was in existence when it wasn't even on the drawing board. He so passionately wanted there to be a nuclear defense.[5]

If for Reagan SDI was a dream, for the Soviet Union, in the words of Alexander Bessmertnykh, it was "a horror." SDI, the Soviets feared, would give the United States a strategic advantage—a first strike capability. Theoretically, the United States could launch an attack against the Soviet Union taking out most of their ICBMs, and then deploy its SDI defense shield against the crippled Soviet retaliation.[6]

Soviet Premier Yuri Andropov called SDI "irresponsible and insane," and accused Reagan of "attempting to disarm the Soviet Union in the face of the U.S. nuclear threat."

"We realized we were approaching a very dangerous situation in the strategic balance," Moscow's Ambassador Anatoly Dobrynin later wrote.[7] "Seen against his defense buildup and his announcement of SDI Reagan's rhetoric of prevailing in the Cold War acquired new meaning. Many in the Soviet Union became convinced that the United States was preparing for a first strike."[8]

The Politburo approved the largest peacetime military intelligence operation in Soviet history, known by its codename Operation Ryon, an acronym of the Russian words *Raketno-Yadernoye Napadenie*, Nuclear Missile Attack. In 1983 all KGB residents received urgent and detailed instructions to collect any evidence of plans for an American first strike.[9]

Soviet fears, though understandable, were unfounded—at least for the duration of Ronald Reagan's presidency. Reagan, all who knew him closely agreed, including his biographer Edmund Morris, hated nuclear weapons and deemed nuclear war "unthinkable."

> He was a passionate anti-nuclear idealist. I don't know it this is understood as much as it should be. The very notion of mass destruction by nuclear weapons was deeply abhorrent to him.[10]

He saw SDI as a moral imperative—as a shield, not a sword. But, as his Chief of Staff James Baker told *The American Experience*, he was not unaware of its importance as yet another weapon in his crusade to consign the Soviet Union to the "ash heap of history."

> [Reagan] saw SDI as yet another pressure on the Soviets, something that they could not withstand. . . . Whether it would work or not, it was a heck of a challenge to the Soviet empire, which was having a very difficult time competing economically and otherwise.[11]

And this is where the Soviets really had a problem. The Soviet Union had achieved superpower status on the basis on their nuclear arsenal. Since the 1960s Soviet leaders had devoted an inordinate amount of resources to achieve nuclear parity. Now Reagan threatened to make nuclear weapons "impotent and obsolete." At a point when the Soviet Union was nearing the point of economic exhaustion, a whole new arms race loomed ahead.

Pavel Palazchenko, a Soviet diplomat, explained the dilemma Reagan's Strategic Defense Initiative posed for the Soviet leadership:

> I think it revealed in their minds the impossibility for the Soviet Union to really compete in that area because of our technological inferiority.[12]

SDI not only heightened tensions with the Soviet Union, but also within the Reagan Administration. While the President saw SDI as a moral imperative first, and secondly as a pressure on the Soviets, his Administration was divided between those who believed developing SDI would force the Soviets into a competition they could now win, and those who saw it as a bargaining chip to be traded for Soviet concessions in future arms control negotiations. The "moderates" who believed in trading SDI were lead by Secretary of State George Shultz, while the "hard liners" who were committed to its development were headed by Secretary of Defense Caspar Weinberger. Through 1983 Weinberger had an effective ally in National Security Advisor William Clark, but the equation changed dramatically when Bill Clark was replaced by Robert McFarlane as National Security Advisor in October 1983. McFarlane, like Shultz, believed SDI should be bargained away at the negotiating table.

The two camps would wage a pitched battle during Reagan's second term. But in the fall of 1983, the attention of his Administration would be consumed by escalating global tensions that brought the Soviet-American relationship close to a dangerous breaking point.

On September 1, Soviet pilots shot down a Korean airliner, KAL 007, which had strayed into Soviet air space, killing 269 people. "The world witnessed the Soviet Union that Ronald

Reagan had always warned against," wrote *Newsweek*. "This was the Soviet Union against the world and the moral precepts which guide human relations around people everywhere," Reagan told the nation on September 5. "It was an act of barbarism, born of a society which wantonly disregards individual rights and the value of human life and seeks constantly to expand and dominate other nations."[13]

On October 21, a car bomb, driven by a suicidal Muslim extremist, crashed against the U.S. marine barracks in Lebanon, killing 241 members of the American peacekeeping force. It was an event Reagan would later remember as "the saddest day in my life," and one for which he bore great responsibility.[14]

On October 25, 5,000 troops U.S. invaded Grenada. The presence of thirty Soviet advisors and hundreds of Cuban soldiers and workers, proved to the Reagan Administration that the Caribbean island was being transformed into a Communist beachhead.[15]

On October 27, in a televised address, Reagan linked the downing of KAL 007, the terrorist attack in Beirut and the invasion of Grenada into a blanket accusation of Soviet aggression throughout the world.

> The events . . . though oceans apart, are closely related. Not only has Moscow assisted and encouraged violence . . . but it provides direct support through a network of surrogates and terrorists. . . .
>
> You know, there was a time when our national security was based on a standing army here within our own borders, and shore batteries of artillery along our coast. . . . Today our national security can be threatened in faraway places. It's up to all us to be aware of the strategic importance of such places and to be able to identify them.

In response to Reagan's actions and harsh words, the Soviet press compared Reagan to Hitler and called him a "madman." "If anybody ever had any illusions about the possibility of an evolution to the better in the policy of the present American Administration, these illusions are completely dispelled now," Soviet Premier Yuri Andropov is reported to have said.

While superpower relations worsened, tensions in Europe were reaching new heights. As the date for the deployment of the Pershing missiles approached, opposition in Europe intensified. The world grew more anxious. The deployment of the Pershings loomed as the next—and some feared final—stage in the escalation of tensions between the United States and the Soviet Union, begun when Reagan rejected détente in his first press conference in January 1981.

> The escalating tension that developed out of his successive speeches—his declaration that the Soviet Union was the focus of evil in the world, his announcements of the SDI initiatives, his actions that year in Grenada, the disastrous debacle of the 007 Korean airliner—the tensions were mounting to such an intolerable point that fall that to go ahead and deploy missiles in Europe was like the final spark that was going to light the tinder.[16]

> The shooting down of the airliner had shown how close we were to miscalculation and how much of a hair trigger certainly the Soviet Fighter Command was on. And it didn't take a real stretch of the imagination to see that things could get worse and that there could be other incidents. And I think we were close to not necessarily war, but we were really close to a kind of a breakdown that could have led to war.[17]

On November 20, days before the Pershing missiles were to arrive in Europe, 100 million Americans watched "The Day After," an ABC television movie which depicted the effects of nuclear war in Lawrence, Kansas. The film reflected as well as heightened the growing anxiety among Americans about the escalating superpower tensions.

Earlier that month, Reagan had seen a preview of the film. "It was a scenario," he wrote, "that could lead to the end of civilization as we knew it. It left me very depressed."[18]

Despite of its emotional impact, "The Day After" had no effect on the President's decision to go ahead with deployment.

On November 23, the controversial Pershing II missiles arrived in Germany.

In protest, the Soviets walked out of the ongoing Geneva talks, vowing not to return as long as the Pershings were on the ground. For the first time in twenty years the two superpowers would not be engaged in arms negotiations. This cherished symbol of superpower stability in an uncertain and dangerous world was now gone. It was the lowest point in Soviet-American relations since the Cuban missile crisis in October 1962.

"There was a feeling of tragedy in the air," recalled Soviet diplomat Alexander Bessmertnykh. "All of us who were dealing with the United States were feeling that maybe the relationship would [deteriorate] even further."[19]

The superpowers, some predicted, were on "the brink of nuclear war." Six world leaders joined in stating that the world was heading toward suicide. Even Pope John Paul II, an ardent foe of Communism, warned that "we were moving from a postwar era to a prewar phase."[20]

Reagan was far more sanguine about the Soviets' decision to walk out of Geneva. "They'd left the ballpark, but I didn't think the game was over," he later wrote.[21]

Many applauded Reagan's determination to go ahead with the Pershing II deployment,

> He had the fundamental courage that it took to go ahead with that. And that was unmistakable from the point of view of any Soviet strategist, that what they were dealing with on this side of the water was a very determined President.[22]

> If NATO had decided upon a deployment and had [been] unable to follow through . . . the Soviet Union would have had a new burst of confidence. The Atlantic Alliance would have been cracked and who knows what would have happened . . . and that didn't turn out to be the case in large measure because the President was staying the course.[23]

Years later, Secretary of State George Shultz would call the decision to go ahead with the deployment of the Pershing missiles in Europe one of the two "turning points in the Cold War."[24] The other would be years later, at a hastily called summit in Reykjavik, the capital of Iceland, where Reagan stood fast against Soviet attempts to kill SDI.

NOTES

[1] Martin Anderson, Interview with Author.

[2] Michael Deaver, Interview with Author.

[3] Robert McFarlane, Interview with Austin Hoyt.

[4] William Norton Smith, Interview with Author.

[5] Lou Cannon, Interview with Austin Hoyt.

[6] Soviet fear was heightened by the talk among U.S. strategists about the possibility of fighting "limited nuclear wars." Throughout the 1980s, nuclear strategists were busy developing scenarios where nuclear weapons could be used in the event of international crises, without necessarily triggering a nuclear holocaust.

[7] Anatoly Dobrynin, *In Confidence: Moscow's Ambassador to America's Six Cold War Presidents, 1962–1986* (New York: Times Books, 1995), p. 609.

[8] Alexander Bessmertnykh, Conversation with Josh Clark.

[9] Anatoly Dobrynin, *In Confidence.*

[10] Edmund Morris, Interview with Austin Hoyt.

[11] James Baker III, Interview with Author.

[12] Pavel Palazhenko, Interview with Austin Hoyt.

[13] Andropov responded with some harsh rhetoric of his own. On September 28 he warned that "to turn the battle of ideas into military confrontation would be too costly for the whole of mankind. But those who are blinded by anti-Communism are evidently incapable of grasping this." Quoted in Cannon, *Role of Lifetime*, p. 318.

[14] Reagan had repeatedly ignored the advice of his military commanders that the Marines were an exposed symbol of the American presence in Beirut. He had paid no attention to growing acts of terrorism against Americans, including the bombing of the U.S. Embassy on September 5. Cannon, *Role of Lifetime*, p. 443.

[15] The Reagan Administration had watched with concern as Cubans helped the government of Grenada expand an air strip to accommodate large transport planes. The opportunity to invade came when Marxist Prime Minister Maurice Bishop was overthrown by a fellow Communist in a bloody coup. That made it easier to justify an invasion, since an invasion against the democratically elected Bishop government would have provoked an outcry from his Caribbean and Latin American neighbors.

[16] Edmund Morris, Interview with Austin Hoyt.

[17] Lou Cannon, Interview with Austin Hoyt.

[18] Ronald Reagan, *An American Life*, p. 585.

[19] Alexander Bessmertnykh, Interview with Austin Hoyt.

[20] Quoted in Jay Winnik, *To the Brink*, p. 286.

[21] Ronald Reagan, *An American Life*, p. 586.

[22] Edmund Morris, Interview with Austin Hoyt.

[23] George Will, Interview with Author.

[24] George Shultz, Interview with Austin Hoyt. "We started 1983 with Soviet threats and efforts to decouple the U.S. from European allies. We ended the year with our alliance stronger than ever." George Shultz, *Triumph and Turmoil: My Years as Secretary of State* (New York: Charles Scribner, 1993), p. 377.

CHAPTER 15

Morning in America

In the summer of 1984, with the Pershings deployed, SDI in the works, the economy flourishing, the defense buildup humming along, and anti-Soviet insurgencies thriving the world over, a confident President Reagan stood proudly in front of a war memorial in Normandy, on the French coast.

It was the fortieth anniversary of D-Day, and Reagan had come to honor the U.S. Rangers who had scaled the cliff and silenced the German guns pointed at Omaha Beach, just below:

> We are here to mark that day in history where the Allied Armies joined in battle to reclaim this continent to liberty. . . . Here in Normandy the rescue began. We stand on a lonely, windswept point on the northern shore of France. Today the air is soft, but forty years ago at this moment the air was dense with smoke and the cries of men . . .

At Pointe du Hoc, the landscape of craters and barbed wire has been preserved as a reminder of the horror of war. Looking beyond the remnants of destruction, past the Rangers' memorial, one's eyes rest on a distant horizon, where the blue French sky meets the ruffled waters of the English Channel.

"Visuals"—Deputy Chief of Staff Michael Deaver wrote later about this setting—"I am sure the purists who want their news unfiltered and their heroes unrehearsed, gag on the word 'visuals.' But when every night you have to fill the four corners of that box in America's living rooms, visuals become very important."[1]

The Reagan White House understood that in the television age the power of Reagan's rhetoric depended not only on his message, but also on the surrounding images and events. In Michael Deaver, Reagan had a master of images. Pointe du Hoc would be Deaver's masterpiece.

"I looked at this as the creative side of my work," wrote Deaver. "I do not mean to suggest that the feeling was comparable to directing a major Hollywood production or a Broadway musical. But when you stood at a distance and surveyed the Normandy coast . . . you had a sense of sweep and panorama. . . . In this kind of environment, Ronald Reagan . . . glowed."[2]

> At dawn on the morning of June 6, 1944, 225 American Rangers jumped off the British landing craft and ran to the bottom of these cliffs . . .
>
> Two hundred-twenty-five came here. After two days of fighting, only 90 could still bear arms. . . .

"They wanted a speech like the Gettysburg Address," Peggy Noonan later wrote, "and they kept giving it back to me because the speech was not moving enough. And they kept saying, 'They'll be there, they'll be there.' And finally, I realized what they were saying. The Rangers would be facing Ronald Reagan. And then it came to me . . . ."[3]

> These are the boys of Pointe du Hoc.
>
> These are the men who took the cliffs. These are the champions who helped free a continent; these are the heroes who helped end the war.

As the camera panned the faces of the veterans, tears running down their cheeks, it all came together in one perfect moment: Noonan's words, Deaver's images, Reagan's delivery.

"The Rangers wept. Many of us in the press wept. Even the Secret Service could not hide their feelings," wrote Lou Cannon.[4] The old Hollywood actor never broke the mood.

Thus commenced, on the beaches of Normandy, the great patriotic surge of election year 1984.

Nineteen eighty-four unfolded as one long sequence of televised patriotism: D-Day in Normandy, the summer Olympics in Los Angeles, the Republican Convention in Dallas, and Reagan's campaign appearances, all tied together in an explosion of national pride. Through the summer and into fall, Americans rallied behind two national symbols: the American flag and Ronald Reagan.

"By the artful use of iconography," wrote Richard Darman, "President Reagan strengthened himself, the Presidency, and America's traditional sense of self. [His] use of symbols helped reconnect America with its own mythology. . . . The mood of the country was lifted."[5]

This was the revival of the American spirit, the restoration of national pride and self-confidence Ronald Reagan had promised in his inaugural address in 1981.

On August 23, 1984, the Republican party met at Dallas to select a candidate for 1984. With Reagan's nomination a foregone conclusion, the Republican Convention became a celebration of Ronald Reagan and of the accomplishments of his first term.

There was no nomination speech at Dallas. The President was introduced by an eighteen-minute film called "A New Beginning." Juxtaposing images of America, of events in the Reagan presidency—real and created for the occasion—and comments by the President himself, "A New Beginning" celebrated Ronald Reagan and the accomplishments of his Presidency.

That evening in Dallas the mood was ecstatic. As Reagan spoke the crowd chanted: "Four More Years, Four More Years," and repeated the cheer made famous weeks before at the Los Angeles Olympics: "USA! USA!"

Riding the crest of patriotism Reagan proclaimed from the podium: "America is standing tall."

The Reagan campaign against Democratic nominee Walter Mondale was, in essence, a series of television commercials celebrating the accomplishments of Reagan's first term. The spots had not been intended as the campaign's centerpiece, but as Mondale failed to chip away at Reagan's popularity, campaign strategists saw no need to go beyond the "feel good" spots.[6] They were broadcast well into the fall.

The campaign ads evoked an ideal America—the rural heartland, small towns, hard working people, farms and churches—bathed in soft honey-colored light and underscored by a message of hope and optimism :

> It's morning again in America. Today more men and women will go to work than ever before in our country's history. With interest rates and inflation down more people are buying new homes. And our new families can have confidence in the future. America today is prouder and stronger and better. Why would we want to return to where we were less than four short years ago?

Critics accused Reagan of manipulating voters through the use of images and symbols of a mythic place that no longer existed—if it ever did. But while the "feel good" campaign ads would have been laughed off the screen in 1982, in the midst of the recession, in 1984 they resonated with voters.[7]

> We'd come through the darkness of the night. We'd come through the economic crisis and the recession of '82. We're now to a point where we'd rebuilt the defenses of the country. The military, basically, felt good about themselves again, which they clearly didn't in 1980. The American country felt good about itself again, which it clearly didn't in 1980.[8]

Reagan detractors pointed out that in 1984 it was not morning in America for everyone. The average income of the poorest one-fifth of all families had declined by nearly 8 percent during Reagan's first term.[9] They also called attention to the fact that the good times were being bought "on the credit card" at the expense of a growing deficit.

But their concerns mostly fell on deaf ears. Just as Reagan had predicted in late 1981 when he faced the inevitability of spiraling deficits: "if inflation is down, business is up, jobs are up—even if the deficit is bigger—the man on the street will say, 'Okay, things are better.'"

Reagan's popularity reached deeper than his association with "economic good times." "A strange alchemy had developed between Ronald Reagan and the American people," noted Jane Mayer of *The Washington Post*:

> It was visible in the tear-streaked faces of the cheerleaders who lined his parade routes . . . in the southern Democrats who set aside traditions held since the Civil War and flocked to the party of Lincoln. . . . Voters had an extraordinary affection for him . . . They were inspired

by his optimism, and they responded to his warmth and humor. . . . They thought he had backbone. . . .[10]

Reagan's appeal amazed even his opponents:

> He didn't know anybody by name. He didn't even know his own HUD Secretary, Sam Pierce. He called him Mr. Mayor when he met him one time. I mean, a man like that who is so unfamiliar with the individuals he has to deal with, you would think was an idiot, but he wasn't because Ronald Reagan knew one person and . . . this person is the American people. Ronald Reagan lives in Bel Air and he hangs around with the Bloomingdales, [yet] somehow he still evokes the guy that goes to the Knights of Columbus and plays cards on Friday night. That guy who struggles every day just to make it through the week, who worries about the value of his property going down, who worries about never having a vacation, who's afraid he might get sick and lose his health insurance. That guy thought Ronald Reagan was his guy. Thought Ronald Reagan was looking out for him. That's an amazing political power. But he knew who he was talking to, and he talked to them.[11]

The one issue on which Ronald Reagan had failed to win over the American public was on his arms buildup. In 1984, most voters still feared his proximity to the nuclear button.

An episode in August as Reagan prepared to deliver a radio broadcast underscored public nervousness about the president's possible use of nuclear weapons. Unaware he was on the air Reagan joked into an open microphone:

> My fellow Americans, I'm pleased to tell you today that I've signed legislation that will outlaw Russia forever. We begin bombing in five minutes.

The "gaffe" cut into Reagan's margin over Mondale by 7 points.

Except for the radio episode, Reagan coasted through his re-election campaign. Assured of victory, his staff felt there was no need to expose the candidate to a grueling schedule or to risk another costly Reagan gaffe. Most of his appearances were set-pieces with set speeches delivered to pre-selected audiences. The strict security measures implemented since the 1981 assassination attempt kept voters at a distance.

But without a real fight, Reagan tended to lose his edge. Lyn Nofziger, who had witnessed Reagan's performance in three campaigns, observed that:

> Reagan likes a challenge . . . he was an athlete, as a kid. He played football; he was a competitive swimmer. . . . By nature, he's competitive, he always reacted to a challenge. As a matter of fact, when he didn't have a challenge, is is when he kind of laid back and let the world go by.[12]

That Reagan was not "fighting fit" as election day approached became painfully clear in his first debate against Walter Mondale, on October 7. The Great Communicator stumbled during an exchange. But it was his closing statement that might have been most costly.

In response to moderator Barbara Walters' instructions, the President said, "I'm all confused now." He then proceeded to combine rebuttal and a close, bits of facts and notes, appearing, at times, incoherent.

"The Great Communicator," who in 1980 had devastated Jimmy Carter with a single line, had blown a public performance.

Nancy later described the debate as "a nightmare. Right from the start he was tense, muddled and off-stride. He lacked authority. He stumbled. . . . It was painful to watch. . . . As we were leaving Ronnie said to me, 'I was terrible.'"[13]

She blamed her husband's failure on the debate team and, especially on Richard Darman who she felt had "brutalized" him, overwhelming him with too many facts and information. Writer Gary Wills offered a different interpretation of what Nancy meant by "brutalizing."

> It was not just that her husband had been overwhelmed by information, but that he had been browbeaten, his confidence undermined by his advisors who had let him know that he was not in command of his facts. An actor without confidence cannot deliver a good performance, and Nancy had been in Hollywood long enough to know this.[14]

Darman later defended himself, arguing that the President was not over-, but under-prepared.

> The First Lady . . . kept Baker and me from getting him to rehearse his closing statement" . . . he wrote. "She stopped our final briefing at Camp David, so she and the President could have a leisurely lunch and an afternoon ride. And on the day of the debate . . . she wouldn't let any of us near him.[15]

For a moment Reagan had come perilously close to the caricature of the aging befuddled fellow the press had glimpsed in

1980 when a series of "gaffes" cost him to lose ground against incumbent Jimmy Carter. *The Wall Street Journal* raised the possibility that Reagan was unfit to govern: "Reagan Debate Performance Invites Open Speculation On His Ability To Serve," the paper headlined.

For the next ten days the issue of Reagan's age dominated the elections and the press. TV networks dug up old clips of Reagan nodding off at the Vatican in 1982, and groping for an answer on August 1, 1984, when a reporter asked what the United States could do to bring the Soviets back to the bargaining table.[16]

At the next debate on October 21, *Baltimore Sun* journalist Henry Trewhitt confronted the age issue head on:

> **Trewhitt:** Mr President. . . . You already are the oldest President in history, and some of your staff say you were tired after your most recent encounter with Mr. Mondale. I recall that President Kennedy had to go for days on end with very little sleep during the Cuban missile crisis. Is there any doubt in your mind that you would be able to function in such circumstances?"
>
> **Reagan:** Not at all, Mr. Trewhitt. And I want you to know that also I will not make age an issue of this campaign. I am not going to exploit for political purposes my opponent's youth and inexperience.
>
> **Trewhitt:** Mr. President, I would like to head for the fence and catch that one before it goes over.

For most Americans, Reagan's quip put to rest "the age issue" and with it any serious concerns about the incumbent's fitness for a second term. But for one of the most perceptive observers of Ronald Reagan, the candidate's level of engagement in the campaign, raised another, more worrisome concern.

Watching the presidential race, Lou Cannon, who covered Reagan's 1984 campaign for *The Washington Post*, saw a candidate increasingly isolated from the voters and the business of politics.

"During a period he is supposedly taking his case to the American people," he wrote, "Reagan is being deliberately isolated by a staff that wants to take no risk. How isolated would he be in a second term, when he and his staff would be beyond the reach of the voters?"[17]

Reagan routed Walter Mondale, winning 59 percent of the popular vote. He swept 49 states. "We can read," Tip O'Neill would later tell Reagan. "In my 50 years in public life, I've never seen a man more popular than you with the American people."

> If there's one constant in American presidential politics it's that landslides are poison to the winner. I mean, Roosevelt's landslide, he packs the Supreme Court. Johnson's landslide, we go to war in Vietnam. Nixon's landslide, we have the Watergate cover-up. Landslides are just murderous for the winner. I mean, because there's so much power in that place. . . . Then you've got to look out.[18]

In the next four years Reagan would see his best days as President and his worst, without the help and counsel of his oldest friends and advisors. Michael Deaver, who had been with Reagan since he was governor, would soon leave government to form his own public relations firm. Edwin Meese who had been with Reagan just as long became Attorney General. Chief of Staff James Baker became Treasury Secretary, switching jobs with Donald Regan, who became the new Chief of Staff.

No one left in the White House had a history with Reagan.

They had not been through his campaigns, most of them had not served in his first term. Donald Regan even brought his own staff from the Treasury Department.

Chief political strategist Ed Rollins worried about the changes in the Reagan White House:

> I was always convinced that the President would wake up someday and say where have all my friends gone. . . . They weren't in the White House day in and day out controlling what he saw or the information flow that he had.[19]

"For the leading man, it was merely a change of cast and directors," wrote Lou Cannon. "And while none of these people might by themselves have been indispensable, the loss of all of them within a few months proved a heavy blow to the Reagan presidency."[20]

"I started to feel a kind of disorientation," wrote Peggy Noonan. "I would wonder, 'Who's in charge here?' I could never understand where power was in that White House; it kept moving. I'd see men in suits huddled in a hall twenty paces from the Oval Office and I'd think, 'There it is. They're making the decisions.' But the next day they were gone, and the hall was empty. At the center of it all, at the center of the absence was Ronald Reagan."[21]

NOTES

[1] Michael Deaver, *Behind the Scenes* (New York: William Morrow & Company, 1989), pp. 141–142.

[2] *Ibid.*

[3] Peggy Noonan, *What I Saw at the Revolution*, pp. 87–89.

[4] Lou Cannon, *Role of a Lifetime*, p. 484.

[5] Richard Darman, *Who's In Control*, p. 123.

[6] Michael Deaver, Interview with Author.

[7] Lou Cannon, *Role of a Lifetime*, p. 514.

[8] Ed Rollins, Interview with Austin Hoyt.

[9] A 1984 study by the Urban Institute showed that average annual income had risen 3.5 percent in Reagan's first term, about $700 per year, in 1982 dollars. Family income for the typical middle-class family rose from $18,857 to $19,034, about 1 percent, in the first term. But average income for the top fifth went from $37,618 to $40,888, nearly 9 percent. Meanwhile, the poorest Americans had languished, with the average income for the bottom fifth declining from $6,913 to $6,391, or nearly 8 percent. Of course, these numbers reflect in large part the vast difficulties caused by the Reagan recession, but also point up who bore the biggest brunt of the recession (the bottom fifth). By 1984, more than 13 million children lived in poverty, more than when LBJ launched his War on Poverty in 1965. Government programs benefiting families making less than $10,000 were cut eight percent in the first term, while those for families making more than $40,000 went unchanged. Lou Cannon, *The Role of A Lifetime*, p. 516.

[10] Jane Mayer and Doyle McManus, *Landslide: The Unmaking of a President 1984–1988* (Boston: Houghton Mifflin, 1990). Conversation with Author, Washington D.C.

[11] Christopher Matthews, Interview with Author.

[12] Lyn Nofziger, Interview with Author.

[13] Nancy Reagan, *My Turn*, p. 266

[14] Gary Wills, *Reagan's America*, Chapter 21, pp. 327–236.

According to Wills's account, preparation time for the next debate was cut back from 5 to 2 days, and Roger Ailes, "Dr. Feelgood" a man who specializes in in coaching businessmen and others to speak in public, was brought in to oversee the practice and prepare Reagan psychologically.

[15] Richard Darman, *Who's In Control.* p. 131.

[16] Lou Cannon, *Role of a Lifetime*, p. 544.

[17] Lou Cannon, "Overzealous Aides Misuse Secret Service, Media and the Boss. *The Washington Post*, September 3, 1984. Quoted in Cannon, *Role of a Lifetime*, p. 538.

[18] Lou Cannon, Interview with Austin Hoyt.

[19] Ed Rollins, Interview with Austin Hoyt.

[20] Lou Cannon, *Role of a Lifetime*, p. 560.

[21] Peggy Noonan, *What I Saw at the Revolution*, p. 153.

CHAPTER 16

Geneva: When the Aging Lion Met the Young Tiger

R onald Reagan's second presidential term began with an intimate ceremony at the White House. At 73, he was the oldest President in history to take the oath of office. He was also one of the most popular. That very day he announced what seemed to be a startling change in his Soviet policy. He would seek a summit meeting with Soviet leader Konstantin Chernenko.

The decision had been made by Reagan and his closest advisors on New Year's Day at the Palm Springs home of Walter Annenberg in response to a letter by Soviet Premier Konstantin Chernenko. In that letter, Chernenko stated that the Soviet Union was willing to reconvene to talk about arms reductions and what he called "the militarization of outer-space."[1]

Reagan would never meet Konstantin Chernenko. The third Soviet Premier in three years, he died the following April. Mikhail Gorbachev was now the man in the Kremlin. Only 54 years old, vital, alert, intelligent and cosmopolitan, Gorbachev represented an unmistakable contrast to the bloated geronto-crats who had led the Soviet Union for decades. To the world, this vibrant new leader, with his talk of far-reaching economic and political reforms, and his less ideological approach to world affairs, seemed to symbolize a new era for the Soviet Union and a new opportunity for a thaw in the Cold War. Gorbachev had

been groomed by former Premier Yuri Andropov, some believe
as the Soviet system's response to Ronald Reagan.

> When Andropov had to come to terms with his own
> physical decline, the knowledge that he was a dying
> man, plus the knowledge that Ronald Reagan was a
> much more formidable adversary than had originally
> been assumed—that he was not an old stupid ideologue,
> but that he was actually very canny and determined—
> these two perceptions on Andropov's part, brought out,
> I believe, the selection of Mikhail Gorbachev to be his
> successor. Andropov started grooming Gorbachev in
> 1983 as the only likely Soviet leader who would be able
> to handle this formidable, adamantine anti-Communist
> on the other side of the Atlantic.[2]

In 1985, Gorbachev quickly became aware that he had
assumed power in a Soviet Union whose economy could not
produce goods or food for its people, where corruption was rampant, and alcoholism a national scourge. In such circumstances, the last thing that any Soviet leader wanted, especially
one bent on reform, was to spend scarce resources in an arms
race, or try to match American development of a super-
expensive, ultra-high-tech strategic defense system.

Soviet Deputy Foreign Minister Alexander Bessmertnykh
told *The American Experience*,

> I think that . . . economic side of the arms race was
> very much on Gorbachev's mind. When Gorbachev
> came to power in Moscow in 1985, the economic sta-
> tistics already indicated that the economy was not
> doing so well. So when you were talking about SDI
> and arms control, the economic element of the neces-

sity to go . . . with . . . reductions was . . . in my view,
the number-one preoccupation of Gorbachev.[3]

On the other side of the Atlantic, Reagan was coming under
pressure as well. His military buildup had been advocated under
the slogan "peace through strength," and the Pentagon was
busily spending taxpayers' dollars at a rate of nearly $30 million
an hour. Since the fall of 1983 the escalating tensions between
the superpowers had scared many into thinking about the real
possibility of nuclear war. Opinion polls continued to show
that while the public, for the most part, backed the President's
"peace through strength" policy, they also wanted Reagan to be
more flexible in his dealings with the Soviet Union. "The issue
of peace kept showing up in our polls. We never could get rid
of it," Richard Wirthlin recalled.[4]

If there was ever an opportune time to seek a relaxation of
tensions, this was it.

For a decade, Ronald Reagan had publicly and privately
expressed his hatred of nuclear weapons. His close advisor Martin Anderson recalls a conversation aboard the campaign plane
in the 1970s when Reagan suggested that strategic negotiations
should go beyond arms control (Strategic Arms Limitations
Talks, SALT) and aim for arms reductions (Strategic Arms
Reductions Talks, START). "When he began to talk of a dream
he had that someday we might live in a world free of all nuclear
missiles, we just smiled."[5]

But if Reagan had a dream of a nuclear-free world, he had
little faith in treaties. He felt that Soviet Union had used the
SALT agreements as a smokescreen behind which to continue what he called a "one-sided" arms race. Throughout his
first term, he had shown little interest in arms control negotiations while increasing spending on nuclear weapons to an
all-time high.

"He had come to office as a hardline confrontationist who saw no reasonable or justifiable purpose in giving the Russians quarter or in engaging in dialogue with a country he considered "our sworn enemy," wrote Reagan's third National Security Advisor Robert McFarlane."[6] But beginning in 1983, McFarlane, Secretary of State George Shultz and Michael Deaver joined forces to convince the President that the time had come to make good on his public promise to "build up in order to build down," by signing treaties codifying reductions in nuclear weapons.

"I thought the time had come to re-engage the Soviets in meaningful negotiations," Secretary of State George Shultz wrote. "I kept telling President Reagan that I shared his dislike for nuclear weapons, but that he had to realize they couldn't be uninvented. We had to negotiate."

Shultz, McFarlane, and the other "moderates" had a most effective ally in the First Lady. Nancy Reagan had been instrumental to Ronald Reagan's success. She protected and supported him. "She accepted almost total responsibility for their family and home, and remained his closest advisor in public life," Michael Deaver wrote.[7] "[Nancy]," confirmed Ed Rollins, "felt that the arms buildup had gone too far and that his place in history was very important."[8]

Columnist George Will, a close friend of Nancy's, told *The American Experience* that "Nancy had her eye on Ronald Reagan after 1989, that is, where he would stand in history."

> And she knew that Presidents get their standing in
> history not by balancing the budget or reining in this or
> that program, but by the questions of war and peace.[9]

In her autobiography, *My Turn*, Nancy admitted to her concern with her husband's reputation:

For years, it had troubled me that my husband was always being portrayed by his opponents as a "warmonger." I knew that "warmonger" was never a fair description . . . but I also felt that calling the Soviet Union an evil empire was not particularly helpful in establishing a dialogue with the other side. The world had become too small for the two superpowers not to be on speaking terms.[10] I encouraged Ronnie to meet Gorbachev as soon as possible especially when I realized that some people in the Administration did not favor any real talks. So yes, I did push him a little.[11]

"She knows when and how hard to apply pressure," wrote Michael Deaver, "waging a quiet campaign, planting a thought, recruiting others to push it along."[12]

In February 1983, Secretary of State George Shultz—with the help of the First Lady and Michael Deaver—convinced Ronald Reagan to meet privately with Soviet Ambassador Anatoly Dobrynin. "Mike and Nancy were anxious for an outbreak of world peace. They thought by getting Dobrynin into the East Wing peace would prevail," said Reagan's then National Security Advisor Bill Clark.[13]

Though the meeting did not lead to the outbreak of world peace, it was an important first step. Reagan asked Dobrynin to intercede on behalf of a family of Pentecostals who had sought exiled at the U.S. Embassy in Moscow and were awaiting permission to emigrate. Through Dobrynin's influence, months later, they were allowed to leave. Reagan first direct exchange with the Soviet Union had proved successful.

By 1985, with America economically and militarily strong and Reagan more popular than ever, the President had little to lose and perhaps much to gain from talking to the Soviets. Though initially spurred by his wife, Shultz and Deaver, negotiations with the Soviets appealed to the nuclear abolitionist within him and to his sense of optimism.

> The notion that "we can now moderate our rhetoric, Mr. President, and perhaps start giving these people a little encouragement," is the kind of notion that he would love. Because he did like to resolve conflict. I think he knew very well that . . . he had brought the world pretty close to a [nuclear] standoff. He realized that he had pushed his adversary as far against the wall as he could. And he sensed that having made his theatrical strokes—made his declaration of intent, made the resistance of the United States to Communism abundantly clear—he then felt that the ground was ready for conciliatory gestures.[14]

"I had come to believe that if we were ever going to break down the barriers of mistrust that divided our countries we had to begin by establishing a personal relationship of between the leaders of the two most powerful nations on earth. I knew there were great differences between our two countries," Reagan wrote. "Yet the stakes were too high for us not to try to find a common ground where we could meet and reduce the risk of Armageddon."[15]

On July 1, Gorbachev agreed to meet Reagan that November in Geneva.

Reagan was no stranger to negotiation. In his Hollywood days when he was president of the Screen Actors Guild he had sat across the negotiating table with the toughest studio moguls. He had been elected for six successive terms and gained a stellar reputation. Charlton Heston, who succeeded Reagan as SAG president, remembers:

He was an extremely effective negotiator, which is not quite the same as being tough. He could be adamant, he could be resistant . . . but he never raised his voice, he always spoke in warm terms to whoever he was arm wrestling with but he could express his position and support it, very effectively. I learned a great deal about negotiating, about arguing, which is what negotiating comes down to by watching him.[16]

But before Reagan got the chance to test his skills on his Soviet enemy, he would have to use them with his own conservative friends.

Conservative Republicans for 50 years had tended to denigrate the importance of personal diplomacy. It's the legacy of the Yalta Conference. They thought FDR had sold us out and then we sold out China. We were always selling out someone and the sale was usually by a President who thought that, if only he could get in a room with his Soviet counterpart, his charm and his arguments would prevail. And Reagan clearly believed that he could do that—that the aura of his personality and of his arguments and above all, of his sincerity, would impress themselves upon the Soviets.[17]

By then, the influence of Conservatives in the Reagan White House had sharply diminished. Gone were Richard Allen, Bill Clark, and Alexander Haig, among others. They had either been cast out by scandal, excessive zeal, and, some argue, pressure from the First Lady. The last stronghold of conservative opinion was the Defense Department, led by Caspar Weinberger and his assistant Richard Perle. Weinberger weighed in. In a letter written to Reagan just one week before the summit, he urged him not to compromise on SDI, hold the Soviets accountable on cheating, resist words or promises, and stick to U.S. interests.[18] Leaked to the press, the letter exposed the rift between "moderates" and "hardliners" within the Reagan Administration.

Weinberger's concerns were shared by the American delegation at Geneva. As Reagan prepared to receive Gorbachev, Edmund Morris recalls sensing a "great fear, a palpable sense of fear throughout the delegation that this young, formidably intelligent, aggressive and fast-moving Soviet leader (whose charming smile was said to hide teeth of iron) was going to run rings around our gentle, slightly doddering, aging President. Up to the moment Reagan came downstairs . . . to his first meeting with Gorbachev, the American delegation was afraid that he was going to be outsmarted, outmaneuvered and diplomatically perhaps destroyed."[19]

"He was in his mid seventies and perhaps wasn't as robust as he might have been twenty years earlier," Donald Regan told *The American Experience*, "so there was this thing of the aging lion against the young tiger.[20]

But Geneva was a performance, and the old actor knew he was about to play "the role of a lifetime."[21] Those who witnessed the first encounter between Reagan and Gorbachev recall a scene worthy of a first-rate Hollywood film.

Edmund Morris, who as official biographer witnessed Reagan's performance at Geneva, vividly recalls the moment:

> It was supremely dramatic. I can still see it in slow motion. This great gleaming black [Russian limousine] comes whispering around the corner on the gravel, crunches to a halt. Down the stairs comes this great gliding blue-suited unbelievably self-confident and calm President, without a coat on in the freezing air.

And out of the big Russian limousine comes this awkward, heavily overcoated, heavily scarved, hatted Communist leader, who fumbled with his scarf and fumbled with his coat as he approached this great benign presence. And they met at the foot of the stairs. Reagan towered over Gorbachev. Reagan smiled down at him and then gently choreographed him up the stairs. And the grace with which he did the gesture . . . his absolute lack of apprehension or fear, you could just feel the tension evaporating in the freezing air.[22]

Chief of Staff Donald Regan breathed a sigh of relief.

That set the tone of the meeting. This was no aging lion being eaten up by a young tiger. This was an older man showing a little sympathy for somebody we want to be friendly with.[23]

The Russians Sergei Tarasenko told *The American Experience* in Moscow, knew immediately that Soviets had been upstaged.

We came to the porch and I saw President Reagan coming out to greet Gorbachev in well-tailored suit, looking young with good haircut, you know, maybe he was made-up a little bit, but skillfully, he projected an image of young, dynamic leader. And Gorbachev came out of this tank-like limo, black limo, in standard Politburo hat, in scarf, in autumn overcoat, heavy overcoat, looking like old guy . . . it reminds me of the actors playing KGB people in bad American films, you know. Stereotype of KGB agent. And so I said to myself that we have lost the first, this photo opportunity, we have lost this first round.[24]

Reagan had received Gorbachev with customary grace and courtesy, but as the two men engaged in discussion, Reagan's long-held hatred of the Soviet Union came to the surface. "I took Gorbachev through the long history of Soviet aggression," Reagan later wrote, "citing chapter and verse of the Soviet Union's expansionist policy since 1917. I wanted to explain why the free world had good reason to put up its guard against the Soviet bloc."[25]

> His language was brutal. From the transcripts I've read, he would say things like, "Let me tell you, Mr. General Secretary, why we fear you and why we despise your system." Now that in a diplomatic meeting is extremely confrontational language. To say that to the leader is asking for him to walk out. He was scarily confrontational.[26]

Gorbachev revealed to us that he was put off by Reagan's tone.

> He lectured me as though I was a suspect or maybe a student, and I cut him short. I said, "Mr. President, you are not a prosecutor. I am not the accused. You are not a teacher. I am not a student.[27]

Having staked his moral ground, Ronald Reagan felt it was now time to diffuse tensions. He suggested that he and Gorbachev meet in private, at an informal and comfortable boat house away from the pressures of their delegations. "I . . . sensed that he was willing to listen," he later wrote, "and that possibly he sensed, as I did, that on both sides of the Iron Curtain there were myths and misconceptions that contributed to misunderstanding."[28]

Like others Presidents before him, Ronald Reagan, as Conservatives had feared, thought he could win over his enemy with the power of his personal appeal. Henry Kissinger, the master of "realpolitik," felt Reagan was being naive. "In typical American fashion Reagan was convinced that Communist intransigence was based more on ignorance than on congenital ill will, more on misunderstanding than on purposeful hostility," he wrote. "As if seventy-five years of Communist hostility could be removed by personal appeal."[29] Maybe not. But Reagan was sure going to try.

As they walked toward the boathouse on the shore of Lake Leman, the two men chatted about Reagan's movie career—the first time they had talked as human beings. "As we sat in stuffed chairs beside the hearth, I said, 'Mr. General Secretary, here we are, two men born in obscure rural hamlets, both poor and from humble beginnings. Now we are the leaders of our countries, and probably the only two men who can start WWIII, and possible the only two men . . . who can bring peace to the world. . . .'"[30]

"Gorbachev immediately started to like Reagan," recalls Alexander Bessmertnykh, "and that was a very surprising thing. I think Reagan had something which was so dear to Gorbachev and that was sincerity."[31] "I think that people don't reckon with my father's power of charm and just personal persuasiveness," Ron told us. You know, when he kind of turns the high beams on, even somebody like Gorbachev tends to melt."[32] As they walked back to rejoin their delegations, Reagan invited Gorbachev to Washington. Gorbachev reciprocated with an invitation to Moscow.

When the two leaders got down to business the next day, no amount of good will, and no exercise of personal charm could alone bridge the distance between the two negotiators. Reagan had come to Geneva to try to convince Gorbachev to reduce nuclear weapons. Gorbachev had come to Geneva to try to convince Reagan to kill SDI. The Soviets had expected a very different Ronald Reagan than the one Gorbachev now faced across the negotiating table. Sergei Tarasenko explained to us how Reagan was perceived:

> I read that . . . he has a limited attention span, that he is not particularly interested in complicated things. He takes maybe half a page of these idiot cards, you know, to the position papers and talking points, whatever they are called. But what I noticed during this personal observation, he was unattentive when the subject presents no interest to him. He let it go, slip by. But as soon as say, Shevardnadze or Gorbachev touched some point of interest to the President he will immediately comes out with extremely good, spontaneous delivery, he would deliver a good piece, strong on conviction, strong on facts, emotionally charged. So he was another guy immediately.[33]

"The two men debated each other with a passion rarely witnessed between heads of state."[34]

Gorbachev began by stressing the interrelationship between cuts in offensive arms and SDI.

"No, no," responded Reagan. "SDI will help rid the world of the scourge of nuclear weapons. The current doctrine is uncivilized. People want defense and they look at the sky and think what might happen if missiles suddenly appear and blow up everything in our country. They don't want that." "The missiles are not flying," Gorbachev impatiently retorted. "The Soviet Union wants to stop SDI before it happens."

The negotiations quickly reached a deadlock. Day Two would be a replay.

Reagan: We are at the point where the two sides are going to have to get beyond suspicions. We are trying, the United States, to see if there is a way to end the world's nightmare of nuclear weapons.

Gorbachev: We're prepared to compromise. We can talk about a separate INF[35] agreement. We can talk about deep cuts in strategic weapons. But SDI has to come to an end.

There was a long pause.

I believe the silence lasted only a minute or so, but he just sat there staring at Reagan across the polished table, realizing that he couldn't budge him any further. And after this interminable silence, a minute in diplomatic terms is like a year of suspense, [Gorbachev] threw down his pencil and said, Mr. President, I'm very sorry that you feel the way you do, but I can see that I'm not going to change your mind.[36]

Reagan left Geneva with SDI intact, an agreement to seek 50 percent reductions in nuclear weapons, a communiqué which read "a nuclear war cannot be won and must never be fought," and a commitment from Gorbachev to hold two more summits, one in Washington and one in Moscow.

Gorbachev later told *The American Experience*:

The world was waiting. The world wouldn't have forgiven us if after these tremendous years of worry— years of tremendous worry about what was happening, about the flight in to the abyss. We could not have left Geneva without saying something that would give people hope.[37]

Geneva had produced few concrete results, but it was there that the ice of the Cold War began to melt. A rapport had been established between Reagan and Gorbachev which would deepen in the years to come.

> I think the big discovery of Geneva is that Gorbachev and Reagan had some rapport . . . Reagan really liked Gorbachev. It is quite clear in retrospect that Reagan and Gorbachev hit it off as no U.S. and Soviet leader had done since Roosevelt and Stalin.[38]
>
> There was a huge sigh of relief all around the world. Reagan went to NATO immediately after leaving Geneva and reported on the summit to the leaders of NATO, and you could just feel their delight . . . that all these tensions had been building up over the last forty years were being dissipated.[39]

Soviet dissident Andrei Sakharov, then living under house arrest in the Soviet Union, reportedly told his wife: "Today for the first time since the Cold War began we seem to be getting closer to peace, to the resolution of our difficulties."[40]

Gorbachev returned home knowing he could do business with the man the Soviet press had once compared to Hitler. He had made concessions at Geneva. He had agreed to enter into an arms reduction process without any assurances on SDI, and he had given Reagan a public relations victory by allowing him to shed his image of a nuclear cowboy. Gorbachev would now have to turn his attention to his country's growing domestic problems. The Soviet empire was in great economic, political and social stress. Without major reforms it could not continue to compete with the United States. Its superpower status was at risk.

Reagan returned home a winner. On November 25, after

going without sleep for twenty-four hours, Reagan addressed a joint session of Congress. "I haven't gotten such a reception since I was shot," Reagan quipped.

"The enthusiastic cheering and stomping in the chamber of the House of Representatives that night as I delivered my report from Geneva spoke for all peoples of the world who shared a hope for lasting peace in the nuclear age,"[41] Reagan later wrote. "There was much more to be done, but we laid a foundation at Geneva . . ."[42]

The image of Ronald Reagan as a trigger-happy cowboy was fading. A more flattering one—Ronald Reagan, the peace-maker—had emerged.

NOTES

[1] Robert McFarlane, *Special Trust*. Cadell and Davies, p. 291.

[2] Edmund Morris, Interview with Austin Hoyt. When Andropov became General Secretary, Gorbachev became a serious future contender for the very top position.

[3] Alexander Bessmertnykh, Conversation with Josh Clark.

[4] Richard Wirthlin. Interview with Author.

[5] Martin Anderson, *Revolution*, Hoover Institution Press, CA, 1990.

[6] McFarlane, *Special Trust*, p. 295.

[7] Michael Deaver, *Behind the Scenes*, p. 39.

[8] Edward Rollins, Interview with Austin Hoyt.

[9] George Will, Interview with Austin Hoyt.

[10] Nancy Reagan, *My Turn*, p. 64.

[11] *Ibid*, p. 337.

[12] Michael Deaver, *Behind the Scenes*, p. 39.

[13] Cannon, *Role of a Lifetime*, p. 312.

[14] Edmund Morris, Interview with Austin Hoyt.

[15] Ronald Reagan, *An American Life*. p. 14.

[16] Charlton Heston, Interview with Author.

[17] Richard Norton Smith, Interview with Author.

[18] Jay Winnik, *On the Brink*. p. 384.

[19] Edmund Morris, Interview with Austin Hoyt.

[20] Donald Regan, Interview with Austin Hoyt.

[21] I have borrowed this phrase from Lou Cannon, whose second volume on Ronald Reagan is titled *The Role of a Lifetime*.

[22] Edmund Morris, Interview with Austin Hoyt.

[23] Donald Regan, Interview with Austin Hoyt.

[24] Sergei Tarasenko, Interview with Austin Hoyt.

[25] Ronald Reagan, *An American Life*, p. 635.

[26] Edmund Morris, Interview with Austin Hoyt.

[27] Mikhail Gorbachev, Interview with Austin Hoyt.

[28] Reagan, *An American Life*, p. 14.

[29] Henry Kissinger, *Diplomacy*, pp. 768–769.

[30] Ronald Reagan, *An American Life*, p. 636.

[31] Interview with Alexander Bessmertnykh. At the time, Mr. Bessmertnykh was the director of U.S.A. Affairs at the Soviet Foreign Ministry. From 1986 to 1987, he was deputy foreign minister of the Soviet Union, and subsequently became Foreign Minister.

[32] Ronald Prescott Reagan, Interview with Austin Hoyt.

[33] Sergei Tarasenko, Interview with Austin Hoyt.

[34] Jay Winnik, *On the Brink*, pp. 394–399. The following reconstruction is derived from Winnik, and from our own conversations with witnesses at the summit.

[35] Intermediate Nuclear Forces, that is, nuclear weapons stationed in Europe.

[36] Edmund Morris, Interview with Austin Hoyt.

[37] Mikhail Gorbachev, Interview with Austin Hoyt.

[38] Lou Cannon, Interview with Austin Hoyt.

[39] Edmund Morris, Interview with Austin Hoyt.

[40] *Ibid.*

[41] Ronald Reagan, *An American Life*, p. 15.

[42] Ronald Reagan, *An American Life*, p. 641.

CHAPTER 17

Lady Liberty's Leading Man

Ronald Reagan had launched his 1980 presidential campaign against the backdrop of a Statue of Liberty worn and tattered by neglect. Six years later, on a clear, cool July 4th evening, he stood on the deck of the aircraft carrier *John F. Kennedy* and pushed a button which sent a laser a mile across New York harbor to light the refurbished symbol of the American promise. As the beam pierced the cool summer air bathing Lady Liberty in red, white and blue, the skies above erupted in the biggest display of fireworks in history.

Liberty Weekend, the celebration of the centennial of the Statue of Liberty, was a three-day, $32-million extravaganza "with the Statue of Liberty serving as leading lady and Ronald Reagan cast in the male lead."[1]

> The things that unite us, America's past of which we are so proud, our hopes and aspirations for the future of the world and this much loved country. These things far outweigh what little divides us. Tonight we pledge ourselves to each other and to the cause of human freedom, the cause that has given light to the land and hope to the world.

"Ronald Reagan has found the American sweet spot," *Time* wrote. "He is a Prospero of American memories, a magician who carries a bright, ideal America like a holograph and projects its image in the air . . . a sort of masterpiece of Ameri-

can magic—apparently one of the simplest creatures alive
. . . yet a character of . . . complexities that connect him
with the myths and powers of his country in an unprecedented way."[2]

"Reagan is brilliant at creating a kind of rapport with the
country," Professor Robert Dallek admiringly commented,
"appealing to its better angels, appealing to the native optimism which is so much a part of our culture and our tradition."[3]

This oldest of American presidents, whose memory spanned
most of the twentieth century, boasted a 68-percent approval rating, and an unprecedented 82 percent among young voters.

He and the nation had much to celebrate.

The recovery begun in 1983 had accelerated into an economic boom. Growing at a rate of 3.5 percent per year, the
nation's economy churned out more than $20 trillion in goods
and services under Reagan's watch, 65 percent more per year
than when Carter left in 1981.[4]

More than 18 million new jobs were created. Since 1980 the
prime rate had been cut by one-third. From 12.5 percent, inflation dropped to 4.4 percent. Unemployment decreased from
7.1 percent to 5.5 percent.[5]

The number of millionaires in the country shot up nine-fold,
from 4,414 in 1980 to 34,944.[6] Median family income saw its
largest increase since 1972. Even the poor, who had been hard
hit by the recession, shared modestly in the recovery. But when
measured against the surrounding prosperity their gains were,
in fact, negligible.[7]

Most Americans were feeling affluent and went on a shop-
ping spree. Between 1983 and 1988, consumers bought 105
million color television sets, 88 million cars and trucks, 63 million VCRs, 62 million microwave ovens, 57 million washers
and dryers, 46 million refrigerators and freezers, 31 million
cordless phones and 30 million telephone answering

machines.[8] A "yuppie"(young urban professional) culture sprouted in major cities. More than any other group, these young, well paid professionals—who spent a fortune on champagne, gourmet foods, luxury cars, state-of-the-art electronics, and trips to exotic destinations—defined the 1980s as a decade of excess and conspicuous consumption.

Personal income tax rates fell dramatically. The tax rate of America's wealthiest decreased from 70 percent to 28 percent. Their share of taxes, however, doubled. Federal tax revenues soared—as supply-siders had predicted. In 1982, total federal receipts were $618 billion. By 1986, they were pushing $1 trillion.[9]

Economists still debate what caused the economic expansion which began in 1983 and, save for a brief lapse, has lasted through the late 1990s. But Reagan, who had been blamed for the 1982 recession and paid a high price for "staying the course," took credit for the recovery.

"The tax cut . . . allowed people to accumulate money to start new businesses . . . not only enriching their own lives but adding to the national wealth and helping to send a wave of prosperity across the land," Reagan wrote. "Reduced interference by the government also helped."[10] As George Will told *The American Experience,*

> We got ninety-three consecutive months of economic expansion. The economy grew the equivalent of grafting onto our economy the West German economy. That's how fast it grew in the 1980s. Huge job creation. Just astonishing. While job creation in Europe was flat for the decade. Reaganomics worked.[11]

But was it Reaganomics—that is, lower taxes and less government interference—which fueled the economic expansion?

Christopher Matthews told *The American Experience* he does not believe it was.

> You had a recovery [beginning] in 1983 that was dramatic. It was almost as dramatic as the recession itself—I think driven by consumer demand, driven by cut—lower taxes. In a way, it was the kind of thing Jack Kennedy would have done, just cut taxes that'll increase consumer spending. It wasn't supply-side, it wasn't cut taxes, therefore increase saving, therefore increase investment, therefore increase productivity. That's the way it was sold, but in effect, it was good old time Hubert Humphrey liberalism, cut taxes, increase the deficit, drive the economy through higher consumer demand. And it worked.[12]

In 1986, Reagan was not only enjoying success at home, but also abroad. Months before, in Geneva, Reagan had shed his "nuclear cowboy" image, embarking on a process to ease tensions with the Soviet Union. But his "secret war" against Soviet expansion had intensified and was beginning to pay handsome dividends. Everywhere in the world, Communism was on the retreat.

In Poland, the government declared a general amnesty and freed all political prisoners. Years later, Solidarity leader President of Poland Lech Walesa would tell how Ronald Reagan and his policies "gave strength and sustenance" to Solidarity during the darkest days of repression.[13]

In Afghanistan the Soviet Union was paying a high price for its invasion. Reagan had expanded the objectives of his Administration from harassing the Soviets in Afghanistan into forcing them out.[14] Armed with Stinger missiles provided by the United States, the Mujahadeen rebels inflicted unacceptable losses on the Soviet Army.[15]

And in June 1986, after years of bitter political fighting, the House of Representatives approved a bill to restore aid the "Contras" fighting the Sandinista government in Nicaragua.

Support for the "Contras," or "freedom fighters" as he preferred to call them, was Ronald Reagan's favorite cause. It was also one of the most unpopular initiatives of his Administration. A majority of the American public feared that growing U.S. involvement in Central America could mire the nation into "another Vietnam." Reagan's allegations that the Sandinistas were a spearhead of Communist expansion in Central America were blunted by a sophisticated campaign mounted by the Sandinistas. The Nicaraguan government exploited the sympathy of many Americans for their role in overthrowing the repressive regime of Anastasio Somoza and portrayed themselves as social democrats endowed with a popular mandate, and the victims of American imperialism.[16]

At first the Administration portrayed its aid to the "Contras" as an effort to interdict Nicaraguan aid to rebels in neighboring El Salvador. But as the "ragtag" band of followers of the deposed dictator Anastasio Somoza, joined by peasants and disaffected Nicaraguans, swelled to an army of 7,500, the "contra war" turned into an all out effort to overthrow the Sandinista, or at least pressure them into holding democratic elections.[17] Tip O'Neill, frustrated in just about every other initiative, made it his cause to block aid to the Contras, whom he described as "an army of racketeers, bandits and murderers."[18]

In December 1982, emboldened by their gains in the November mid-term Congressional elections, House Democrats passed the Boland Amendment prohibiting the CIA and the Department of Defense from furnishing military equipment, training or support to anyone "for the purpose of overthrowing the government of Nicaragua." In 1984, Congress strengthened the Boland Amendment, making it virtually impossible for the Administration to aid the Contras in any way.

When he learned of the decision, "Reagan was red-faced with disgust and so angry he could barely speak."[19] According to Bud McFarlane, Reagan told him: "We've got to find a way to keep doing this, Bud. . . . I want you to do whatever you have to do to help these people keep body and soul together. Do everything you can."[20]

Reagan's staff had succeeded in keeping the "Contras" together "body and soul," in ways which stretched, if not violated Congressional law. Reagan's "freedom fighters" could now pursue their war with full American backing.[21] The length to which members of the Reagan Administration went to fill the gap would later come back to haunt them.

Reagan's domestic and international successes brought him recognition from every quarter. In September 1986, *Fortune* magazine ran a cover story praising Reagan for restoring confidence in the institution of the presidency. "One extraordinarily important if little-noted element of the Reagan legacy, is already established. He has proved once again that the presidency can be managed."[22] *Fortune* praised Reagan's ability to delegate, and held his management style as an example to company CEOs. But *Fortune* overlooked the fact that Reagan's management style and his tendency to delegate was a double-edged sword.

The way Reagan governed, which reminded his advisor Marty Anderson of a "Turkish pasha,"[23] rendered him too dependent on those around him. "When his staff was good, talented, wise and loyal . . . it worked brilliantly," observed Martin Anderson. "But when his staff is ordinary . . . and loyal more to themselves than to Reagan—then mediocrity ruled."[34]

Chief of Staff Don Regan, those close to Reagan agree, had proved unable to fill the vacuum left by the departure of Reagan's White House "troika" early in his second term.

> The first term we had Baker and Deaver and Meese. . . . They would brings things to the President. And they would fully engage in the discussion and the dialogue with him. Don Regan had a tendency to keep staff away from the President and basically have staff brief him and he would go into the President himself.[25]

"Ronald Reagan's operating style has always been 'bring me all the options,'" explained his daughter Maureen. "Lay them on the table. Get your best advocates. I want to hear them argue about it and then hopefully I will make the right decision. Which meant that now he wasn't gonna get all of that. That was [now taking] place in front of the Chief of Staff who then decided what the President was going to see. I thought 'wait a minute. There's something very wrong.' He was limiting the President's access to ideas . . . inhibiting the President's ability to make decisions."[26]

It was around this time that Maureen witnessed a change in her father's mood:

> [I] sensed a discomfort in him. I knew that he was coming upstairs quieter at night, where he used to come up with great stories about some decision that had been made and who was arguing what. Now, it was all just kind of quiet. And, we'd have to draw it out of him, you know, kind of what happened during the day and there was just a kind of sadness about it. All the things that he had that had energized his presidency, the zealous-

ness of the debate between protagonists on a particular issue—it was all gone, it was all missing.[27]

Cut off from the American people by the security measures imposed in the wake of his assassination attempt, and from the lively debate of his advisors, aging and tired, Reagan grew increasingly uninterested in his job. By 1986 only those closest to Reagan knew that the President, at the height of his prestige, had become little more than a figure-head, detached from the affairs of government. Biographer Edmund Morris, while poring through Reagan's papers, discovered this evidence:

> A good way of tracking how much a President is doing is looking at the papers that come through his hands and seeing how much they engage his attention. And in the first years of Reagan's presidency he is constantly checking these points off, writing comments, thinking about them. But as the years proceed you see he is less and less interested. They just become check marks. Check marks. Check marks. He was saving his facilities as old men do for the really important, vital events.[28]

Two of those really important, vital events were just around the corner. One—the summit at Reykjavik—would prove his "finest hour"; the other—the Iran-Contra scandal—would forever tarnish his reputation.

NOTES

[1] Lou Cannon, *Role of A Lifetime*, p. 655.

[2] *Time*, July 7, 1986, p. 12.

[3] Robert Dallek, Interview with Author.

[4] Anderson, *Revolution*, p. 175.

[5] Lou Cannon, *Role of a Lifetime*, p. 20

[6] Cannon, *Role of a Lifetime*, pp. 22–23.

[7] In 1981 when Reagan took office the poverty rate was 14 percent. After climb-

ing to 15.2 percent during the recession, it dropped to 12.8 percent by 1989. For those who remained below the poverty line the financial gains were marginal. In 1981 average income was $6,913, by 1989 it was $6,994. Irving J. Sloan, Editor *Ronald W. Reagan, 1911–* (New York: Oceana Publications, 1990). Lou Cannon, *President Reagan*, p. 516; Edwin Rubenstein, *Right Data* (National Review, New York, 1994), p. 36

[8] Lou Cannon, *Role of a Lifetime*, p. 24.

[9] Martin Anderson, *Revolution*. p. 176.

[10] Ronald Reagan, *An American Life*, p. 349.

[11] George Will, Interview with Author.

[12] Christopher Matthews, Interview with Author.

[13] Jay Winnik, *On the Brink*. p. 596.

[14] In March 1985, Reagan signed NSDD 166 to seek the defeat and removal of Soviet troops in Afghanistan. Knott, "Reagan's Critics," p. 72.

[15] Victory 270; Reagan's Critics, *National Interest*, Summer 1966, p. 72.

[16] It is by now a matter of record that Reagan's assessment of the Sandinistas was largely correct, and the American public was in fact, duped. Despite their own propaganda in the United States, and the image their supporters constructed, the Sandinistas made no secret of their intentions. "Our historic project," they wrote in 1982, was to seek "an authentic unity with the fraternal people of Central America . . . to lead the way to coordinating efforts to achieve national liberation and establish a new system without imperialist domination." (Historic Program of the FSLN, Sandinistas Speak, NY. and London Pathfinder Press, 1982, p, 13.) While liberal Americans saw them as folk heroes, and hoped for democracy in Nicaragua, the Sandinistas gradually and deliberately endeavored to transform Nicaragua into a "second Cuba." They nationalized land and private property, took over radio and television, imposed press censorship, established Cuban-style neighborhood committees to keep watch on the population, and, under direct guidance from the Cuban military, built the largest army in Central America under their strict political control.

[17] At their peak the Contras grew to 15,000.

[18] Tip O'Neill, *Man of the House*, p. 370. O'Neill's assessment of the "contras" was no more accurate than Reagan's romantic view of the rebel army as "freedom fighters." The "contras" were, in fact, a coalition force, in which members of the defeated Somoza National Guard made common cause with angry peasants and democratic idealists who felt betrayed by the Sandinistas, and fought a ruthless war against an equally ruthless and militarily superior enemy—often at the expense of innocent Nicaraguans.

[19] Jay Winnik, *On the Brink*, p. 418.

[20] *Ibid.*

[21] Not only did the Contras gain weapons, logistics support and advice but also a great psychological boost. They would not be betrayed by Ronald Reagan in the Nicaraguan jungles like anti-Communist Cubans had been betrayed by John F. Kennedy on the beaches of the Bay of Pigs.

[22] Ann Reilly Dowd, "What Managers Can Learn from President Reagan," *Fortune*, September 15, 1986. p. 41.

[23] For a more complete treatment of Reagan's management style, see Chapter 9.

[24] Martin Anderson, *Revolution*, p. 292.

[25] Ed Rollins, Interview with Austin Hoyt.

[26] Maureen Reagan, *First Daughter*, p. 365, and interview with Author.

[27] Maureen Reagan, Interview with Author.

[28] Edmund Morris, Interview with Austin Hoyt.

CHAPTER 18

His Finest Hour

Soviet Foreign Minister Edward Shevardnadze came to the Oval Office one day in September 1986 with a letter from Mikhail Gorbachev. It was an invitation to meet with him in London or in Reykjavik, Iceland, for "preliminary" discussions on arms control, stalled since the Geneva summit one year before.

In the letter, Gorbachev also took the opportunity to accuse the United States of escalating a recent incident in U.S.-Soviet relations to the level of a crisis. "It is as if a pretext was deliberately sought to aggravate Soviet-American relations to increase tensions."[1]

Gorbachev was referring to U.S. reaction to the KGB's apprehension of *US News & World Report* Moscow correspondent Nicholas Daniloff on trumped-up charges of espionage. Daniloff's arrest was seen as a customary KGB tactic. Days before, the United States had arrested a Soviet spy, Genadi Zakharov, and now the Soviets were offering Daniloff in a prisoner exchange. Reagan declined the offer, and instead threatened to expel 25 KGB-agent members of the Soviet UN delegation from the United States.

The summit initiative was portrayed as an effort to ease tensions in the wake of the Daniloff affair. But the real purpose behind the offer was to ambush the President. Gorbachev hoped that if Reagan came to a summit rushed and unprepared, he could be tricked into giving up SDI. Sergei Tarasenko,

Assistant to the Foreign Minister, admitted as much in an interview with *The American Experience*:

> I guess to catch President off-guard. To propose to him a package beyond all the expectations. To talk real big. . . . That was [Gorbachev's] idea. Why we shall discuss all these small things. Let's come up with a big idea and sell it. . . . To kill SDI. That [is], the bigger [the] bait on our side . . . the more probability that the American side will sacrifice SDI.[2]

Unaware of Gorbachev's hidden agenda, Reagan agreed to meet him in Reykjavik. His acceptance of Gorbachev's invitation created quite a stir in Washington. By then, the rift within the Reagan Administration between those who wanted the President to use SDI as a bargaining chip—mainly George Shultz and his State Department—and those who wanted to preserve SDI at any cost had grown into a pitched battle. Secretary of Defense Caspar Weinberger wanted to develop SDI without delay. He worried that Reagan, now approaching the end of his presidency, was so eager to achieve a breakthrough in arms reductions that he might be seduced into bargaining SDI away. His concerns were echoed by conservatives outside the Administration who sensed Reagan was being lured by their old enemy, détente.[3]

"I was most unhappy before he went to Reykjavik," recalled George Will.

> I remember shortly before he went to Iceland; I think it was shortly before he went, he called me at home, and he said, "I'm not enjoying reading you as much as I once did," and I said, "I'm not enjoying watching you be President as much as I once did."[4]

Reagan's old friend and former advisor, Lyn Nofziger, paid a visit to the President at the White House just before Reykjavik.

> There was a lot of worry in conservative circles in this town that [Reagan] might be convinced by some of his own people to go too easy and to kind of give away the store and that he wasn't going to be properly prepared. So . . . I went over to the White House, and they said, "He wants to see you in the living quarters." So I went on up to the living quarters, and we said hello and one thing or another, and I said, "Well Mr. President, I'm here because there's a lot of people worried that you're going to go to Reykjavik and give away the store." And he said, "Lynwood"—he always called me Lynwood, which is not my name—he said, "Lynwood, I don't want you ever to worry about that." He said, "I still have the scars on my back from when I fought the Communists in Hollywood." He said, "Don't ever worry about it."[5]

Before his departure, Reagan underplayed the importance of the encounter about to take place. It will be "a private meeting between the two of us. . . . We will have no large staffs, nor is it planned that we will sign substantive agreements." But soon after the delegations sat down to talk, it was obvious that Gorbachev had something much bigger in mind.

"Gorbachev," Secretary of State Shultz later wrote, "laid gifts at our feet."[6] The Soviet leader suddenly appeared willing to respond to long-held U.S. concerns. He accepted the U.S. INF proposal, the same "Zero Option" which the Soviets had rejected in 1983 when U.S. deployment of the Pershing missiles in Europe had strained superpower relations to the breaking point. He proposed a 50-percent cut in heavy missiles, the same missiles which in the late 1970s had given rise to concern about a possible "window of vulnerability." And he promised to let the ABM Treaty banning deployment of defense systems lapse after ten years, not twenty as he had earlier insisted.

He even made a major concession on human rights, agreeing, for the first time, that the issue would be a legitimate, recognized item on the superpower agenda. Secretary of State George Shultz still regards the concession as "a breakthrough":

> When you're breaking through on the nature of the relations between a government and its people, you're really getting a lot deeper than perhaps you think.[7]

Caught by surprise, the U.S. delegations worked all night to draft a response to Gorbachev's surprising proposals. The next day, the Americans delivered their reply to the Russians. They accepted the proposed 50-percent cut in heavy missiles, and though INF was still snagged in technical details, the negotiators were close to an agreement which would remove the Pershing and SS-20 missiles threatening Europe. "George and I couldn't believe what was happening," Reagan later wrote. "We were getting amazing agreements."

> As the day went on, I felt something momentous was occurring. . . . As evening approached I said to myself, "Look what we have accomplished . . . the most massive weapons reduction in history.' . . . Then Gorbachev threw us a curve. With a smile on his face he said, "This all depends, of course, on your giving up SDI." I couldn't believe it.[8]

Suddenly it became clear why Gorbachev had been so forthcoming with concessions.

The two men stared at each other. Gorbachev finally said, "We've accomplished nothing. Let's go home." But he did not move. The two leaders decided to give it one more shot. They instructed their advisors to summarize the progress made so far—to see if there was a way around SDI.

They reconvened at 3:25 in the afternoon. Reagan opened the session with an offer to adhere to the ABM Treaty for ten years. Over the first five years ballistic missiles would be reduced 50 percent. Both sides would abide by the treaty for another five years, during which time all ballistic missiles would be eliminated. At that point, both superpowers would be free to deploy SDI. Reagan even offered to share SDI technology with the Soviets.

Gorbachev countered with an offer to eliminate not just ballistic missiles, but *all* offensive missiles. But he insisted that under the ABM Treaty, SDI research be confined to the laboratory.

At this point, Secretary of State George Shultz suggested a recess. The two leaders rejoined their expectant delegations. Gorbachev was still hopeful he might convince Reagan to exchange SDI for arms reductions. Deputy Foreign Minister Bessmertnykh remembered:

> We were receiving him there in a small room and he said, "If Reagan accepts, the world will be a new one. Things will change historically."[9]

But before he could accept Gorbachev's dazzling offers, Reagan needed to know whether confining research to the laboratory would kill SDI, or whether the United States could work around that limitation and still achieve a strategic defense. As Richard Perle related the details of the meeting to *The American Experience*, Reagan got conflicting advice when he posed the question to his advisors at Reykjavik.

Some of the people present urged him to go forward and thought that there were ways we could work around these limitations. . . . I expressed the categorical view that there was no way you could see the program through to a successful conclusion if we accepted the constraints that Gorbachev had in mind. . . . And upon hearing that, [Reagan] turned to Don Regan, his Chief of Staff, and said, "If we agree to the Gorbachev limitations, won't we be doing that simply so we can leave here with an agreement?" And it was a rhetorical question, of course, and you knew the moment he put it, that he'd made his decision.[10]

As far as Reagan was concerned, the summit was over. The seasoned negotiator already knew that there was no room for compromise.

He wanted to get out of there and be home. He wanted to be home for dinner that night if at all possible, and with the change of hours if he left in the early afternoon, he could be home in Washington for dinner. . . . And [I said] to him, "Hang in there, Mr. President, I think we're winning."[11]

At 5:30, Gorbachev and Reagan met once again. In the heated atmosphere all bets were off. For ninety minutes the two leaders engaged in a high-stakes poker game while the fate of the world hung in the balance.

Gorbachev reiterated his proposal to eliminate *all* offensive missiles. Reagan retorted, why not *all* nuclear weapons? For a few moments in Reykjavik, the dazzling illusion of a nuclear-free world hung in the air, seemingly within reach of the leaders of the two nuclear superpowers.

Never mind that Western Europe depended on nuclear weapons to deter the massive Red Army. Never mind that other countries possessed nuclear weapons out of the reach of superpower agreements. Never mind the difficulties of verifying compliance.

It's easy to say that President Reagan was anti-Communist or anti-something. No, he was a romantic . . . he really was maybe the last romantic of this generation.[12]

Gorbachev also had a romantic abolitionist vision of nuclear weapons. And you've got the two leaders of these two powerful countries running way beyond their arms controllers and their defense ministries and their State Departments and saying, "Let's get rid of nuclear weapons."[13]

But Gorbachev's notion of a nuclear-free world was a world without SDI. To deploy a space defense would consume resources the Soviets needed to survive. Not to compete would allow the United States a strategic victory in the Cold War. He insisted that for the ten-year duration of the ABM Treaty, SDI research be confined to the laboratory. "I cannot do without the word laboratory," he told Reagan. "It's laboratory or goodbye."[14]

Gorbachev fell silent, and Reagan . . . got up from the table and walked out. . . . And Reagan looked very stern, [his] lips were pursed. You could see the man was very emotional. . . . He got into the car and his shoulders slumped . . . and he said, "Don, we were that close," and he held up his left hand, just finger and thumb, "that much. [Gorbachev] kept insisting that we had to do away with SDI, and I couldn't do that. I promised the American people I would not give in on that. I cannot do it." . . . And I've never seen a guy so beat in all my life.[15]

At Reykjavik, Reagan had stood his ground, sacrificing his dream of nuclear arms reductions to preserve his dream of SDI. "There is no way we're going to give up research to find a defense weapon against nuclear missiles," Reagan later wrote. ". . . SDI was an insurance policy to guarantee the Soviets kept [their] commitments."[16]

Richard Perle later called the President's performance "extraordinary."

He had tremendous stamina. He had a compass that worked from beginning to end. I detected in Gorbachev a panicky sense, and at various times, among some of our own delegation. But the President was just steady, steady, steady, from beginning to end. He wasn't swept away by the concessions that were offered early on. . . . When the hooker was revealed, he was balanced. His judgment was solid.[17]

Soviet Deputy Foreign Minister Alexander Bessmertnykh agreed:

He was a good negotiator, very strong, very persuasive, and sometimes he was very aggressive. And in Reykjavik, I think he was at his best. I have never seen him so good as a negotiating partner. . . . At the final part of the summit without briefing papers, they were talking directly to each other, so each leader showed his own intellectual ability, and Reagan was very good.[18]

Gorbachev had overplayed his hand. By underestimating Reagan, he joined the long list of adversaries who had crashed against his determination.

> He was the most unhappy man I've ever seen, Gorbachev was. Because again, they felt that they had a historic solution just so close to them, and they didn't get it. And he was very angry. When we were driving in the car, in the car to the hotel, he was kind of, you know, he was explosive. . . . But then . . . he probably started to think about the reaction of Soviet public opinion. If he followed [his] initial emotional line, then his mission to Reykjavik would be considered a failure.[19]

The Soviet leader put on a good face for the press. He blamed Reagan's insistence on maintaining SDI on the "military industrial complex," adding that, "the atmosphere of the meeting had been friendly," and that aside from SDI, "our positions have never been so close."[20]

> I said to the reporters that indeed Reykjavik was a breakthrough. . . . I said Reykjavik will eventually produce results.[21]

Some members of the American delegation found it harder to hide their disappointment. "The mood was bad," recalls Sam Donaldson. "Reagan . . . looking grim, and then Don Regan saying the Soviets were just trying to trap the United States,

and George Shultz, the Secretary of State, acting like his dog
died."[22]

> Shultz came and gave this emotional press confer-
> ence. [He] was near tears. Shultz conveyed the sense
> that we had almost reached this historic agreement and
> it had eluded us at the last moment.[23]

Not everyone in the U.S. delegation shared Shultz's disappointment.

> That was considered a great tragedy by the State
> Department. It was considered a great victory by those
> of us who wanted strategic defense and wanted the
> United States to appear . . . firm.[24]

Richard Perle later claimed, "I knew as we left Reykjavik
that this had been an enormous success for the President."

> I was astounded that people thought otherwise.
> Because Gorbachev had made concessions he was never
> able to recapture. He went back to Moscow without
> having stopped SDI, but having for the first time agreed
> [in principle] to very sharp reduction in strategic offen-
> sive forces which we had argued for, and having agreed
> essentially to eliminate their SS-20 missiles, which had
> been the focal point of the U.S.-Soviet relationship up
> until that moment.[25]

Though himself deeply disappointed, Reagan found solace in
the support of his conservative friends. Speechwriter Tony
Dolan, the pen behind Reagan's "Evil Empire" speech and

other fierce Reagan rhetorical attacks on the Soviet Union, was on the plane heading home from Reykjavik.

> We were on the plane and . . . Reagan emerged from his quarters. We were going on the air the next night, and everybody had their contribution to the speech draft, and in the middle of all this chaos, I just sort of scribbled out a note to Reagan saying he had done exactly what the American people had always wanted their President to do. He [had] stood up to the Russians, and for the sake of his own fame or some . . . illusionary peace effort, he hadn't sacrificed what he believed in . . . and he'd done the brave thing. And I gave it to him. I expected he'd put it in his pocket and just sort of read it a little later and send it back out to me . . . instead he stood there and read it with all this going on around him in the aisle of Air Force One, and when he looked up his eyes were filled with tears.[26]

Back in the United States, the press blamed Reagan for walking away from the most sweeping offer of arms reduction in history, for sinking a summit by being stubborn on Star Wars. "No Deal: Star Wars Sinks the Summit," headlined *Time*. "Reagan-Gorbachev Summit Talks Collapse as SDI Wipes Out Other Gains," bannered *The Washington Post*.

But the American people gave high marks to their President. A *New York Times*-CBS poll taken the week after Reykjavik showed an 11-point increase in the percentage of Americans who thought Ronald Reagan was doing a good job handling the Soviet Union.[27] A majority believed their President when he told them, "we made progress in Iceland."

In London, Prime Minister Margaret Thatcher breathed a sigh of relief. In his high stakes *"mano a mano"* with Gorbachev,

Reagan had overlooked the fact that the security of Europe still depended on nuclear weapons. As Thatcher told *The American Experience*,

> Was I relieved. Goodness me, I was. A world without nuclear weapons meant the Soviet Union would have colossal superiority of conventional weapons and how could we monitor a world without nuclear weapons? We couldn't.[28]

Mikhail Gorbachev had tried to put a positive spin on the summit. So did Ronald Reagan once he returned to Washington. But it would be years before the pivotal significance of Reykjavik was fully understood.

"Without Reykjavik," Gorbachev told *The American Experience*, "the process that was eventually started and that brought about . . . one treaty and further treaties . . . would not have been possible. Reykjavik is really the top of the hill. And from that top, we saw a great deal."[29]

He conveyed this sentiment to George Shultz during a visit to Stanford University, after they were both out of office. According to Shultz,

> I said to him, when you entered office and when I entered office, the Cold War could not have been colder, and when we left, it was basically over. "What do you think was the turning point?" And he said, without any hesitation, just like that, he said, "Reykjavik." And I said, "Why?" expecting him to talk about missiles and stuff like that. He said, "Because for the first time the two leaders really had a deep conversation about everything. We really exchanged views, and not just

about peripheral things, about the central things, and that was what was important about Reykjavik."[30]

NOTES

[1] Letter quoted in Ronald Reagan, *An American Life*, p. 669.

[2] Sergei Tarasenko, Interview with Austin Hoyt.

[3] Representative Jack Kemp. Quoted in Winnik, *On The Brink*, p. 503.

[4] George Will, Interview with Author.

[5] Lyn Nofziger, Interview with Author.

[6] George Shultz, *Triumph and Tragedy*, p. 760.

[7] George Shultz, Interview with Austin Hoyt.

[8] Ronald Reagan, *An American Life*, p. 677.

[9] Alexander Bessmertnykh, Interview with Austin Hoyt.

[10] Richard Perle, Interview with Austin Hoyt.

[11] Donald Regan, Interview with Austin Hoyt.

[12] Sergei Tarasenko, Interview with Austin Hoyt.

[13] Lou Cannon, Interview with Austin Hoyt.

[14] Jay Winnik, *To the Brink*, p. 517.

[15] Donald Regan, Interview with Austin Hoyt.

[16] Ronald Reagan, *An American Life*, p. 679.

[17] Richard Perle, Interview with Austin Hoyt.

[18] Alexander Bessmertnykh, Interview with Austin Hoyt.

[19] Alexander Bessmertnykh, Interview with Austin Hoyt.

[20] Mikhail Gorbachev, Press Conference in Reykjavik, October 12, 1986, in Mikhail Gorbachev, *Reykjavik: Results and Lessons* (Sphynx Press: 1987), pp. 11–42.

[21] Mikhail Gorbachev, Interview with Austin Hoyt.

[22] Sam Donaldson, Interview with Author. Later on, Shultz regretted having displayed his emotions so openly.

[23] Lou Cannon, Interview with Austin Hoyt.

[24] Caspar Weinberger, Interview with Austin Hoyt.

[25] Richard Perle, Interview with Austin Hoyt.

[26] Tony Dolan, Interview with Author.

[27] Lou Cannon, *Role of a Lifetime*, p. 770.

[28] Margaret Thatcher, Interview with Austin Hoyt.

[29] Mikhail Gorbachev, Interview with Austin Hoyt.

[30] George Shultz, Interview with Austin Hoyt.

CHAPTER 20

Iran-Contra: The Darkest Time

On November 3, 1986, the Lebanese magazine *Al Shiraa* broke the news that National Security Advisor Robert McFarlane and four other Americans had visited Tehran that September. Their secret mission: to negotiate the release of hostages held by terrorists in Lebanon in exchange for weapons for Iran's military, then at war with Iraq. The Speaker of the Iranian Parliament, Ali Akbar Rafsanjani, confirmed the report the next day.

The Lebanese article marked the beginning of the scandal that would come to be known as Iran-Contra. It would shake the Reagan Administration to its foundations and reveal the deficiencies of the Reagan White House and shortcomings in the President's character.

By the time it was all over, eight defendants, including NSC staffer Colonel Oliver North and his boss, National Security Advisor John Poindexter—who had replaced Robert McFarlane—were handed convictions.[1] Chief of Staff Donald Regan was forced to resign. CIA Director Bill Casey died of a brain tumor. Robert McFarlane attempted suicide. But perhaps the most significant casualty of Iran-Contra was Reagan's reputation. "Iran-Contra forever tarnished the credibility Reagan had nurtured and preserved as an actor and politician. He would never again bask in the unquestioned trust of the American people as he had done in the red glare of Liberty Weekend."[2]

Since the early months of his Administration, President Reagan had supported a Nicaraguan insurgent group—the

Contras—in a covert war against the Marxist Sandinista government. Since 1984, he had also fought Congress, increasingly unwilling to fund the "Contra war."

In the Middle East, the U.S. had become the target of a terrorist campaign unleashed by Muslim extremists. Two-hundred and forty-one U.S. soldiers were killed when a truck carrying a bomb crashed through the gates of the U.S. Marine barracks in Beirut in November 1983. And Shiite terrorists had kidnapped and continued to hold hostage seven U.S. citizens, including William Buckley, the CIA station chief in Beirut.

Keeping the Contras alive in Central America and freeing the U.S. hostages in the Middle East became obsessions for Ronald Reagan. "No problem was more frustrating to me than trying to get the American hostages home," he later wrote. "Almost every morning, at my national security briefings, I began by asking the same question: 'Any progress on the hostages?' . . . As President, as far as I was concerned, I had the duty to get those Americans home. . . . I didn't want to rest or stop exploring any possible avenue until they were home safe with their families."[3]

It was on July 18, 1985, while Reagan was recovering from colon cancer surgery at Bethesda Naval Hospital, that his National Security Advisor Robert McFarlane first told him of a secret request by Iran to buy American weapons. McFarlane argued it was time to improve relations with Iran by courting moderates who might succeed the Ayatollah Khomeini and might also help free U.S. hostages in Beirut. "His reaction," McFarlane told *The American Experience*, "was that yes, if we could open a dialogue with people who might succeed Khomeni, that would be good. When the possibility of the release of the hostages was added, he was even more enthusiastic."[4] That the hostages were foremost in Reagan's mind is evidenced by a diary entry on July 17, the day before McFarlane's visit. "Some strange soundings are coming from some Iranians," Reagan wrote. "Bud M. will be here tomorrow to talk about it. It could be a breakthrough on getting our seven kidnap victims back."[5] As George Will told *The American Experience*:

> This is the soft side of Ronald Reagan. He was really bothered by the hostages. It would take a harder man than Ronald Reagan to say what a President ought to say, which is, "Sorry, this is a big country, and big countries have casualties, and we just have to regard those people as for the moment, casualties. Put them out of your mind." Ronald Reagan had a hard time being hard.[6]

In the words of Lou Cannon,

> The hostages brought out one side of Reagan's character not too many people knew. Reagan could show an intense, almost passionate commitment to causes he visualized in personal terms. He could identify with these guys in their cells. Reagan would start describing these agonies, imagined agonies. He had just enormous empathy. This is where Reagan is like all of us. He's a surrogate for America. He feels what ordinary Americans are feeling. This is where his feelings, which had carried him to the heights, dashed him to the depths.[7]

Selling weapons to Tehran violated an official U.S. embargo against Iran and would surely give the impression that the President was negotiating with terrorists. The operation would have to be conducted in secret. Israel, who backed Iran in the war against Iraq, would send the weapons, and the United States would replenish Israeli stocks.[8]

A meeting was held on August 6 to discuss the initiative. The Administration was divided.[9] Secretary of State George Shultz and Secretary of Defense Caspar Weinberger put aside their differences over U.S. Soviet policy and joined forces in arguing strongly against the initiative. It could hurt U.S. relations with European and Middle Eastern allies who had joined in the embargo against Iran, and it could create incentives for the taking of more hostages. Ultimately, the President's credibility could be severely damaged if the secret deal were ever discovered.

But National Security Advisor "Bud" McFarlane was eager to initiate a relaxation of tensions with Iran as a first step toward improving the U.S. position in the Middle East. And CIA Director William Casey was determined to free his operative, Bill Buckley, whom he believed was being held captive along with the other hostages in Lebanon.

Reagan sided with McFarlane and Casey. His empathy with the hostages overrode all other considerations. A few days after the meeting, Reagan authorized the sale of Israeli weapons and other military spare parts to Iran. That same month, he signed a law banning arms sales to terrorist nations, and approved a tough new anti-terrorist law.

Between the first shipment of 100 anti-tank missiles to Iran on August 20, 1985, and the first public disclosures in *Al Shiraa* in November 1986, the Iranians received more than 1,500 missiles. Three U.S. hostages were released in exchange, and then promptly replaced by new American prisoners in what Shultz had predicted would be a "hostage bazaar."

At first, Reagan questioned the credibility of the news story. Barraged by questions during press conference on November 6, he pleaded: "Could I suggest an appeal to all of you in regard to this—the speculation, the commenting and all on a story that come out of the Middle East and that has no foundation?"[10]

But on November 13, ten days after *Al Shiraa's* disclosure, Reagan went on television to explain that the shipment of weapons to Iran had been part of an effort to improve relations with that strategically important nation. But he denied that the arms had been traded for the release of hostages.

> In spite of the wildly speculative and false stories of arms for hostages and alleged ransom payments, we did not—repeat did not—trade weapons or anything else for hostages nor will we.

"Reagan had absolutely convinced himself that he was not dealing with the kidnappers," Lou Cannon told *The American Experience*.

> He had promised that he would never deal with the people who had taken the Americans hostage. He had convinced himself that he was dealing with these Iran-ian moderates. Reagan is a classic model of the success-ful child of an alcoholic: he doesn't hear things and doesn't see things that he doesn't want to hear and see. And that's the thing you learn, you learn that as a child, and Reagan learned it.[11]

"Ronald Reagan doesn't see the world that you and I see," added Sam Donaldson.

> He sees a world through rose-colored glasses. It's a wonderful world. But it's not the real world that exists out there. And so, he didn't want to see a world in which he had traded arms for hostages.[12]

The next day, a poll published by the *Los Angeles Times*

showed that only 14 percent of the American people believed the President when he said that he had not traded arms for hostages. As Donald Regan described it, "He flushed and pursed his lips when he talked about it. He thought that he was telling the truth. Why didn't the people believe him?"[13]

> Reagan always said that the television reveals you. That you can't fool the camera. Reagan understood this better than most people. And when he gave this report, he was so completely unconvincing. He was so defensive and so Nixonian. It's the only time in my life I ever thought Reagan gave a speech that he sounded like Nixon, you know, lashing out and snarly. And people just knew something was wrong.[14]

> He had let down the pride of America by dealing with the people who had humiliated us all. In violation of every principle he'd ever stood for, he had traded with the enemy, had sent arms to the same cadre of people who had blown up our Marines in Beirut. The American middle had been confounded by this patriotic President who had won on standing tall, who was found to be paying tribute to the enemy.[15]

Reagan's greatest asset, his honesty, was in question. At a press conference on November 19, reporters, who had up to that point treated Ronald Reagan with a degree of deference, hammered him with questions.

> **Helen Thomas:** Mr. President, how would you assess the credibility of your own Administration in light of the prolonged deception of Congress and the

public in terms of your secret dealings with Iran, the disinformation?[16]

Bill Plante: The record shows that every time an American hostage was released, there had been a major shipment of arms just before that. Are we all to believe that is just a coincidence?[17]

The President dodged questions and fumbled answers. "This whole irresponsible press bilge about hostages and Iran has gotten out of hand," Reagan wrote in his diary.[18] He was feeling under siege, and it was about to get much worse.

November 24, the Monday before Thanksgiving, Chief of Staff Donald Regan received an early morning telephone call from Attorney General Edwin Meese, who had been looking into the Iran affair. His investigation, Meese told Regan, had discovered, "things the President does not know." Meese demanded to see the President immediately.

The three men met at 11 A.M. in the Oval Office.

Meese informed the President that his investigation had revealed that the Iranians had paid $30 million for the weapons, but the U.S. government had only received $12 million. No one was sure where the other $18 million had gone. A member of the NSC staff, Lieutenant Colonel Oliver North, had admitted to Meese over the weekend that he had diverted some of those funds to the Nicaraguan Contras in ways which circumvented the law forbidding the Reagan Administration from aiding the Nicaraguan resistance. [19]

To the men conducting the secret operation this was the "ultimate" irony, the Ayatollah Khomeini paying for the "Contra War." But to the three men meeting that morning, the diversion of funds spelled political disaster. As Meese told *The American Experience:*

> Here you had two different operations, each of which had a certain amount of contentiousness and about which there was considerable opposition on Capitol Hill. And now the two had been joined together. It was kind of like putting together a match and gasoline.[20]

Reagan sensed the danger. "The President actually turned white," recalls Don Regan.

> He blanched and said, "What could have been going through their minds? Why would they do this?" He was very definite there should be every precaution taken that no one would think that there was any cover-up or any attempt to conceal whatever wrong-doing we might find, and immediately ordered Meese to "get to the bottom of this."

The next day, the President and his Attorney General stood before an expectant press corps still preoccupied with getting Reagan to admit to the arms-for-hostages deal. Reagan began by defending the rightness of his Iran policy.

> As I have stated previously, I believe our policy goals toward Iran were well founded. However, the information brought to my attention yesterday convinced me that in one aspect, implementation of that policy was seriously flawed.

Then Reagan turned the microphone over to Meese. It was then that Meese revealed the findings of the diversion of funds from the arms sales to Iran into the war chest of the Contras.

From then on, the press and the nation sought the answer to one question: What had the President known?

Either way it was damning. If Reagan knew of the diversion of funds, he could be impeached. If he did not, the fact that he was not told was a chilling thought of a rudderless, leaderless White House.[21]

Reagan pleaded ignorance at the press conference. "The only person in the United States government who knew precisely about this was Lieutenant Colonel North," he said.

The next day, Reagan accepted the resignation of his National Security Advisor John Poindexter and fired NSC staffer U.S. Marine Colonel Oliver North, the "point man" in the operation. North was bitter. He thought he was doing "all he could" to implement the President's policies of keeping the contras "alive body and soul." "I deeply believe that I had the authority of the President to do it," North later told investigators.[22]

Throughout his first term, Ronald Reagan waged a secret and highly effective offensive against the Soviet Union and its proxies around the globe—an offensive that proved so successful that many observers would give it significant credit for America's eventual victory in the Cold War. But now some of the very same secret operations which had helped undermine the Soviet Union were threatening to undo the Reagan presidency.

Bill Casey at the CIA, and the NSC had conducted a secret war against the Soviet Union with the President's full authorization. But by the second term, they were running their own foreign policy without regard to the Cabinet and all the other usual foreign policy channels. When you are involved in those kinds of deals, and you are not accountable to anyone, the boundaries between the legal and the illegal, the appropriate and the inappropriate, tend to blur.[23]

"Our credibility is shot," wrote Secretary of State George Shultz. "We've taken refuge in tricky technicalities of language to avoid confronting the reality that we lied to the American people . . . We are revealed to have been dealing with some of the sleaziest international characters around."[24]

Nearly fifteen years after Richard Nixon's darkest days, the ghost of scandal once again hovered above Washington. "This presidency is over," columnist Charles Krauthammer wrote. "1987 will be a Watergate year and the following an election year." Between the appearance of the article in *Al Shiraa* and December 1, 1986, Reagan's approval rating dropped from 67 to 46 percent. It was the sharpest drop ever recorded.

The President sank into a deep depression. "It went right to his soul to see his character being questioned every day," Nancy remembered.[25] Reagan's son, Ron, paid a visit to his Dad.

> I went to the White House because it was clear that he was going through some sort of crisis, and I just felt that, you know, as his son, as a family member, that I ought to be there, somebody ought to be there, somebody ought to buck him up and help him get through this. It was the first time I'd really seen him with the wind completely out of his sails.[26]

Edmund Morris, who as official biographer had the opportunity to observe the President closely, remembers feeling, for the first time, "that [Reagan] was not able to handle anything that came at him again. He wasn't quite up to handling a crisis of that dimension."[27]

Reagan appointed a commission headed by Senator John

Tower to explore the details of the Iran-Contra operation. The investigation was impeded by two facts: Oliver North had shredded most documents, and William Casey, the man most likely to know all the answers—including how much the President knew—was dying of a brain tumor.

The Iran-Contra crisis engulfed the Administration in mutual recriminations and fierce infighting. A power struggle ensued between the First Lady and Chief of Staff Donald Regan. "Don was not my favorite person in the White House," the First Lady wrote in her memoirs. "He liked the word 'chief' in his title [Chief of Staff], but he never really understood that his title also included the word 'staff.'"[28] "He was miscast as a Chief of Staff," Ed Rollins told *The American Experience*.

> [He] never thought of himself as staff. He thought of himself as Deputy President. Said to me one day, "I can make 85 percent of the decisions the President makes," and I said to him, "Don, I just ran a campaign in 50 states. I didn't see your name on the ballot anywhere."[29]

It was not only Don Regan's imperiousness that put off Nancy Reagan. She felt the Chief of Staff was was openly disrespectful of her husband, and not sufficiently concerned with his health.[30] The first confrontation had been over Don Regan's insistence that the President receive McFarlane and Shultz only two days after his colon cancer operation in October 1985. Now, in the depths of the Iran-Contra scandal, Don Regan wanted to get the President out on the road and in front of the press to work his magic on the American people.

Nancy opposed Regan's plans. Her husband had just undergone a delicate prostate operation. She felt he was in no shape to undertake a grueling schedule. She also feared for his life. Nancy's astrologer, Joan Quigley, had warned that "the alignment of Uranus and Saturn raised the danger of assassination." Ever since Reagan survived John Hinkley's bullet in 1981, Nancy had checked Reagan's schedule with Quigley. Press conferences would have to be scheduled on "good days" and that December, according to Quigley's reading of the stars, most days were bad. The First Lady was not about to take chances.

Don Regan told *The American Experience:*

> The media was in full cry for Reagan's scalp, and the hotter it got, the more she decided that either the people in the White House staff weren't reacting correctly, or they weren't smart enough to know how to handle it. Well, I was the guy on that. The staff under me was doing its best, but unfortunately, we couldn't get the President to go out. She insisted that he couldn't go out to make speeches. He couldn't get out in front of himself, and we just had to keep the press away from him.[31]

But there was more to the Regan problem than a dispute over Reagan's health. Many of Reagan's old advisors felt Regan had not served the President well, and that he should bear some of the blame for the lack of accountability in the Reagan White House. They also felt the Administration needed a fresh start under "new management."

Old friends Stuart Spencer and Michael Deaver paid a visit to the President to try to convince him to fire Regan. Deaver spoke: "The media is not going to let you go on. You have to make a bold move. You have to get rid of somebody, because you've got to do something that says, 'This is an action I'm taking and I'm gonna go on.' Reagan got very angry. 'I'll be dammed if I'm going to throw someone overboard to save my own ass,' he said."

Deaver then appealed to Reagan's patriotism. "'It's not your

ass, Ron. It's the country's ass.' He looked at me very quietly
and said, 'You know what I think about this country.'"[32]

The opportunity to drop the ax was not long in coming. One
evening, at the end at the end of a long day, Donald Regan
hung up on the First Lady.

> She was incessantly calling me. One day, I got home
> late from the office. No dinner. It was after nine o'clock.
> I was just starting to eat when she called. We went back
> and forth and back and forth, and I was on the phone fif-
> teen or twenty minutes, and we were getting nowhere.
> Finally, I was just so disgusted, I hung up.[33]

> Don Regan for some reason took the point of view
> that Nancy Reagan wasn't important. That was wrong
> from the standpoint of the President. He could set all
> these other things along the line, but when you hung up
> on his wife—you didn't treat his women that way.[34]

The next day, February 27, Don Regan heard on CNN that
the President had chosen former Senator Howard Baker to
replace him as Chief of Staff.

That same day, the Tower Commission met with the President to discuss its findings.

"On more than one occasion," the Commission had found,
"an aircraft loaded with weapons sat on a runway, awaiting
word that hostages had been freed." Yet Reagan still refused to
admit that he had traded arms for hostages.

The Commission found no evidence linking the President
to the diversion of funds to the Contras, but it placed responsibility for that debacle squarely on his shoulders. "The President," Senator Tower reported, "clearly did not understand
the nature of [the] operation, who was involved or what was

happening . . . . He did not force his policies to undergo the most critical review . . . and at no time did he insist on accountability." Reagan's testimony to the Tower board had been disappointing: "I'm trying to recall events that happened eighteen months ago," he wrote in a memorandum dated February 20, "I'm afraid that I let myself be influenced by other's recollections, not my own. . . . My answer therefore and the simple truth is that I don't remember, period."

Reagan's growing disengagement from the day-to-day operations of his White House, the commission confirmed, had created the atmosphere which made possible the diversion of funds from the sale of weapons to Iran to the Contras in Nicaragua.

> He was old and he was tired. He'd gotten used to saying yes and checking the decision boxes that were presented to him. He was beginning to take advice rather too easily. He was beginning to let go. And when a President begins to let go, that's when the wildly ambitious little men who work for him tend to get carried away with their own designs.[35]

The report also scolded Chief of Staff Donald Regan. "He must bear primary responsibility for the chaos that descended upon the White House."

In her conversation with *The American Experience*, Maureen Reagan went beyond the findings of the Commission, placing primary blame on Chief of Staff Donald Regan and his take-charge style, which cut off President Reagan from policy-making.

> I think it was the seed of Iran-Contra. I really truly believe this. Once the word got out that options to the President were being limited, it gave a carte blanche to

everybody down the line. I don't think that even Mr. Regan was at that point seeing all the options because the person down below would limit the person above them, it would limit the person above them, and finally, by the time it got to the President, it was [very narrow]. And I think that's what happened in the NSC.[36]

The Monday after the Tower Report, a new team would take over the operations of the Reagan White House. A transition team chosen by the new Chief of Staff Howard Baker would keep order over the weekend.

What Baker's transition team was told by Don Regan's White House staff that weekend was shocking. According to Regan's team, Reagan was "inattentive, inept, and lazy," and Baker should be prepared to invoke the 25th Amendment to relieve him of his duties.[37]

Howard Baker called a meeting the next morning. As Edmund Morris, who watched the morning session, recalled,

> The Baker team decided to have a meeting with [Reagan] Monday morning, their first official meeting with the President, and to cluster around the table in the Cabinet Room and watch him very, very closely to see how he behaved, to see if he was indeed losing his mental grip. They positioned themselves very strategically around the table so they could watch him from various angles, listen to him and check his movements and listen to his words and look into his eyes. And I was there when this meeting took place. And Reagan who was, of course, completely unaware that they were launching a death watch on him, came in stimulated by all these new people and performed splendidly.[38]

Howard Baker came out of the meeting having made up his mind about Ronald Reagan:

> I came away convinced not only was he fully in command, fully competent, but he was not being well served by the arrangements in the White House. But he was fully capable of discharging that job in a very, very effective way.[39]

Kenneth Duberstein, the new Deputy Chief of Staff, believed Reagan's problems stemmed less from his loss of abilities and more from his loss of confidence.

> He had lost some confidence because he had been badgered so badly, and you had a responsibility to help him restore his confidence, his belief that he could get things done, that he could communicate with the American people and they would understand and agree with him. That he was telling the truth, and credibility and integrity were foremost in his mind. And so, in those initial months . . . we focused a lot on making him feel good about himself, and [having him explain] to the American people where he wanted to lead America again, not based on Iran-Contra, but in spite of Iran-Contra.[40]

One of Howard Baker's first tasks in trying to get the presidency back on track was to get Reagan to admit publicly that he had made a mistake in trading arms for hostages. He found an ally in Nancy Reagan. "That's where Nancy Reagan really shines," said Lou Cannon.

She understood that he needed this public credibility. That's her great role. She went beyond protecting
him to really leading him to this bitter cup of apology
that he had to drink from.[41]

On March 3, 1987, Reagan addressed the nation from the
Oval Office.

A few months ago, I told the American people I did
not trade arms for hostages. My heart and my best
intentions still tell me that's true, but the facts and the
evidence tell me it is not. As the Tower Board reported,
what began as a strategic opening to Iran deteriorated,
in its implementation, into trading arms for hostages.
This runs counter to my own beliefs. There are reasons
why it happened, but no excuses. It was a mistake.

Overnight, Reagan's approval rating rebounded from 42 percent to 51 percent.

Once he apologized to the American people, and
the American people more or less forgave him, you
know—I mean not totally—he never got back quite
the luster, [but] he was able to govern and to be at ease
with himself.[42]

A year later, Don Regan got his revenge. In his book, *For the
Record,* he revealed, for the first time, that the First Lady consulted an astrologer. Howard Baker recalls breaking the news to
the President.

I said, "Mr. President, we will have a press flap about
this, and I think I should talk to the First Lady." He

said, "I think you should." I said, "Would you set it up?"
And he said, "Why don't you set it up?" And I did. I
called her, and I went upstairs and took the galleys with
me, and couldn't figure out what I was, how I was going
to open the conversation, but finally I just blurted out,
"Nancy, Don Regan says here that you talked to an
astrologer." And she said, "Well, I did."[43]

Baker's fear of a "press-flap" was well founded. A few days
after Regan's book was published, the *New York Post* carried a
headline which read "Astrologer Runs the Country." In her
memoirs, published shortly after the Reagans left the White
House, Nancy remorselessly admitted to her consultations with
Joan Quigley. "The idea of consulting an astrologer never
struck me as particularly strange. . . . I have spent most of my
life in the company of show-business people who were superstitious. . . . When someone consulted an astrologer, nobody
thought much about it."[44]

In the twilight of his life, tired and battered, Reagan had yet
to face the worst year of his Presidency. In May 1987, Congress
opened hearings on Iran-Contra and Reagan was called upon
to testify. He had trouble keeping his story straight. Partly
because he was genuinely confused, but partly because while he
denied any knowledge of the diversion of funds, he also
objected to being portrayed as "uninformed about everything."
"I was definitely involved in decisions about support to the
freedom fighters," he said. "It was my idea to begin with."[45]

The spectacle of the Iran-Contra hearings was only one of
many scandals which were calling into question the integrity of
the Reagan Administration. While the Iran-Contra hearings
were taking place, many of Reagan top aides were under investigation for influence peddling and other ethical transgressions.
Attorney General Edwin Meese, who had been with Reagan

since the early days of Sacramento and been part of his original
White House "troika," was investigated for conflict of interest.
He had allegedly helped a friend at the Wedtech Corporation
secure U.S. government backing for an oil pipeline from Iraq to
Jordan. Michael Deaver, the former Deputy Chief of Staff, who
had been Reagan's trusted aide since 1966, was being prose-
cuted for influence-peddling on behalf of his public relations
firm. He was found guilty of lying to Congress. Lyn Nofziger,
another loyal California aide, and briefly White House Director of Political Affairs, was convicted of influence-peddling.
His conviction was overturned on appeal.

Reagan's trusting nature, his hands-off management style,
and his tendency to focus only on a few issues were blamed for
what became known as "the sleaze factor." "Ethics in government," said James Baker, "was not something in [Reagan's] big
picture."[46]

A vulnerable Reagan became an irresistible target for the
press. The Reagan family, long suspected of being less than perfect, was exposed as being beyond dysfunctional. Despite his
amiability, Reagan was described as an emotionally distant
father disinterested in his children and the affairs of his family.

"Not a hint of Ozzie and Harriet has crept into this First
Family," wrote reporter Gloria Borger for *U.S. News & World
Report* in an article titled "A Feuding First Family."

> Indeed, the opposite often seems to be the case for
> the Ronald Reagans . . . who have become known for
> their public feuds and a penchant to exploit their clan
> membership.

Reagan's son Ron appeared in a public-service announcement criticizing his father's neglect of the AIDS crisis, which
by 1987 had taken 50,000 lives. "The U.S. government is not

moving fast enough to stop the spread of AIDS," he said. He opposed the Administration's call for mandatory testing and scoffed at the inadequacy of the Administration's prevention plan. "Write to your Congressman," he told viewers, adding with a sly smile, "or write to someone higher up."

Patti brought shame on the family when she published a novel about the life of the rebellious daughter of a Republican with "hardy good looks" who becomes governor of California and then President. In the novel, the politician has a fiercely protective wife who wears red wool suits. She followed it with a "tell-all" autobiography, *The Way I See It*, in which she described a horrid childhood of full of abuse and rejection. She depicted her father as an emotionally distant man, unwilling to confront his wife, and her mother as a woman addicted to pre-scription drugs, who slapped her almost every day. Faye Dun-away's portrayal of Joan Crawford as an abusive mother in the film "Mommy Dearest" paled in comparison to Patti's descrip-tion of Nancy.

Then on October 19, 1987, the stock market plunged 26 percent. Black Monday, as the day would go down in history, was "the climactic moment in one of the gloomiest weeks of the Reagan presidency."[47] Reagan was still beleaguered by Iran-Contra, the so-called "sleaze factor," the perception that he had killed any progress toward arms reductions at Reykjavik, and the feud with his children. And for the prior two weeks he had lived with the news that Nancy had breast cancer and would have to undergo surgery. On October 17, two days before the market crash, she had a mastectomy at Bethesda Military Hospital.

Though the market began rebounding within the week, Black Monday brought to the surface lingering questions about the economic soundness of the Reagan economic boom. Tax revenues had doubled under Reagan's watch, but they could not keep pace with the budget, which had nearly tripled—sending the deficit skyrocketing to over $1 trillion. The government borrowed one dollar for every five it spent. America, once the world's creditor, had become, for the first time since 1914, a debtor nation.

The poor had made modest gains, but the gap between rich and poor became a chasm. The homeless, whose numbers had grown to exceed the population of Atlanta, were a disturbing sight, especially when set against the ostentatious display of wealth by millionaires like Donald Trump. New York Democratic Governor Mario Cuomo would later comment that, "at his worst Reagan made the denial of compassion respectable."[48]

Biographer Edmund Morris would later gain insight into Reagan's state of mind in the midst of this time of turmoil:

> Around October of 1987, [Reagan] writes in his diary, "Dick and Patty came after dinner and things immediately livened up as soon as they arrived." That's on a Friday night. The following day, he writes in his diary. "Oh, I was mistaken. They didn't come down until lunch time today." He's talking about his wife's brother and wife. The schedule said, "Dr. and Mrs. Richard Davis will be joining the first family after dinner tonight."
>
> So Reagan writes it down after dinner as though they showed up. He says, "Things livened up when they came." In other words, he was so divorced from reality at that time that he didn't even realize that these people did not show up. Which is funny, but it's also scary.[49]

NOTES

[1] Their convictions were later overturned.

[2] Lou Cannon, *Role of a Lifetime*, p. 719.

[3] Ronald Reagan, *An American Life*, p. 513.

[4] Robert McFarlane, Interview with Austin Hoyt.

[5] Ronald Reagan, quoted in Lou Cannon, *Role of a Lifetime*, p. 613.

[6] George Will, Interview with Author.

[7] Lou Cannon, *Role of a Lifetime*, p. 738.

[8] Eventually the operation would expand to include powerful Middle Eastern arms merchants, and all sorts of other shady characters from the underworld of arms dealing.

[9] The sequence of events leading to the Iran initiative is by now well known. The following account is based on Lou Cannon, *Role of a Lifetime*, Robert McFarlane, *Special Trust*, and the production team's interviews with the participants.

[10] Ronald Reagan, November 6, 1986.

[11] Lou Cannon, Interview with Austin Hoyt.

[12] Sam Donaldson, Interview with Author.

[13] Donald Regan, *For the Record.*

[14] Lou Cannon, Interview with Austin Hoyt

[15] Christopher Matthews, Interview with Author.

[16] Helen Thomas, November 19, 1986 Press Conference.

[17] Bill Plante, November 19, 1986 Press Conference.

[18] Ronald Reagan, *An American Life*, p. 528.

[19] But special prosecutor Walsh after a five-year investigation got no convictions—or even indictments—for violations of the Boland amendment which was, according to Meese and Boyden Gray, full of legal loopholes. Convictions had to do with the cover-up, lying to Congress.

[20] Edwin Meese, Interview with Austin Hoyt.

[21] Lou Cannon, *Role of a Lifetime.*

[22] North's testimony, April 6, 1987, cited in Lawrence E. Walsh, *Firewall* (New York: W.W. Norton, 1997), p. 203.

[23] Martin Anderson, Conversation with Author.

[24] George Shultz, *Turmoil and Triumph.*

[25] Nancy Reagan, *My Turn*, p. 320.

[26] Ronald Prescott Reagan, Interview with Austin Hoyt.

[27] Edmund Morris, Interview with Austin Hoyt.

[28] Nancy Reagan, *My Turn*, p. 313.

[29] Ed Rollins. Interview with Austin Hoyt. When we later confronted Don Regan with Ed Rollins's remark, his response was, "balderdash."

[30] On November 14, Reagan had told *The New York Times*, "Some of us are like a shovel brigade that follows a parade on Main Street cleaning up."

[31] Don Regan, Interview with Austin Hoyt.

[32] Stuart Spencer and Michael Deaver, Interview with Author.

[33] Donald Regan, Interview with Austin Hoyt.

[34] Stuart Spencer, Interview with Author.

[35] Edmund Morris, Interview with Austin Hoyt.

[36] Maureen Reagan, Interview with Author.

[37] Jane Mayer, *Landslide*, p. ix, confirmed by Austin Hoyt in conversation with Jim Cannon, who led the transition team.

[38] Edmund Morris, Interview with Austin Hoyt.

[39] Senator Howard Baker, Interview with Austin Hoyt.

[40] Interview with Kenneth Duberstein, Deputy Chief of Staff.

[41] Lou Cannon, Interview with Austin Hoyt

[42] Lou Cannon, Interview with Austin Hoyt.

[43] Howard Baker, Interview with Austin Hoyt.

[44] Nancy Reagan, *My Turn*, pp. 50–51.

[45] Lou Cannon, *Role of a Lifetime*, p. 717.

[46] Quoted in Lou Cannon, *Role of a Lifetime*, p. 795.

[47] David Hoffman, "Reagan's Presidency: One of Its Gloomiest Weeks," *The Washington Post*, October 20, 1987.

[48] *Newsweek*, January 9, 1989, p. 18.

[49] Edmund Morris, Interview with Austin Hoyt.

CHAPTER 20

Peace in Our Time

In the midst of the domestic turmoil, in December 1987, Ronald Reagan received Mikhail Gorbachev in Washington. It was to be the third summit meeting between the two leaders, and the one which would produce concrete results.

Gorbachev came to sign the INF Treaty, which would eliminate all Soviet SS-20 and NATO Pershing II intermediate-range missiles in Europe. This was part of Reagan's "zero option," which the Soviet leaders had scorned six years before, the same proposal Gorbachev had rejected at Reykjavik when Reagan refused to give in on SDI. Now, he was accepting the "zero option" on Reagan's terms—SDI and all.

There is some evidence that by this time, the Soviets believed that the SDI concept was technically flawed, and therefore, not as big a threat as they had earlier feared.[1] But regardless of the prospects of SDI, the Soviets had little choice other than to sign an arms reduction agreement which would unmistakably signal progress in the relations between East and West.

Since 1981, when Reagan first took office, the balance of forces had changed dramatically in favor of the United States. While the Soviet economy continued its downward slide, the U.S. economy had reawakened with the force of a juggernaut.[2] Everywhere in the world, the Soviets were on the retreat. Gorbachev desperately needed breathing space and a period of international tranquility if his dual reform program of *glasnost* and *perestroika* was to have any chance of success. The very survival of the Soviet Union required accommodation with the

United States and its allies. At stake were access to Western technology and credit. A year earlier, in November 1986, Gorbachev had committed the Soviet Union to "new thinking," abandoning the ideology of the 'class struggle' in favor of a commitment to "global interdependence." This was a surrender of one of the fundamental tenets of Marxism-Leninism. No longer would the Soviet Union be the "midwife" to what they once deemed the historically inevitable triumph of Communism through the world.

Reagan's policy of exploiting Soviet economic and geopolitical vulnerabilities had paid off. By de-coupling INF from SDI, "the Soviets had blinked," Reagan wrote in his diary.[3]

For Reagan, beleaguered by Iran-Contra and other scandals, the Washington summit was a welcome respite, just the opportunity he needed to turn his Presidency around. For Nancy the Washington summit was more than that. The summit would secure Ronald Reagan's reputation in history as a peacemaker. In time-honored fashion, a President dogged by domestic political scandal would attempt to repair his reputation by playing the role of world statesman. With the help of Gorbachev—the leader of the "evil empire"—and his usual good luck, Reagan was going to fight his way back to the summit of popular opinion as his presidency neared its end.

But it was Gorbachev who was the star of the Washington summit. The capital was gripped by what *Washington Post* columnist Tom Shales called "Gorby Fever." Wherever he went, crowds lined the streets to catch a glimpse of this Soviet leader, the first to come to the United States on what was truly a mission of peace. Even the Russians were "startled by the Soviet leader's popularity in the United States."[4] If the old actor was put off by his co-star's billing, he didn't let on. When asked by a reporter if he felt upstaged by Gorbachev, he responded, "Good Lord, no, I starred with Errol Flynn."[5]

Reagan's own performance at the negotiation sessions, as witnessed by his closest advisors, was at times stellar and at times disappointing.

Chief of Staff Howard Baker and his deputy Kenneth Duberstein recalled the first session between Gorbachev and Reagan the afternoon of the first day of the summit, when Ronald Reagan used his humor with great effectiveness.

"[Gorbachev] came prepared to dominate the Washington summit." Baker told us.

> . . . We had the arrival ceremony, the arrival luncheon—which is always a mistake because you eat too much—and by the time we got to the plenary session in the cabinet room, everybody's sort of groggy. And we'd no more than sat down at the cabinet table, a big, long oval table, when Gorbachev pulled out his little black book and just started out in a rapid-fire, machine gun-like presentation of his points. And I could look at his book from across, and I saw it was all written in hand, some in red ink, some in green ink, some in black ink. It was pretty clear, to me at least, that he must have prepared that book himself. But anyway, he was just unrelenting. And we just all sat there sort of stunned, and Ronald Reagan just sat there without any expression on his face. And after about fifteen minutes, I got squirmy in my seat, looked over at George Shultz, who looked like he was about to expire because Gorbachev was dominating this first plenary session. And then I heard Ronald Reagan say, "Mr. President, I heard a story the other day I'd like to tell." And some of us froze in our seats because there were some Russian stories that he used to tell, that really I didn't think were going to fit. But he told a nice story about Gorbachev driving a car

and being stopped by two policemen, [and] the [first] policeman [asked the other], "Who was it?" [and the other said] "I don't know, but Gorbachev was driving him." Ronald Reagan told it with consummate skill, and it broke the place up. It survived translation, and Gorbachev laughed. And then it switched the whole thing. It broke the tension, and then Reagan started on his agenda. Now that's the first time I'd ever seen him use his humor—and he had wonderful wit—use his humor as a technique. But he did that, he changed the direction of the first plenary session, in that meeting.[6]

"Ronald Reagan had thrown off [Gorbachev's] rhythm," observed Duberstein,

and we got back on to our talking points, our arguments, rather than letting Gorbachev dominate it. And it must have been terribly frustrating, and people would say, "But that's not sophisticated." And you know something? Maybe it's not, but it's also the genius of Ronald Reagan, 'cause he had the presence to say, "Okay, let's turn the page."[7]

At a later session, however, Secretary of State Shultz lived through some difficult moments when the President embarrassed himself and the other members of his Administration:

We started out kind of informally, and Gorbachev said something like, "We have some real problems in our economy and I'm trying to do something about them through *perestroika*, and I'd like to tell you about these problems and hear what you have to say about them." And I thought, "Terrific, that's a great thing to talk about." And then President Reagan, for some reason, told [an offensive joke about Gorbachev's economic failures] that sort of killed the subject.[8] And I thought it was a gigantic mistake to do that. Anyway, Gorbachev then said, "Well, let's talk about conventional arms," which was a subject that the President hadn't focused on very much and hadn't really prepared in his mind. And so this discussion started, and it put him in a bad position because he had to defer to me all the time to respond. . . . Gorbachev would say things, raise questions, and the President didn't know the answers. Being a candid kind of guy, he didn't try to fake it. He said, "Well, George . . .," so it wound up as a kind of dialogue between me and Gorbachev. So the meeting kind of meandered to an unsatisfactory close, and then it was over and we saw Gorbachev. And then, Colin Powell [Reagan's sixth and last National Security advisor] and I came back in to the Oval Office, and I gave the President hell. I said, "We don't want to have that happen again, and here's what happened and it was bad. And so let's not have any more of these big meetings."[9]

From then on, Reagan would be kept on a tight rein, under the supervision and control of his close advisors. He would have to stick to his talking points. There would be no more inspired initiatives and no more jokes.

Regardless of Reagan's spotty performance, the Washington summit was widely regarded as a great achievement. The INF Treaty was the first in the history to reduce the number of nuclear weapons. It was hailed as a major step toward peace and better relations between the Soviet Union and the United States.[10] For Reagan, it was a first step away from Armageddon.

During a rainswept exchange at the White House South

Lawn on December 10, an elated Reagan told the press the summit had been "a clear success."

"It was historic," recalled Howard Baker,

> . . . and I remember him expressing his pleasure that it was done, and I remember him pushing me hard for how the Senate was going to treat it. What he did was say, "See, they underestimated me again. They thought that they could persuade me, they could beat me, and by staying the course, I brought Gorbachev and the Soviets to the table. I got the INF Treaty.[11]

Lou Cannon, who in 1979 had heard Ronald Reagan predict that the Soviet Union was too weak economically to continue to wage an arms race, felt Reagan's insight had been vindicated.

> What you see in the INF Treaty was that Reagan's perception . . . had been correct. . . . The Russians didn't have the economic resources to stay the course. That's why they folded. They didn't fold because . . . they [were] weak or stupid. They just didn't have the resources. . . . They had to cut back, they had to cut down. . . . In a sense, the INF Treaty [was] a kind of ratification of economic reality.[12]

Soviet Ambassador to the United States Anatoly Dobrynin corroborated Cannon's observation when in 1995 he wrote:

> There is no escaping the fact that under this pressure Moscow gradually revised its views on general strategic parity and its approach to the negotiations on limiting nuclear missiles. In short, the Soviet leadership had to

accept the zero option as it applied to its own SS-20s as the most suitable under the circumstances, although at the end of the day it meant that billions of rubles had been wasted because of our own hasty decision to deploy the missiles in the first place.[13]

Not everyone agreed that INF had been a success. Hardline conservatives felt betrayed by what they considered Reagan's surrender. Before the summit, New Right leader Paul Weyrich had called Reagan a "weakened President, weakened in spirit as well as in clout, and not in a position to make judgments about Gorbachev at this time."[14] After the summit, William F. Buckley wrote "[Reagan] disappointed me on the INF Treaty. I simply could not understand his enthusiasm for a treaty that minimized the number of weapons, but wasn't tied to the larger question of whether Europe was safer or not." Reagan was called a "useful idiot for Soviet propaganda," and "an apologist for Gorbachev." George Will accused the President of accelerating America's "intellectual disarmament" and "succumbing fully to the arms control chimera," and predicted that the INF Treaty would go down in history as "the moment the United States lost the Cold War."[15]

In retrospect, as Edmund Morris told us, their judgment proved hasty.

> It was a historic achievement, and [Reagan] was very pleased and happy about it. But I think he regarded it as an interim step in the progression he was making toward his real goal, which was the elimination of totalitarianism from the surface of the earth.[16]

In May 1988, at the invitation of Mikhail Gorbachev, Reagan went to Moscow for a fourth summit with Gorbachev. Just days before his trip, he had won two important victories. In April, the Soviet Union had signed an agreement at Geneva committing to begin withdrawing from Afghanistan no later than May 15. Two days before his trip, the Senate ratified his INF Treaty by a decisive 93 to 5 vote.

In 1987, Washington had caught "Gorby fever." Now it was Reagan's turn to bask in the adulation of Muscovites. Everywhere his motorcade went, people lined the streets to cheer him. He was mobbed during a trip to the Moscow street market, the Arbat.[17] The Reagans and the Gorbachevs shared the Royal Box at the Bolshoi. Before the performance, the American national anthem was played along with the Soviet anthem for the first time. During a stop at Red Square, when asked whether he still believed the Soviet Union was an evil empire, he answered, "That was another time, another era."

To the relief of Americans and Soviets alike, Gorbachev and Reagan, the former enemies who now called each other "friend," were collaborating to bring the Cold War to an end. Lou Cannon, who covered the Moscow summit for *The Washington Post*, recalled the mood:

> I think the Moscow summit was . . . a ratification of their mutual desire for peace. When they walked together through Red Square with all of these people wandering through—some of whom were sent by the Communist Party and some of whom just happened to be there—I think you had a sense that the world was going to be okay.[18]

Reagan, feeling politically and personally rejuvenated, had brought his own agenda to Moscow. He would make clear that the achievement of peace would not be at the expense of his pursuit of freedom—freedom of religion, freedom to immigrate, and freedom of speech.

If, as Lou Cannon wrote, "Reagan's trip had been carefully scripted,"[19] the script, according to Edmund Morris, followed closely the themes to which Reagan was most deeply committed.

> The one thing that Reagan was more passionate about than anything other was the unsupportable phenomenon of totalitarian power enslaving a large part of the world's population. In other words, what he was really looking forward to was the collapse of Soviet Communism. He wanted to see the Wall come down. He wanted to see free elections and freedom and liberty and Christianity in Russia. It's as simple as that.[20]

In a visit to Berlin the previous year, Reagan had challenged Gorbachev to push his reforms further. Standing at the Brandenburg Gate within view of the Berlin Wall, he had said:

> General Secretary Gorbachev, if you seek peace, if you seek prosperity for the Soviet Union and Eastern Europe, if you seek liberalization, come here to this gate! Mr. Gorbachev, open this gate! Mr. Gorbachev, tear down this wall!

In Moscow, Reagan did not let up. Secretary George Shultz marvelled to *The American Experience* at Reagan's staying power and his commitment to his anti-Communist crusade:

> Here we come to the Moscow summit. It's the end of his Presidency really, and this is a big thing, and we're getting along with the Soviets. So we're coming to the Moscow summit, and there is a couple who were in need

of medical attention and also wanted to emigrate and
they got Ronald Reagan's attention. So he let it be
known to the Soviets that rather than do what they
wanted, which was, after he arrived at the airport, be
transported to the Kremlin and then there would be a big
ceremony with Gorbachev, [Reagan] said, "On the way
to the Kremlin, what I'm going to do is go to the apartment of this couple that you're not allowing to emigrate
and visit with them." With 2,000 press along, you know.
By this time they knew Ronald Reagan well enough to
know that if he said that was what he was going to do, he
would do it. He did not make idle threats. They sent
Bessmertnykh, who was a very high-ranking guy, to
Helsinki, where we were before we came to Moscow, and
Bessmertnykh brought a message. He said, "If the President visits that couple, we can assure you they will never
be allowed to emigrate. But if he doesn't, then probably
their cases will receive favorable attention." And we said
to [Bessmertnykh], "We take that as a commitment and
on the basis of that commitment, the President will go
directly to the Kremlin." And we followed through and
[the couple was] allowed to emigrate about four weeks or
so after the summit meeting.[21]

The second day of their Moscow visit, the Reagans held a
dinner for 100 dissidents at Spasso House, the residence of the
American Ambassador. "I came here hoping to do what I could
to give you strength," Reagan told his guests. "Yet I already know
that it is you who have strengthened me. . . . On human rights,
on the fundamental dignity of the human person, there can be
no relenting. For now, we must work for more. Always more."
Later that evening, at a state dinner in the Kremlin, Gorbachev expressed his annoyance by reminding Reagan that

nations "should get along without interfering in [each other's] domestic affairs."[22]

At the Danilov monastery, the spiritual home for the Eastern Orthodox religion in Moscow, Reagan expressed his hope for greater religious freedom in the Soviet Union.

> Our people feel keenly when religious freedom is denied to anyone anywhere and hope with you that all the many Soviet religious communities will soon be able to practice their religion freely and instruct their children in the fundamentals of their faith.

But Reagan left his best performance for last. At Moscow State University, beneath the cold marble stare of a gigantic bust of Lenin, Reagan preached his gospel of freedom to a selected audience of Moscow's best students:

> Freedom is the right to question and change the established way of doing things . . . It is the continuing revolution of the marketplace. It is the right to put forth an idea, scoffed at by critics, and watch it catch fire among the people. It is the right to dream . . . Freedom is the recognition that no single person, no single authority or government, has a monopoly on the truth. . . .
>
> Your generation is living in one of the most exciting, hopeful times in Soviet history. It is a time when the first breath of freedom stirs the air. When the accumulated spiritual energies of a long silence yearn to break free.
>
> In this Moscow spring, we may be allowed that hope—that freedom, like the fresh green sapling planted over Tolstoy's grave, will blossom forth at last.[23]

In 1981, Ronald Reagan had rejected détente, and committed himself to a strategy to undermine a vulnerable Soviet Union. Eight years later, relations between the superpowers had stabilized into a familiar pattern: the Soviet Union was once again a legitimate competitor, and arms control had regained its place as the centerpiece of the superpower relationship, with the difference that the emphasis was now on arms reductions, not just arms limitations. In 1989, by the time Ronald Reagan left the White House, Washington and Moscow were enjoying better relations than at any time since the World War II grand alliance against Hitler.

Only six years earlier Reagan had described the Soviet-American competition as "a struggle between Christianity and godless Communism." Now he was allowing Gorbachev the "period of tranquility" the Soviet leader needed for his reforms to work, for Communism, in whatever its new guise, to survive.

But what no one knew, or dared predict in 1988, was that the Soviet empire would unravel completely within the next three years.

By early 1989, the Soviet Union had pulled out of Afghanistan. In June 1989, Lech Walesa was elected President of Poland. Gorbachev refused to intervene. The other Soviet-dominated regimes of Eastern Europe—in Hungary, Czechoslovakia, Bulgaria, Romania—collapsed like a house of cards. In November 1989, the Berlin Wall came down. Three months later, the Sandinistas were voted out of power in the first free elections in Nicaragua. Mikhail Gorbachev's reforms could not arrest the disintegration of the Soviet empire—a disintegration hastened by Reagan's economic and military pressure. On Christmas Day, 1991, Gorbachev dissolved the Soviet Union.

Communism, once regarded by its progenitors as the inevitable wave of the future, had been consigned to "the ash heap of history."[24]

How much credit goes to Reagan will be debated for years to come.

Conservatives, many of the same people who, as late 1988, argued that Reagan had become an apologist for Gorbachev, and had fallen for the "chimera of arms control," today give him much credit for winning the Cold War.

> The Soviet Union in a sense died of ignorance. It didn't know what things ought to cost. Didn't have a price system. Didn't have markets and eventually that brings you down. You can run a tribe that way. You can't run a continental Eurasian landmass that way. Just imploded. So there's a sense in which internal contradictions brought it down but I think that was hastened by the pressure, moral, rhetorical, military and economic, put on consciously by Ronald Reagan.[25]

Others believe that external pressures were, at best, marginal to the implosion of the Soviet system.

> The fate of the Soviet Union was decided inside our country, in which no small part was played by Mikhail Gorbachev himself. All great powers from the Roman to the British empire have disintegrated because of internal strife, and not because of pressure from abroad. Nobody won the Cold War, and both sides paid a great price, but the end of the Cold War is our common victory.[26]

For forty years, through the policy of containment, the United States stood watch, confronting the Soviet Union at every turn. Only in the 1970s, in the wake of Vietnam, did America relinquish its vigilance. Leonid Brezhnev seized that opportunity to

expand Soviet military power and geopolitical influence, bank-
rupting the already precarious and inefficient Soviet economy in
the process. It was in that context that Ronald Reagan, a committed anti-Communist, decided to confront the Soviet Union.
Appealing to America's sense of mission, he rallied the nation
behind his battle against the "evil empire," and dealt the final
blow to a system doomed by history and by its own mistakes.
Gorbachev, along with Reagan, deserves credit for bringing what
might have been a deadly final confrontation to a peaceful end.

Reagan himself paid a word of tribute to his adversary:

> Gorbachev had the intelligence to admit Commu-
> nism was not working, the courage to battle for
> change, and, ultimately, the wisdom to introduce the
> beginnings of democracy, individual freedom and free
> enterprise.[27]

Christopher Matthews perhaps put it best when he described
the end of the Cold War in these terms:

> The United States rightly, in good times and bad,
> stood up against the global Communist movement, led
> by Moscow, starting in 1946 under the Truman Doc-
> trine, when we backed the Marshall Plan . . . [and]
> when we challenged the Soviets in Korea and Vietnam
> and all around the world. [But] Ronald Reagan was
> there for the kill.[28]

Reagan critic and well-known columnist Anthony Lewis,
while not denying Reagan credit for "being in power at the
time the Cold War was approaching its end," believes that Reagan's end-game strategy came at too high a price.

We paid a terrible price for that, and we are continuing to pay it, and our children are going to pay it,
because we ran up budget deficits cumulatively larger
than everything from the beginning of this country to
that date—which makes the ability of the national government in this country to govern very limited.[29]

That outcome might not have bothered Reagan. Though he
would clearly have preferred a balanced budget—one of his
campaign promises in 1980—the deficit turned out to be an
effective way to reduce the size of government. Ironically, as
George Will told *The American Experience*, Reagan's biggest
failure brought about the fulfillment of one of his fondest
dreams.

There was a theory here. It's called "starving the
beast," and Stockman wrote it out explicitly, and
Ronald Reagan said it explicitly. If you want to stop the
government, take away the money. I can't prove this,
but I think it. I think Ronald Reagan said. . . . "I can
live with a deficit because the deficit will squeeze the
government and drive all political choices after that. [It
will] change the conversation of the country." And he
did. The conversation of our political life has ever since
been driven by the brute fact that the government is
out of money.[30]

NOTES

[1] Bessmertnykh, Interview with Author. "By that time, our intelligence and all
the reports we had indicated the SDI [was] not realistic from the technical point of
view. It looked frightening initially, but it wouldn't work. It could produce some by-
products like laser weapons in space or something like that, but never a system cov-
ering the whole nation . . . so he was not so nervous about it.

[2] In 1990, Soviet officials acknowledged that the Soviet economy was indeed in
shambles. Soviet output was only one-fourth that of the United States, and 25 per-

cent of the gross national product went to defense, four times as high as in the United States even accounting for Reagan's defense buildup. Martin Anderson, *Revolution*, pp. xxxv–xxxvi.

[3] Ronald Reagan, *An American Life*, p. 696.

[4] Lou Cannon, *Role of Lifetime*, p. 777.

[5] Reagan was referring to his 1941 film "Santa Fe Trail." Given what we know about Reagan's experience with Flynn's egocentric antics on the set, Reagan's line could have had a double meaning. One, he did not mind being upstaged. Two, he was used to being upstaged by egomaniacs.

[6] Howard Baker, Interview with Austin Hoyt.

[7] Kenneth Duberstein, Interview with Austin Hoyt.

[8] The joke in question told the story of an American traveling to the Soviet Union. On his way to Kennedy Airport he asked his cab driver, a university student, what he wanted to do after graduation, to which the driver responded "I haven't decided yet." When he arrived in Moscow his driver was also a university student. The American asked him what he wanted to do when he finished school, to which the Russian responded, "I haven't been told yet."

[9] George Shultz, Interview with Austin Hoyt.

[10] The treaty involved the elimination of an entire class of nuclear weapons. The Soviets would have to destroy four times as many warheads as the Americans.

[11] Howard Baker, Interview with Austin Hoyt.

[12] Lou Cannon, Interview With Austin Hoyt.

[13] Anatoly Dobrynin, *In Confidence*.

[14] Quoted in Lou Cannon, *Role of A Lifetime*, p. 778.

[15] Richard Darman, *Who's In Control*, pp. 181–182. Even "moderate" analysts worried that the INF treaty was a first step toward the eventual de-nuclearization of Europe and the erosion of the NATO alliance. Henry Kissinger expressed "grave doubts" about its consequences to the eventual de-coupling of Germany from the Nato alliance. Henry Kissinger, *Diplomacy*, p.784. British Prime Minister Margaret Thatcher also worried the treaty could accelerate the trend toward German neutrality, an objective the Soviet Union had long pursued. Margaret Thatcher, *The Downing Street Years* (London: Harper Collins, 1993), p. 771.

[16] Edmund Morris, Interview with Austin Hoyt.

[17] The Americans were appalled at the rough treatment of the people who surrounded Reagan at the Arbat. Later Reagan wrote in his diary, "I've never seen such brutal manhandling as they did on their own people who were in no way getting out of hand. Boy, what a reminder that I was in a Communist country; perestroika or not, some things hadn't changed." Reagan, *An American Life*, p. 709.

[18] Lou Cannon, Interview with Austin Hoyt

[19] Lou Cannon and Don Oberdorfer, "The Scripting of the Moscow Summit", *The Washington Post*, June 9, 1988.

[20] Edmund Morris, Interview with Austin Hoyt.

[21] George Shultz, Interview with Austin Hoyt.

[22] Nancy Reagan, *My Turn*, p. 355.

[23] The Speech had been written by Tony Dolan, author of "the Westminster Speech" and "the Evil Empire" speech.

[24] The phrase was used by Reagan his 1982 "Westminster Speech."

[25] George Will, Interview with Author.

[26] Anatoly Dobrynin, *In Confidence*, pp. 610–612.

[27] Ronald Reagan, *An American Life*, p. 708.

[28] Christopher Matthews. Interview with Author. Henry Kissinger, while giving Ronald Reagan credit for being "the turning point," concluded that the end of the Cold War resulted from "the confluence of forty years of American bipartisan effort and seventy years of Communist ossification." Kissinger, *Diplomacy*, p. 802.

[29] Anthony Lewis, Interview with Austin Hoyt.

[30] George Will, Interview with Author.

CHAPTER 21

Sunset

Ronald Reagan was the first President to serve two terms in office since Dwight D. Eisenhower, and he left the White House with the highest approval rating of any President since Franklin Delano Roosevelt.[1]

From the Oval Office, on January 11, Reagan said farewell to his staff and to the nation in a speech which touched the themes which had driven his presidency, and his public life.

> I've spoken of the shining city all my political life, but I don't know if I quite communicated what I saw when I said it. . . . And how stands the city on this winter night? More prosperous, more secure, and happier than it was eight years ago. . . . But more than that. . . . She's still a beacon, still a magnet for all who must have freedom . . . and her glow has held steady, no matter what the course.

On January 20, after watching his Vice President George Bush take the oath of office, he boarded for the last time the plane which had been Air Force One. The now former President remembered thinking: "Today there would be no last minute changes in a speech text . . . no conferences with the National Security Advisor, no air-to-ground telephone calls to Cabinet members. . . . Today I could take time to look at the window and admire the breathtaking beauty of our land."[2] The Reagans were going back to California—going home.

At seventy-eight, Reagan still had time to enjoy his "Ranch in the Sky"; he could still ride, clear brush, cut tree branches, open vistas. According to his ranch aide Dennis Leblanc:

> Probably when he was eighty, eighty-one, he was still using the chain saws. But I believe he started concentrating more on the pole saw. I don't know if age entered into it or not, or if he just liked reaching high.[3]

Though Reagan felt he had mended much of what was broken in America, he could not mend his own broken home. "We've reached out to Patti since I left the White House," he wrote, "but so far she's made it plain to me that she thinks I am wrong and that she is against everything I stand for."[4]

On February 4, 1994, after years of silence, Patti called her father to wish him a happy eighty-third birthday.

> I sort of got this overwhelming feeling that I should go see my father. I had started to write *Angels Don't Die*, about the spiritual gifts that he had imparted to me throughout my life. And so he was very much on my mind. And I didn't even know if my parents were in town or if they were home. And I called, and he answered the phone, and he was there alone. And I went up and saw him and told him about the book that I was writing, told him how much he had enriched my life with his spirituality and by teaching me, really quite simply, to talk to God. And he was very moved by my telling him that because he had always wondered, as he said, "what my faith was."[5]

Though Patti may not have known it, there was little time to spare. At his eighty-third birthday tribute, many of the guests, including his friend former British Prime Minister Margaret Thatcher, noticed him falter.

> I remember we met beforehand to do all the photographs, which we usually do. And he was very quiet and not very communicative at all. And Nancy had to lead him to the platform holding him by the hand. And when she put up her hand to wave, immediately she said to Ron, "Wave." And he did. And I had thought that he was probably very tired.[6]

Reagan looked dazed, confused, and very old, as he struggled to find his words. For a moment, Nancy seemed worried and pained.

> Frankly, for a minute there, I was a bit concerned that after all these years away from Washington, you would not recognize me.

Reagan spoke haltingly, his voice, Reagan's physician John Hutton noticed, "was not its usual strong, exacting voice. And then suddenly it was as if a switch had gone on, and his old elegance was right back."[7]

> I can't tell you how thrilled Nancy and I are to be here with you tonight to celebrate, as Margaret said, the forty-fourth anniversary of my thirty-ninth birthday.

The relief on Nancy's face was visible. Her husband, diminished by illness and old age, had risen to the occasion one more time.

But Reagan's eighty-third birthday performance would be his last. That evening the former President retreated into the dimmer world his mind now frequently inhabited.

Dr. Hutton told *The American Experience:*

> After this was all over, we went back to the hotel, and he said, "I, I'm going to have to have a little help. I'm a little confused. I don't know where I am."[8]

When the news that President Reagan was afflicted with Alzheimer's disease became public in 1994, speculation was rampant about exactly when the illness had begun.[9] Some felt the signs had already been visible in 1984 when his dismal performance in a campaign debate with Walter Mondale prompted *The Wall Street Journal* to headline, "Reagan Performance Opens Speculation on His Ability to Serve." Others pointed to his forgetful and confused account of the events surrounding Iran-Contra. And what about the report Reagan's staff gave Howard Baker, telling him the President was unfit to govern and that he should invoke the 25th Amendment? Were these not evidence of the early onset of the disease?

Had Reagan's Alzheimer's been hidden from the public? It would not have been the first time that the illness of a nation's leader was the subject of a cover-up. What about Woodrow Wilson, who was in a wheelchair, disabled by a stroke while his wife and close aides maintained the appearance that he was in charge? And Winston Churchill, whose nearly fatal stroke was kept hidden from the British public while his son ran the government? And Franklin Delano Roosevelt, who, unbeknownst to the American people, attended the Yalta Conference—where the fate of the postwar world was to be decided—already a dying man?

Reagan's doctors, in public disclosures of Reagan's medical history, have tried to dispel any doubts about the President's mental competence while in office, and to quell speculation about a cover-up.

Reagan's mother Nelle and his brother Neil were both victims of Alzheimer's, so Reagan was always watchful of his own mental competence. He expected to be tested for failing memory and had pledged to resign if such signs appeared at any time.[10]

Dr. Lawrence C. Mohr, one of Reagan's White House physicians, recalled that one day, during his last two years as President, Reagan walked into his office and said: "I have three things that I want to tell you today. The first is that I seem to be having a little problem with my memory. I cannot remember the other two." As Dr. Mohr saw it, Reagan's quip was his way of expressing his anxiety about his occasional short-term memory lapses.[11]

While the line between mere forgetfulness and the onset of Alzheimer's is a fuzzy one, each of Reagan's four primary White House physicians told *The New York Times* that they had seen no evidence that the President had crossed the line while at the White House.[12]

The earliest any of the doctors recalls noticing Reagan's illness is September 13, 1992, after he gave a campaign speech on behalf of George Bush. Dr. Mohr, who saw Reagan after the speech, noticed

> He was distant and seemed preoccupied, which was unusual because Reagan was a person who was engaged when he talked to you. At the end of the conversation Mr. Reagan asked me, "What am I supposed to do next?"[13]

A battery of tests conducted at the Mayo Clinic the next year confirmed that Ronald Reagan had indeed developed Alzheimer's disease.

For many families, the loss of a loved one to Alzheimer's is a devastating blow. Ron Reagan told *The American Experience* that for him, the pain was somewhat eased by the feeling that he had already lost his father years before:

> I think all of us went through some period in our lives where we missed him while he was still there. And kind of banged our head against that wall, you know, why can't we get any closer? Why can't there be more of a rapport? But after you accept that there just isn't going to be, then you make your peace with that. It's an awful tragedy of course, Alzheimer's is a terrible thing, you wouldn't wish it on your worst enemy. But some of the pain maybe is lessened by the fact that . . . things haven't changed that much in a way. We're not missing something that we had to begin with.[14]

Though Reagan continued to do his best to usher in the Conservative revolution by doing radio spots on behalf of fellow Republicans in 1994—the year the Republicans finally captured the House of Representatives—it became increasingly clear to him and to those around him that he could no longer go on in his new role as elder statesman.

Dr. John Hutton remembers the moment Reagan decided to go public with his illness:

> He was very frustrated. . . . He realized that it was becoming even difficult to make tapes which he used to make for political friends, and we finally had to abandon making those, at which time he said, "I've got to somehow reach out and tell people that I can't do this anymore."[15]

Ronald Reagan left public life with characteristic courage, honesty and optimism. In a letter dated November 5, 1994, he wrote:

My Fellow Americans,

I have recently been told that I am one of the millions of Americans who will be afflicted with Alzheimer's Disease.

Upon hearing this news, Nancy and I had to decide whether as private citizens we would keep this a private matter or whether we would make this news known in a public way.

We feel it is important to share it with you. In opening our hearts, we hope this might promote a greater awareness of this condition.

Unfortunately as Alzheimer's Disease progresses, the family often bears a heavy burden. I only wish there was some way I could spare Nancy from this painful experience.

When the Lord calls me home, whenever that may be, I will leave with the greatest love for this country of ours and eternal optimism for its future.

I now begin the journey that will lead me into the sunset of my life.

I know that for America there will always be a bright dawn ahead.

Thank you my friends. May God always bless you.

Sincerely,
Ronald Reagan.

Reagan retreated into his private world to live the last years of his life. He stopped going to the ranch—the property is for sale—but has kept a daily routine. As late as October 1997, he still put on a suit and was driven to his Century City office where he greeted the occasional visitor. He played some golf at the Los Angeles Country club, and as far as we know is still in good health. But his physical vigor cannot arrest the relentless advance of the illness of forgetting.

With the dust of history only beginning to settle, *The American Experience*, in making the "Reagan" documentary, asked friends and critics for an early assessment of Ronald Reagan's legacy: "How will Ronald Reagan be remembered?"

James Baker III: I think he'll be remembered as a man who presided with grace and dignity over a very difficult time in domestic and foreign policy. . . . As a President who really made a difference.

Kenneth Duberstein: I think his legacy is that he ended the Cold War, . . . that he returned optimism to America . . . that he fundamentally changed the debate in Washington and throughout the country from bigger government to less government.

Anthony Lewis: You can't deny credit to a President who was in power at a time when the Cold War was, approaching its end—can't deny that credit. On the other hand, the theory . . . that we could spend the Soviets into oblivion by increasing our military budget, is a very flawed theory, because we paid a terrible price for that, and we are continuing to pay it, and our children are going to pay it, because we ran up budget deficits cumulatively larger than everything from the beginning of this country to that date.

George Will: I believe Ronald Reagan was as great as a President can be who doesn't have a nation threatened by crisis. Washington, founding of a country. Lincoln, preserving the country. Woodrow Wilson and Franklin Roosevelt, leading the country in great wars. Roosevelt having the Depression also. These are crises of a magnitude that pulled them to greatness. Ronald Reagan didn't have quite that kind of crisis. I think it was Somerset Maugham who was once asked where he stood in the ranks of literature. He said, "I'm at the very front rank of the second rank," and maybe that's where Ronald Reagan is.

Richard Norton Smith: We already know that he's the largest President of the 20th century, since Franklin Roosevelt. Much as every President, since Franklin Roosevelt, before Reagan were themselves limited in their actions by the Roosevelt legacy. It will be interesting to see how long the Reagan legacy defines the parameters of the American presidency.

Whatever history makes of him will be of paramount importance to future generations. But the judgment of history no longer has any meaning for Ronald Reagan.

At Christmas in 1995, a visitor brought Reagan a special gift, a porcelain replica of the White House to place in his fish tank at his office in Los Angeles. Reagan seemed bewildered as he looked at this gift. "I must take it home," Reagan said. "I have to show Nancy because I know I had some relationship to this place. I just can't remember exactly what it was."

NOTES

[1] Gallup poll showed Reagan's approval rating was 63 percent, Roosevelt's 68 percent.

[2] Ronald Reagan, *An American Life*, p. 725.

[3] Dennis Le Blanc, Interview with Austin Hoyt.

[4] Ronald Reagan, *An American Life*.

[5] Patti Davis, Interview with Austin Hoyt. Patti had already contracted with

Playboy to pose nude and would film a sexually explicit video. She saw no conflict between her spirituality and these activities. Since Reagan's illness, she has made up with her mother.

[6] The Baroness Margaret Thatcher, Interview with Austin Hoyt.

[7] *Ibid.*

[8] Dr. John E. Hutton Jr., Interview with Austin Hoyt.

[9] Alzheimer's is a progressive form of dementia afflicting with increasing frequency people over 60. As it advances, abnormal deposits of protein destroy the nerve cells erasing memory.

[10] Lawrence K. Altman, "A President Falls Into a World Apart," *The New York Times*, October 5, 1987. p. 34.

[11] *Ibid.*

[12] *Ibid.*

[13] *Ibid.*

[14] Ronald Prescott Reagan, Interview with Austin Hoyt.

[15] Dr. John E. Hutton Jr., Interview with Austin Hoyt.

Index

ABM Treaty 218, 282, 283, 285
abortion 125, 145-146
AFDC, Aid to Families with Dependent Children 108, 110
Afghanistan 199, 203, 204, 272-3, 322, 326
AFL-CIO convention 157
Africa 197-9
Allen, Richard 200, 202, 259-60
Alzheimer's Disease 334-9
    letter 338
Anderson, John 147
Anderson, Martin 16, 22, 23, 116, 121, 139, 145, 217-8 , 255, 274
Andreas, Dwayne 174
Andropov, Yuri 233, 237, 254
Angola 198-9, 204
Annenberg, Walter 253
anti-communism 9, 18, 21, 65, 81, 122, 199, 203-4, 254, 285, 323-4, 328
anti-nuclear movement, Europe 209, 211
Armageddon 22, 120, 166, 213, 217-20, 258, 319
arms control 197-8, 235, 255, 265, 279, 282, 285, 315-16, 321, 326
arms-for-hostages 293-308
arms race 214, 218, 220-33, 254-5, 320
Arnow, Max 41
Asia 198-9
assassination attempt 157, 160-172, 247, 276
astrologer 101, 169, 302-3, 308-9
Ayres, Lew 67

B-1 bomber 202
B-52 bomber 202

Baker, Howard 123, 147, 189-90, 304, 306-7, 317-8, 320, 335
Baker, James 21, 145-146, 148, 149, 153, 162, 234, 250, 275, 310, 339
balanced budget 103, 115, 146, 151, 183-4, 329
Barletta, John 13, 177
Barnett, Barney 14, 178-179
Bellamann, Henry 47
Berlin Wall 18, 20, 323, 326
Bessmertnykh, Alexander 13, 200, 202, 214, 233, 238, 254-5, 263, 283, 286-7, 324
big government 18, 21, 83, 87, 92, 115, 144-145
Bishop, Maurice 199
Black Monday 311-2
Boland Amendment 273-4
Borger, Gloria 310
Brady, James 163
Brezhnev, Leonid 327-8
Broder, David 126, 164, 192
Brown, Edmund 90, 92-4, 96-8, 101, 103, 108, 125
Brown, Willie 105-106
Buckley, William F. 87, 321
    National Review 87
Buckley, William (CIA Station Chief, Beirut) 293, 295
budget cuts 103-5, 148, 181-2, 191
Bulgaria 326
"bully pulpit" 20-1, 155
Bush, George 17, 123, 147, 148, 332, 336

Caddell, Patrick 126-8
Caldicott, Dr. Helen 21, 207-8
Cambodia 198-9
Camp David 77, 248

Cannon, Lou 13, 17, 19, 22, 38, 42, 47, 91, 94, 102, 108, 110, 153, 157, 167

Carson, Johnny 143, 160-1

Carter, Jimmy 115, 118, 122, 123, 124, 125, 126, 127, 139, 142, 143, 153, 174, 181-2, 183, 186, 199, 202, 209, 249

   conceded Presidency 128

Castro, Fidel 199

Catalina Island 41

Chambers, Whittaker 87, 121

   Witness 87

Chernenko, Konstantin 253-4

Cheyene Mountain 217

Chicago 26, 27, 37, 70

child nutrition 151, 184

China 259

Churchill, Winston 163, 335

CIA 18, 123, 202-5, 273-4, 292, 295, 300-1

   covert operations 204

Citizens for the Republic 121

Clark, William 68, 103, 235, 257, 259-60

Cleaver, Margaret 32, 36, 37

Colbert, Claudete 185

Cold War 13, 14, 17, 18, 20, 63, 142, 194, 203, 213, 233, 239, 253-4, 266, 285, 290-1, 300, 321, 322, 327-8, 329

college education benefits 151

Committee on the Present Danger 198

Commonwealth Club 97

Conference of Studio Unions, (CSU) 63

Congressional Black Caucus 152

Congressional elections, mid-term 1982 153

Conservative movement 16, 20, 87-90, 110, 118, 122, 125, 139, 143, 146, 192, 259-60, 337

"The Continentals" 77

Contras 204, 273, 274, 293, 298, 300, 305

cruise missiles 17

Cuba 194, 198-9, 204, 236, 238, 248

Cuomo, Mario 312

Czechoslovakia 326

D-Day comemmmorization 241

Dallek, Robert 30, 42, 43, 270

Daniloff, Nicholas 279-80

Danilov monastery 325

Darman, Richard 148, 151, 165, 179, 180, 182, 243-4, 248

Davis, Edith 70, 87

Davis, Loyal 70, 87

Davis, Nancy *see* Reagan, Nancy

Davis, Patti 72, 73, 78, 84, 85-7, 101, 164, 165, 206-7, 208, 311, 333-4

   Angels Don't Die 333

   The Way I See It 311

"The Day After" 238

Deaver, Michael 27, 73, 75, 76, 105, 116, 120, 127, 148, 149, 161, 162, 169, 170, 177, 186, 193, 219, 241-2, 243, 250, 256, 257-8, 275, 303-4, 310

   influence peddling 310

defense 17, 90, 117, 146, 151, 180, 183-4, 200-1, 217, 218, 220-33, 254, 288

   spending 190, 194, 202

deficit 20, 180, 182, 189, 194, 245, 312, 329, 339

Des Moines, Iowa, 37

détente 197-8, 237, 280, 326

Didion, Joan 104

Disciples of Christ 15, 30, 31, 36, 166, 186

Dobrynin, Anatoly 233, 257, 320-1

Dolan, Tony 14, 211-2, 213

Dole, Robert 123

Donaldson, Sam 125, 170, 187, 199-200, 287-8, 296
Duberstein, Kenneth 75, 171, 307, 317, 318, 339

economic program 150, 170-1, 172, 176, 179-80, 183, 189, 190, 194
Edwards, Anne 44
Eisenhower, Dwight D. 16, 48, 83, 87, 332
Ethiopia 198-9
Eureka College 36-8
Europe 209-10, 237, 239, 285, 321
Evangelical convention 212-3
Evil Empire 14, 21, 197, 212-3, 288-9, 316

Feederal Reserve Board 190
"A Feuding First Family" 310
Ford, Gerald 113, 115, 116, 117, 119, 142, 174, 197, 199
Ford, Glenn 70
Fulks, Sarah Jane *see* Wyman, Jane

Gable, Clark 70
Gdansk, Poland 207
"GE Theater" 78, 80-84
    cancelled 83-84
General Electric 42, 78, 81, 88, 89
    Appliance Park 81
Geneva talks 13
Geneva Summit 260-5, 266, 267, 272, 279
Geneva talks 238
glasnost 315-6
Glenn, John 192
Goldwater 20, 87, 89, 91, 92, 214
    Concience of a Conservative 87
Goldwater campaign, co-chairman 87
Gorbachev 13, 17, 253-4, 258, 262-6, 279-82, 287-90, 315-18, 321-23, 326, 328

"Gorby Fever" 316, 322
Graham, Billy 219-20
Graham, Daniel 218
Great Depression 16, 21, 37, 61, 182, 184, 188, 189, 340
Great Society 87, 151
Grenada 199, 236-7
Griffin, Merv 169

Haig, Alexander 145-146, 259-60
Hauck, William 109
Hayek, Frierich 121
Hinkley, John, Jr. 157, 162, 165, 166, 167
Hoffman, Stanley 213
Holden, William 71, 72
Hollywood 41-78, 94, 98, 124, 143, 160
    communists in Hollywood 16, 62, 63, 83
Hollywood Independent Citizens' Committee for the Arts, Sciences and Professions (HICCASP) 62
Hollywood Legion Stadium 62
Holmes, Oliver Wendell 83
homelessness 188, 312
Hoover Institution 22
House Un-American Activities Committee 65, 66
    Strippling 65-6
human rights 324
Humphrey, Hubert 272
Hungary 326
Huston, John 70
Hutton, Dr. John 334, 335, 337

ICBM 233-4
inaugural 143-144, 146
Inaugural Address 49, 189, 243-4
INF Treaty 265, 281-2, 315-6, 319-22
inflation 150, 182-4, 186, 193, 245, 270
Iran 122, 127, 292-5, 298-9, 305

Iran hostage crisis 122
Iran-Contra 276, 292-308, 311, 335
Iraq 310

jelly beans 143, 250
Johnson, Lyndon 87, 89, 142, 151
Jordan 310

KAL-007 235-7
Kemp, Jack 90, 147
Kennedy, Edward 206
Kennedy, John F. 142, 194, 272
KGB 233-4, 279-80
Khomeini, Ayatollah 122, 293-4, 298
Khrushchev, Nikita 194
Kirkpatrick, Jeanne 213
Kissinger, Henry 117, 199, 202, 263
Korea 328
Krauthammer, Charles 301
Kremlin 214, 253-4, 324-5
Kuhn, Jim 77, 80

Laffer, Arthur 147
Lake Arrowhead 61-2
Lake Leman 263
Laos 198-9
Las Vegas 77
Lawton, Helen 30, 34
LeBlanc, Dennis 14, 178-9
Lebanon 292
Lewis, Anthony 17, 328-9, 339
liberalism 151
Liberty weekend 269, 292
Libya 219-20
Little, Rich 143
Louiville, Kentucky 81
"Love is on the Air" 41
Lowell Park 33, 83, 96, 124
    Graybills 34
Lucket, Edith 70 *see also* Davis,
    Edith

MacNamara, Robert 206
MAD, Mutually Assured Destruc-
    tion 198, 218-20
Mansfield, Mike 154
Mason, James 70
March, Frederick 70
Marshal Plan 328
Martin, Mary 70
Matthews, Christopher 13, 23, 152,
    172
McCarthy, Tim 163
McFarlane, Robert 76, 208, 235,
    256, 284, 292, 293-4, 295, 302
Medicaid 185
Medicare 92, 151, 183-4
Meese, Edwin 90, 103, 110, 125,
    148, 149, 162, 250, 275, 298-9,
    309-10
Meiklejohn, Bill 41
Meyer, Herbert 203
Middle East 293, 295-310
military build-up 146, 202, 206, 246,
    255, 339
military service 48-9
"the misery index" 126
Mohr, Dr. Lawrence C. 336
Mondale, Walter 192, 244-6, 247,
    250, 305
Moral Majority 145-6
Moretti, Bob 109, 110
Morris Morris, Edmund 13, 14, 15,
    16, 23, 28, 30, 35, 40, 42, 88, 91,
    124, 125, 167, 188, 199, 202,
    213, 234, 260, 276, 301-2, 306,
    312, 321
Moscow State University 325
Moscow summit 321-2
Moyers, Bill 184-5
Mujahedin 203, 204, 273
MX missile 202

National Association of Manufac-
    turers 83

national debt 20
national security 139
NATO 209, 239, 315
NBC 37
New Deal 87, 125, 150-151
Nicaragua 199, 204, 273, 292-3,
    298, 305, 326
Nixon, Richard 90, 113, 115, 142,
    181-2, 199, 250
Nofziger, Lyn 19, 26, 71, 89, 93, 94,
    95, 97, 102, 106, 113, 114-115,
    121, 179, 188, 197, 281
    influence peddling scandal 310
Noonan, Peggy 81
NORAD 217
North, Oliver 292, 298, 300, 302
NSC 292, 298, 300-1, 306
Nuclear Freeze Movement 206-8
    Central Park rally 206
nuclear weapons 198, 201, 206, 210,
    217, 234-5, 246, 255, 265, 285

O'Brien, Pat 46
O'Neill, Tip 23, 152-153, 157, 172,
    174, 192, 250, 273

Pacific Palisades 95
Palazchenko, Pavel 209
Panama 117
Parker, Dorothy 61
Parliament, British 18
Parr, Jerry 161
Pavlevi, Shah Rehza 122
Pentacostals 257-8
"People Like Us" 184-5
perestroika 315-6, 318-9
Perle, Richard 259-60, 286, 288
Pershing missiles 17, 21, 208-10,
    237-9, 241, 281-2, 315
Physicians for Social Responsibility
    21, 207
Pierce, Sam 246
Plante, Bill 298

Poindexter, John 292, 300
Point du Hoc 49, 241-2
Poland 18, 203-5, 272-3, 326
Politburo 233-4
Pope John Paul II 205, 238
poverty relief 184, 188
Powell, Colin 319
PATCO, Professional Air Traffic
    Controllers Organization 173
Proposition 13 122
public service jobs 151

Quigley, Joan 169-170, 302-3, 309

Rafsanjani, Ali Akbar 292
ranch, Malibu 84
"Rancho del Cielo" 14, 121, 176-80
"Reagan Doctrine" 21
Reagan Library 28
Reagan, farewell address 332
Reagan, Jack 25, 26, 29, 44, 46-7
Reagan, Maureen 44, 77, 85, 97,
    101, 123, 139, 156, 164, 165,
    275-6, 305-6
Reagan, Michael 45
Reagan, Nancy 15, 70, 77, 86, 104,
    111, 119, 120, 144, 162, 163,
    168, 169-70, 185, 214, 248, 256,
    259-60, 301, 302-3, 304, 307-8,
    311, 316, 334
    early relationship with Ron 71-
        72
    films
        "The Doctor and the Girl" 70
        "East Side, West Side" 70
        "It's a Big Country" 70
    protectiveness 73, 74, 256-7,
        308
    Smith College 71
    White House china 185
Reagan, Neil 25, 26, 38
Reagan, Nelle 25, 26, 30, 31, 38, 44,
    46, 186, 199, 336

Reagan, Patricia Anne. See Davis, Patti

Reaganomics 193-4, 271-2

realpolitik 197

recession 16, 37, 183, 184, 186, 189, 191, 245

Rector, James 107

Red Army 285

Regan, Donald 75, 190, 250, 260, 261, 275-6, 284, 287-8, 292, 297, 298, 302, 303, 304, 305-6, 308-9
   For the Record 308-9

religious faith 19, 22, 25, 31, 105, 165, 166-167, 189, 213, 219-20, 333

Republican convention, 1980 123

Republican convention, 1984 243-5
   acceptance speech 123

Republican primaries, 1976 116-118

Republican primaries, 1980 17

Reykjavik summit 17, 239, 276, 279-91, 311, 315-16

Robbins, Anne Francis *see* Reagan, Nancy

Robbins, Kenneth 70

Rock River 28, 33

Rockefeller, Nelson 93, 113

Rollins, Ed 251, 302

Romania 326

Reagan, Ron 13, 21, 26, 84, 85, 104, 118-119, 164, 167, 301, 310-1, 336-7

Roosevelt Franklin D. 143, 150-1, 259, 332, 335, 340

Rubel, Cy 90, 113

Sacramento 91, 103, 104, 181-2

Sakharov, Andrei 266

SALT 255-6

SALT II 208

Salvatori, Henry 90, 113

San Francisco 97

Sandanistas 204, 273, 293, 326

Santa Barbara 41

Savimbi, Jonas 204

school prayer 145-6

Screen Actors Guild (SAG) 16, 63, 65, 66, 83, 200, 259
   Hollywood strike 63
   loyalty affidavit 66
   FBI informant 64, 65

SDI, Strategic Defense Initiative 17, 219-20, 233-6, 238, 240, 261, 265-7, 280-1, 286-90, 316-7

Secret Service 13, 15, 161, 162, 177

Shales, Tom 317

Shamir, Yitzhak 49

Shevardnadze, Edward 264, 279

Shultz, George 14, 76, 235, 239, 256, 257-8, 280, 281-2, 288, 290, 295, 301, 302, 317-9

Sinatra, Frank 98, 143

Smith, Richard Norton 28, 98

Social Security 151, 180, 183-4, 185, 194

"socialized medicine" 83

Solidarity 19, 203, 205, 272-3

Somoza, Anastsio 273

Sorrel, Herb 63. See Wyman, Jane

Soviet Union 17, 122, 126, 142, 145, 146, 147
   expansionism 198, 202, 204, 263, 274
   dissolution 17, 18, 327

Spasso House 325

speeches
   "Encroaching Control" 82
   "A New Beginning" 243-5
   "Our Eroding Freedom" 82
   "The Speech" 88
   "A Time for Choosing" 88, 89

Spencer, Stuart 72, 91, 94, 98, 102

Statue of Liberty 19, 124, 270

"stay the course" 183, 193, 272

START, Strategic Arms Reduction
    Talks 256
Stewart, Jimmy 80, 143
Stockman, David 147, 148, 153,
    180-1, 183-4, 190, 329
supply-side economics 146-7, 151,
    180-1, 272

Tarasenko, Sergei 14, 210, 261, 264
taxes 83, 92, 103, 108, 115, 122,
    126, 145, 146, 148, 180, 182,
    183-4, 190, 194, 271, 272, 311-2
TEFRA 191
Tehran 292, 294-5
Teller, Edward 218
Tennessee Valley Authority 83, 92-
    93
That Printer of Udells 30
Thatcher, Margaret 13, 211, 289-90,
    334
Third Liberation Movement 106
Thomas, Helen 297-8
Todd, Richard 68
Tower Commission 302, 304-5, 308
Tower, John 301-2, 304-5
Tracy, Spencer 70
Treptow, Martin 49
Trewhitt, Henry 249
Truman Doctrine 328
Tuttle, Holmes 90, 113

unemployment 189, 191, 270
unemployment compensation 151
UNITAS 204
University of California 103, 106
U.S. Marine barracks, Beirut 236,
    293, 297

USS John F. Kennedy 19, 269
Vatican 205, 249
Veteran's Administration 83
Vietnam 11, 101, 106, 122, 142,
    197, 198-9, 250, 327-8
Volker, Paul 183, 184, 190, 193

Walesa, Lech 204-5, 272-3, 326
Walters, Barbara 247
War on Poverty 151
Warner Brothers 63, 68
Watergate 115, 250
Wedtech scandal 310
Weinberger, Caspar 180, 181, 184,
    235, 259-60, 280, 295
Welfare 92, 108-111, 185
Welfare Reform Bill 108, 109, 110,
    153
Wells, Dr. Lamar 34
Western Europe 17
WHO 37, 38, 41
"wilderness years" 121
Will, George 20, 22, 27, 28, 32, 72,
    74, 89, 128, 151, 184, 193-4,
    256, 271, 280, 294, 321, 329,
    339-40
Wills, Gary 103, 143, 248
Wilson, Woodrow 335, 340
Wirthlin, Richard 139, 166, 173,
    192, 255
Work Experience Program 110
Wyman, Jane 44, 63, 67, 68, 71, 72
    films
        "Johnny Belinda" 67
        "The Yearling" 67, 115, 118
    film roles
        Baxter, Ma 67

Acknowledgements

This book is the result of two-and-a-half years of hard and dedicated work by a production team at WGBH and the staff at *The American Experience* in Boston. It builds on more than fifty interviews with Reagan family members, friends, aides and adversaries, and on the audio-visual record of Reagan's life and presidency. I owe a great debt to Reagan's distinguished biographers Lou Cannon, who has left few stones unturned through decades devoted to understanding Ronald Reagan, and Edmund Morris, whose biography of Reagan is scheduled to appear this fall. They generously shared with us their observations and conclusions.

Unlike other written works, it is not the product of a lonesome endeavor by its author. It is truly a collaborative work. Austin Hoyt, my partner of ten years at WGBH, was Executive Producer of "Reagan," and wrote and produced the second half of the four-and-a-half hour PBS documentary on which this book is based. Our film editors, Betty Ciccarelli and Bill Lattanzi, made significant contributions to the structuring of the stories. To them, my deepest gratitude.

I'd also like to thank Alison Smith, the director of archive research, for her mighty effort on our behalf; Carla Raimer, production assistant; and Tobee Phipps, the unit manager who attended to the myriad details of a complex television production.

Margaret Drain, Executive Producer of *The American Experience*, courageously read the manuscript and offered many, many useful comments. She and Mark Samels, Senior Producer for *The American Experience*, also did their share of hand-holding.

Judy Crichton, former Executive Producer for *The American Experience*, held my feet to the fire and made a great contribution to the shaping of the story.

To them and the rest of the staff, I owe a great debt.

To my publisher, Peter Kaufman, thank you for being so "up." Your encouragement made a world of difference.

To Peter McGhee, Vice-President of National Productions, my appreciation for your confidence in me.

The phrase "without whom this work could not have been written" is old and overused. Regardless, Carol Lynn Alpert deftly edited this manuscript, and more than shared my burden. Without her, this book could not have been written.

I am also indebted to my friends at WGBH, Elizabeth Deane, Karen Johnson, Sandy Haller, Helen Russell, Paul Taylor and Joseph Tovares. Also to Kyla Herblum and Shelley Borg, who buoyed me through this project.

—Adriana Bosch
Boston, January 1998

Photo Credits

Courtesy of the Ronald Reagan Boyhood home:
>   page 51, football photo;
>   page 54, school play.

Courtesy of the Loveland Community House:
>   page 52-53, beach.

Courtesy of Palmer College:
>   page 55, WHO.

Courtesy of the Motion Picture and Television Archive:
>   page 55, Jane Wyman and family.

Courtesy of the Screen Actors Guild:
>   page 56, all three photos.

Courtesy of Nancy Reagan:
>   page 57, both photos;
>   page 60, both photos;
>   page 255, letter.

Courtesy of the Hall of Electrical History of the Schenectady Museum Association:
>   page 58, middle and bottom photos.

Courtesy of UPI/Corbis-Bettmann:
>   page 59, bottom photo with Goldwater.

Courtesy of Peter Borsari:
>   page 222, bottom, Patti with celebrities.

All other photos are used courtesy of the Ronald Reagan Presedential Library.

About *The American Experience*

"...historical television at its finest...If any history series deserves to be spun off into its own channel, it's *The American Experience*."

—*Atlanta Journal Constitution*

Since its debut in 1988, *The American Experience* has brought stories of the people and events that shaped this country to nearly seven million viewers each week. As television's only regularly scheduled prime-time historical documentary series, *The American Experience* brings to life the incredible characters and epic stories that helped form our nation.

The series has produced more than 100 programs. Among the best known are the presidential portraits, including "TR, The Story of Theodore Roosevelt," "FDR," "Ike," "The Kennedys," "Nixon," "LBJ," "Truman" and "Reagan." "Nobody does presidential biographies better," according to the *Houston Chronicle*.

The American Experience has served public television audiences by drawing them to the great and the untold stories of our nation: biographies such as "Malcolm X: Make It Plain" and "Amelia Earhart"; wrenching tales of natural disasters like "The Johnstown Flood" and "The Great San Francisco Earthquake"; the agony of war in "Battle of the Bulge" and "D-Day"; the struggle of native peoples in "Geronimo" and in the highly acclaimed mini-series, "The Way West"; the hype and glamour of Hollywood in "The Battle over Citizen Kane"; and a tale of human tragedy in "The Donner Party."

The series has been praised as "undoubtedly one of the best shows on television" (*Baltimore Sun*) and described as "among TV's best history teachers" (*USA Today*). Woven together from archival images, photographs, home movies, and original cinematography, the programs are produced by some of the most talented filmmakers in the country with an eye to inform as well as to entertain, to be honest and thoughtful and, most importantly, to bring America's past to life. *The American Experience* has won numerous awards, including eleven Emmys, two duPont-Columbia Journalism Awards, five George Foster Peabody Awards, six Writers' Guild Awards, five Erik Barnouw Awards, and has received six Oscar nominations.

Pulitzer Prize-winning author and historian David McCullough is the series host. Margaret Drain is the executive producer. Mark Samels is senior producer. Joseph Tovares is series editor and director of new media. Susan Mottau is coordinating producer.

For more information about *The American Experience*, visit our website at www.pbs.org/amex.

About the Authors

Adriana Bosch is Series Producer for *The American Experience* documentary film, "Reagan." She is also series producer and writer for "The Churchills," "Eisenhower," "The Americas" and "War and Peace in the Nuclear Age" for WGBH-Boston. Cuban-born, she holds a Ph.D. from the Fletcher School of Law and Diplomacy at Tufts University and is a graduate of Rutgers. She lives in Boston.

Austin Hoyt is Executive Producer of "Reagan." His many previous productions for *The American Experience* include a biography of Andrew Carnegie, "The Richest Man in the World." Winner of an Emmy Award and aWriters Guild of America Award, he is a graduate of Yale University.

David McCullough, winner of the Pulitzer Prize, the National Book Award and the Francis Parkman Prize is the renowned write, historian, lecturer and teacher. His books on biography and history include: *Truman, Mornings on Horseback, The Path Between the Seas, The Great Bridge* and *The Johnstown Flood.*